# Praise for *Stories of Caring School Leadership*

"Captivating, moving, and sincere; a beautiful collection of stories of caring leadership practice. Full of dilemmas around boundaries and privacy, ambiguities and ethics, inequities and responsibility, this book illuminates, instructs, and inspires. It will be an eye-opener for anyone skeptical of the hard and necessary work that is caring and that schools and educators do on a daily basis."

**Milena Batanova**
*Research and Evaluation Manager, Making Caring Common,*
*Harvard Graduate School of Education*

"What an interesting time we are in where a book that feeds the spirit presents a perspective that is both bold and lacking in today's discourse! Our society's future lies in our ability to guide the youngest among us toward social and emotional health. We will have left an indelible mark on society if we are able to cultivate in our future leaders the capacity to be thoughtful, intelligent, kind, and caring. It will take a journey to get there from where we are today. This book should be required reading for the trip."

**John C. Borrero**
*Executive Director, Collaboration for Early Childhood*

"The voices of these inspiring educators and their stories of hope bring to life how 'caring lies at the heart of schooling' (p. xii). We are reminded that the little things are the big things. The stories illuminate the power of caring, loving, holding, listening, and being present—physically and psychologically—to and for each other. The storytellers create a tapestry made up of the textures of care in different forms—helping us move closer together in our relationships and connectedness. Get ready to open your heart and be filled with goosebumps."

**Ellie Drago-Severson**
*Professor of Education Leadership and Adult Learning & Leadership,*
*Teachers College—Columbia University*

"Anyone who has ever worked in a school understands how important caring leadership is for human flourishing. With provocative questions for immediate application, these three highly respected scholars have framed stories that prove that caring leadership is happening in schools right now. The stories told by school leaders themselves are instructive and inspiring. The student artwork is a perfect complement. This book is more than a must-read for educators—it is a pure joy."

**Jon Eckert**
*Professor of Educational Leadership, Baylor University*

"These stories truly capture what is at the heart and soul of good school leadership: authentic and unwavering care. These accounts are inspiring and motivating for anyone beginning, proceeding along, or reflecting on their own journey as a school leader. I'm forever grateful for the gift these authors have given us all. This will be a frequently called upon resource to share with the current and aspiring leaders I support."

**Richard Frank**
*Coach and Consultant, CT3 Education*

T0354263

"The stories in this book remind us that caring is an indispensable quality of teaching and leadership. *Stories of Caring School Leadership* is an essential resource for those charged with supporting students and adults for today's world—and tomorrow's."

**Kevin Gallick**
*Principal, George Washington High School*
*Chicago Public Schools*

"This profound and practical book animates the irreplaceable presence of caring necessary for the learning and development of children and youth. Constructed from practitioners' stories with multiple avenues for access, the moving narratives give examples of why high school parents will flock to conferences, how middle school students were helped to address concerns about a teacher, an elementary child on the autism spectrum was given timely support, an equity committee was formed, and how an organizational context for caring was created."

**Robert Garmston**
*Professor Emeritus, California State University, Sacramento*
*Cofounder of Cognitive Coaching and Adaptive Schools*

"*Stories of Caring School Leadership* brings compassionate, caring leadership to life through poignant stories and inspiring artistic expressions. The National Association of Secondary School Principals is committed to supporting great leaders in every school who are committed to the success of each student. The sharing of student artwork lets the reader peer into the hearts of our most vulnerable and most precious assets—our students. This book 'shows and tells' what school leadership should look like. Congratulations to Mark Smylie, Joe Murphy, and Karen Seashore Louis for bringing authenticity to the vision of school leadership that NASSP finds crucial."

**Beverly J. Hutton**
*Deputy Executive Director, Programs and Services*
*National Association of Secondary School Principals*

"At times both touching and heartbreaking, this book is a rich source for learning that helps us envision equity—truly caring about each individual student and valuing their unique set of experiences, assets, and needs. I connected with so many of these stories, and I applaud the authors for embracing the power of stories to bridge the gap between theory and practice. To lead for equity, we must do the internal work to see and recover from our own biases and assumptions about students, teachers, and families. These stories are a powerful tool for connecting though our shared humanity and for cocreating the culturally responsive and just school experiences that will free our young people to flourish."

**Rebecca D. Kaye**
*Chief of Equity & Accountability*
*Oklahoma City Public Schools*

"This collection of stories presents an authentic picture of what it means to be a school leader today. As I read the book I cried, laughed, nodded, and said aloud, 'Oh, yeah, that happens—sometimes more than we'll ever know.' The storytellers paint a picture of the challenges students face each day that extend beyond their academic success and how school leaders are instrumental in shaping and nurturing schools in which students' very existence and well-being depend on caring school administrators. This book illustrates the many ways leaders cultivate and model caring within their community to extend collective responsibility for student, staff, and family success. These stories show how vital it is for today's school leaders to act with compassion and urgency so that all students, staff members, and community members have advocates, are acknowledged, and feel worthy, valued, and cared for."

**Joellen Killion**
*Senior Adviser*
*Learning Forward, The Professional Learning Association*

"As a teacher and principal for nearly twenty years, I highly recommend this book to all educators needing a return to the well that drew us into the profession in the first place. The premise and stories in the book tap into the common thread that unites all educators but is often overlooked—a care for humanity. Smylie, Murphy, and Louis remind us that an ethos of caring is a resilient, sustainable, effective road to the Rome we seek for our students and communities. The stories in the text are perfect for a mid-afternoon reading with leadership teams, faculty, or preservice teachers as a way to reground ourselves in the work that ultimately matters most."

**Christian Sawyer**
*Principal, Hamilton Middle School*
*Denver Public Schools*

"*Stories of Caring School Leadership* centers us in the reality that our most essential and basic need is to feel known and cared for. It is through our connection to each other that we grow and thrive. This book brings years of research on school leadership to life. It serves as a powerful resource for school leaders as they deepen their commitment to foster caring within their schools. Stories move people and without a doubt the readers of this book will be drawn, moved, and compelled to invest again and again in the students, educators, families, and communities that they serve."

**Sonia Stewart**
*Executive Officer of Organizational Development*
*Metropolitan Nashville Public Schools*

"This book is a treasure trove of meaningful and beautiful stories that illustrate the power of caring between educators, students, and families. The book begins by defining caring in the context of schools, followed by a cogent argument for why we need to understand and practice caring. At the start of each collection of stories, there is a set of focusing questions to deepen the reader's engagement with and reflection on the stories. This book would be valuable for the preparation of school leaders, as well as for self-study and professional development."

**Megan Tschannen-Moran**
*Professor, William & Mary School of Education*

"This collection of stories demonstrates the importance of building caring relationships with children and their families in order to create a school culture where learning can take place. You will find examples of how school leaders show students and their families empathy, kindness, and compassion. This book is a must read for educators who want to see the Professional Standards for Educational Leaders brought to life."

**Jacquelyn Wilson**
*Executive Director, National Policy Board for Educational Leadership*
*Director, Delaware Academy of School Leadership, University of Delaware*

*To*

*Rachel,*
*LC,*
*and*
*Dan*

# Stories of Caring School Leadership

Mark A. Smylie, Joseph F. Murphy, and Karen Seashore Louis

A SAGE Publishing Company

FOR INFORMATION:

Corwin
A SAGE Companyy
2455 Teller Road
Thousand Oaks, California 91320
(800) 233-9936
www.corwin.com

SAGE Publications Ltd.
1 Oliver's Yard
55 City Road
London EC1Y 1SP
United Kingdom

SAGE Publications India Pvt. Ltd.
B 1/I 1 Mohan Cooperative Industrial Area
Mathura Road, New Delhi 110 044
India

SAGE Publications Asia-Pacific Pte. Ltd.
18 Cross Street #10-10/11/12
China Square Central
Singapore 048423

Acquisitions Editor: Ariel Curry
Development Editor: Desirée A. Bartlett
Editorial Assistant: Caroline Timmings
Production Editor: Tori Mirsadjadi
Copy Editor: Megan Markanich
Typesetter: Hurix Digital
Proofreader: Lawrence W. Baker
Cover Designer: Janet Kiesel
Marketing Manager: Sharon Pendergast

*Library of Congress Cataloging-in-Publication Data*

Names: Smylie, Mark A., author. | Murphy, Joseph, 1949- author. | Louis, Karen Seashore, author. | Smylie, Mark A. Caring school leadership.

Title: Stories of caring school leadership / Mark A. Smylie, Joseph F. Murphy, and Karen Seashore Louis.

Description: Thousand Oaks, California : Corwin Press, Inc., 2021. | Includes bibliographical references.

Identifiers: LCCN 2020021916 | ISBN 9781071801826 (paperback) | ISBN 9781071801840 (epub) | ISBN 9781071801857 (epub) | ISBN 9781071801864 (ebook)

Subjects: LCSH: Educational leadership–Psychological aspects. | Caring. | Moral education.

Classification: LCC LB2806 .S5838 2021 | DDC 371.2–dc23

LC record available at https://lccn.loc.gov/2020021916

This book is printed on acid-free paper.

MIX
Paper from responsible sources
FSC www.fsc.org   FSC® C008955

20 21 22 23 24 10 9 8 7 6 5 4 3 2 1

# Contents

## Collection II:
## Stories of Cultivating Schools as Caring Communities

## Collection III:
## Stories of Fostering Caring in Families and Community

# List of Illustrations

# Preface

## This Book and How to Use It

In the many years that the three of us have worked in educational leadership and school improvement, we have come to believe that caring lies at the heart of schooling and promoting the learning and development of children. We have also come to believe that caring is an essential quality of school leadership. We are not alone in our thinking. Abundant evidence from research shows the importance of caring and support, along with high expectations and intellectual rigor, to the academic success of students. Educators know how essential it is for students' learning and well-being that they are in strong, trusting, caring relationships with adults and peers in and beyond school.

In 2020, we wrote a book exploring the concept of caring and its application to school leadership. That book, *Caring School Leadership* (Corwin), surveys writing and research from education, related academic fields and disciplines, and the human service professions. It identifies practices that school leaders might use to be caring in their relationships with students, cultivate their schools as caring communities, and foster caring in families and communities beyond the school. This book of stories is a companion to *Caring School Leadership*. On the pages that follow, we present stories that illustrate concretely many of the practices of caring school leadership discussed in that book.

## Purpose of This Book

The purpose of this book of stories is to illuminate, instruct, and inspire. Through these stories, we portray key elements of caring school leadership practice. We expose aspiring and practicing school leaders to possibilities of practice that might make their leadership more caring. We encourage school leaders to be reflective about their own practice and to challenge themselves to make caring a central quality of their leadership.

The stories in this book are true. They describe events, actions, and interactions that occurred among real people in real places. Many stories are recounted by practicing and retired school leaders. Teachers, parents, and others also tell about their experiences with school leaders. Some stories are autobiographical. Some describe caring leadership observed or experienced. We do not intend for the stories in this book to stand for generalizable evidence of the efficacy of caring school leadership or any particular leadership practice. Instead, we see these stories as existence proofs of the possible.

We assembled this book of stories for several audiences. One audience is aspiring and practicing school leaders. Another audience is those in higher education, professional associations, and other organizations that support the preparation and professional development of school leaders. We also believe that this book of stories can be useful to teachers and school staff, parents, and others for developing caring leadership in schools and for defining expectations for their own school leaders.

We developed this book of stories as a resource for individual principals and other school leaders to read and reflect upon. We consider it a basis for stimulating discussion about caring within school leader preparation and professional development programs. We also see it as a starting point for administrative leaders and teachers to consider together to develop strong and effective school leadership and improve schools for students. We will discuss more specifically how to use this book at the end of this introduction and at the end of the introductions to this book's three collections of stories.

We offer no analyses and no interpretations of the stories herein. We want these stories to speak for themselves. We want you to hear the storytellers' voices, not ours. Importantly, we want you to reflect upon these stories and discuss them with others. We want you to analyze them yourselves, give them your own meaning, and apply them to your own situations and practices.

## Our Starting Point

This book proceeds from our belief in the legitimacy and power of stories for the development and promotion of leadership practice. As writers from psychiatrist Robert Coles to organization and management scholar Henry Mintzberg observe, stories have a way of calling us to consider what is right and true. Stories play an increasingly important role in programs of educational leadership preparation and professional development. Teaching cases are widely promoted as an effective means of helping aspiring and practicing school leaders understand the nature of their work, examine their own practice, and develop new ways to exercise leadership.

Stories also play an important role in informal learning of practicing school leaders. Oral storytelling is a primary means of on-the-job information sharing and knowledge development. So too are stories of programs and practices told through the pages of professional magazines. Stories are an important means of vicarious learning for school leaders. Sometimes ignored by academic scholars who favor more systematically developed quantitative evidence to guide practice, such stories can be powerful sources of new knowledge, legitimation, and motivation among practicing school leaders.

## Elicitation and Selection of Stories

We began eliciting stories of caring school leadership during the early stages of work on our book *Caring School Leadership*. As we spoke with aspiring and practicing principals and other school leaders about caring, we often heard them express their thoughts and experiences through stories. Many of these stories were vivid and profound, capturing action and interaction and revealing both thought and emotion.

At the start, we asked for stories from practicing and aspiring school leaders in university classes we taught. We branched out to seek stories from educators with whom we worked in professional development activities. We went further to collect stories from individual educators we know from our work in schools and from our neighborhoods. We sought stories from principals, associate principals, department chairs, teachers, and others who interact with principals and other school leaders. We did not elicit stories from students, although some of the stories told by adults recall their experiences as students. Student stories hold great promise for a future project on caring in schools and school leadership. Nor did we engage in systematic sampling. Despite this, we ended up with an archive of stories that come from a wide range of schools across many settings. While they may not be considered dispositive evidence of the phenomenon of caring in school leadership, our stories are evidence of actual occurrence and of possibility.

We were fairly general in what we asked of our storytellers. From some, we asked for stories that reflected what *they* mean by caring in school leadership. From others, we asked for stories that reflected *our* developing thinking about the subject, notably key elements that make school leadership caring. As our archive of stories grew, we elicited stories of particular aspects of caring school leadership practice to ensure that we had sufficient numbers of stories to illustrate each arena of practice represented in this book.

We asked our storytellers to tell stories that related in one way or another to students. And most of our stories focus on them. The reason we sought and included several stories of caring for teachers, parents, and families is our belief that caring can beget caring. To be caring of teachers and parents is to model and inspire them to be caring of others, notably students. It is hard to imagine teachers becoming more caring of students if they do not feel cared for themselves, especially by school leaders.

Beyond such guidance, we gave our storytellers liberty to tell the stories they wished to tell. They could share autobiographical stories about their own work and experiences as school leaders. They could share stories of other school leaders. We told them that they could write in first or third person, and we told them that they could use dialogue they remembered. Our only stipulation was that the events in the stories had to have actually happened. We told our storytellers that they did not have to tell of only positive instances of caring. We encouraged them to tell stories of problematic caring or caring gone wrong. Caring is often complex and not always straightforward. However well intended, it can create problems—even harm. We did not want this book to be a collection of only feel-good or happy stories. Of course, there are many positive stories of caring in this book, but there are also negative ones. There are stories of crises and exceptional circumstances. There are also stories of everyday events. Some stories are quite dramatic, while others feel routine. All of the stories—positive and negative, ordinary and extraordinary—speak to the importance of caring in school leadership.

The vast majority of our stories were written by educators. Several were told to us in a class or conversation, and we put them into writing. Several stories are of interactions or incidents that we witnessed and wrote ourselves. In addition, we found and adapted several stories from news sources, magazines, and books.

By the time we began to prepare this book, we had amassed nearly two hundred stories. From this archive, we selected one hundred stories for this book. These stories illustrate important ways in which caring school leadership is practiced. The stories in this book are *not* a comprehensive representation of the untold number of ways that school leaders can be caring in their work. They are but a sampling and what our storytellers chose to share with us. We strongly suggest that when you read and reflect upon these stories, you also think beyond them to other ways that caring can manifest itself in school leadership.

We selected stories from different types of schools and settings. You will read stories from preschools, elementary schools, middle schools, and high schools. You will read stories from urban, suburban, small-town, and rural schools and communities. And you will read stories from public and independent schools, well-resourced and underresourced schools, and economically and racially diverse as well as homogeneous schools. The stories in this book come from across the country. Not surprisingly, most come from regions in which we live and work. About 40 percent of the stories are from the Midwest; 35 percent are from the South and Southeast; and nearly 25 percent are from the East and West Coasts, the Southwest, and the North and Northeast. They come from seventy different school districts or municipalities from New York City to Los Angeles, from Atlanta to Minneapolis, and many points in between. Several stories come from outside the United States from Africa, Canada, and Mexico. Approximately 47 percent of stories come from urban settings, 25 percent come from suburban settings, and 28 percent come from small-town and rural settings.

Our stories are published with the permission of their authors, who are recognized by name in the book's acknowledgments. To protect the privacy of persons in these stories, we do not associate our storytellers' names or school names with the stories themselves. We also removed or altered information that might serve to identify individuals or places. Pseudonyms are used. For the few stories that appeared in published sources, complete removal of identifying information was not possible. To illustrate the variety of schools and locales from which these stories come, we follow the title of each one with a reference to the role of the storyteller (e.g., principal, teacher, parent), the locale (e.g., small town, rural, suburban, urban), and grade level of the school (e.g., elementary, middle, high school).

## Student Artwork

Throughout this book, you will find pieces of student artwork on caring in school. We asked a teacher in an educational summer camp program in Nashville, Tennessee, to engage three diverse groups of elementary school students in a simple exercise. Using a single prompt that we supplied, she asked these students to draw a picture to show how they felt to be cared for in their schools. We requested that she not give her students any additional guidance other than to encourage them to draw anything that came to mind. It did not matter if students felt like drawing a scene depicting people or an abstraction of shapes and colors conveying emotion. The objective was for students to express whatever caring in schools might look like and mean to them. With the help of a high school teacher and a pastoral associate of a church in Oak Park, Illinois, we engaged groups of middle and high school students in similar exercises, asking them to think about caring both in and out of school. Finally, using the same process, Corwin elicited drawings through its website.

We selected nearly thirty of the drawings and placed them throughout the book. These drawings can be thought of as graphic stories of how students perceive caring. The names of our contributing artists and their grade levels are shown beneath their drawings, as are titles we gave to each.

## Organization of This Book

We organized this book as a companion to our book *Caring School Leadership*. While each book stands on its own and each can be read independently, we wanted to make it easy for our audiences to read across both volumes. We wanted readers of *Caring School Leadership* to readily find in this volume stories that illustrate practices discussed in that book. We wanted readers of this book of stories to take up *Caring School Leadership* and find without difficulty discussion of the concept of caring school leadership and of different arenas of caring leadership practice.

To these ends, we arranged this book to parallel the organization of *Caring School Leadership*. We begin this volume by introducing our concept of caring school leadership and describing key elements that make school leadership caring. We also identify and describe three broad arenas of caring school leadership practice that stories in this volume illustrate. These topics are discussed in greater depth in the Preface and in Chapters 1 and 2 of *Caring School Leadership*.

Following this introduction are three collections of stories—one for each of the three general arenas of caring school leadership practice described in *Caring School Leadership*. Collection I contains stories focusing on being caring in relationships with students. Collection II contains stories of cultivating schools as caring communities. And Collection III contains stories of providing care and fostering caring in families and communities beyond the school. The leadership practices illustrated in Collections I, II, and III are discussed in detail in Chapters 3, 4, and 5 of *Caring School Leadership*.

Stories within Collections I and II are grouped by level of school—elementary schools and secondary schools (middle and high schools). Otherwise, stories are presented in no particular order. There are fewer stories in Collection III than in Collections I and II largely because the third arena of caring leadership receives less attention in school leaders' work. As we discuss later, much of school leaders' time and attention is focused inward to their schools rather than outward to families and communities.

Each collection is prefaced by a short introduction that summarizes the elements of caring school leadership practice illustrated by the stories therein. We have numbered all the stories in this book sequentially, and we have indexed them by number in each of the collections according to the primary caring leadership practices they illustrate. We provide this reference system so you can easily find stories in which you may be interested. We made no effort to index all the leadership practices reflected in each of the stories. The practices in most stories are far more numerous and nuanced than we can reference this way.

As we mentioned earlier, we make no effort to analyze, interpret, or convey meaning that we might attribute these stories. It is important for *you* to read, reflect upon, and make meaning of these stories for *your own* understanding and practice. Most of the stories in this volume provide direct lessons on the nature and function of caring in school leadership. Some stories are ambiguous and can be interpreted in different ways. You may find some troubling, and you may disagree with the thinking and actions of the school leader. You may also argue with other readers about what particular stories mean. We include ambiguous and negative stories because, along with positive and straightforward ones, they can be important sources of learning.

## How to Use This Book

There are many ways that you can use this book. You can use it for independent reading and reflection. You can read and think about the stories, beginning with the first one and moving through the book to the last. Or you can flip through the stories, skipping around, reading those stories that are of particular interest to you. You can read this book by yourself, considering a story or two every day as a centering activity. You can form or join a group of school leaders to read and discuss these stories together, exploring with others their meaning, reflecting on your own assumptions and thinking, and considering how they might apply to your own situation and practice.

This book can be used as a resource for programs that prepare aspiring school leaders for service and as a resource for programs of professional development for practicing school leaders. This book can serve as case material for instructors and groups of learners to read, analyze, and apply to their own situations and practice. We strongly recommend working with these stories in groups.

The stories in this book can serve as a foundation for a variety of learning activities. They can be used as examples of practice to be analyzed and discussed, reflected upon individually and in groups, and considered points of comparison to learners' own thinking and practice. These stories can become the basis of role playing, whereby learners assume the roles of persons in the stories and act out the story line as written or as key facts of the story might be changed. Learners can create and improvise extensions of stories, imagining, acting, and discussing what might come next and why. Moreover, these stories can be used to help aspiring and practicing school leaders tell their own stories about particular situations, persons, or contexts. Composing one's own stories and conveying them to others can help learners organize their thoughts, reflect upon their own assumptions and actions, and raise important issues. Sharing stories can stimulate collaborative analysis and joint problem solving. Sharing stories can be both instructive and inspirational. Indeed, there are many other learning activities that might spring from this book of stories.

Last but not least, this book of stories can be used by practicing school leaders in working with faculty, staff, parents, and students. For principals and other school leaders who wish to strengthen caring in their schools and classrooms, these stories can provide sources of learning for all—that is, concrete examples of caring action and interaction that can be thought about, discussed, and perhaps adapted and applied. These stories provide vivid examples of caring school community that schools may wish to cultivate. They provide examples for developing caring school leadership among teachers as well as administrators. Importantly, they can help schools collectively develop shared expectations for caring in administrative and teacher leadership alike. We envision these stories being used in teacher professional development workshops, in professional communities, and in schoolwide improvement sessions. We can see these stories used to remind administrators and teachers of the aims, virtues, and mindsets of caring and the importance to students of cultivating caring school communities. Indeed, we can imagine a principal starting each faculty meeting with a story of caring to recenter the work of the school around a core value. We can imagine these stories serving as a springboard for administrators and staff to tell their own stories to stimulate expanded and deeper caring.

At the end of the introductions to each collection, we provide a set of questions to guide your reading, reflection, and discussion of stories. We crafted these questions so that they may be readily adapted to individual reading and reflection, group discussion, leader preparation and professional development, and joint administrator-staff work in schools. Each set of questions is organized into three subsets. The first subset contains questions to promote general understanding of caring, its key elements, and its expression through action and interaction. The second contains questions to develop understanding of the particular practices within each collection. The third subset contains questions to promote reflection upon and application of practices in the stories to readers' own situations. These questions ask readers to compare their own assumptions, biases, and practices with those reflected in the stories. They ask readers to consider context and how stories might play out similarly or differently in their own situations. They ask readers how they might answer the question that is the title of the long-running ABC television series *What Would You Do?* if presented with situations in the stories.

Our questions were inspired by a number of authors and teachers, such as Gordon Donaldson, Robert Garmston, Parker Palmer, and Donald Schön. We favored questions that direct readers toward understanding and meaning, and that push readers toward personal and professional reflection.

Many writers of teaching case materials propose a rational sequence of steps for case analysis. Generally, these steps begin with understanding the facts and establishing what happened in the case. Readers are then asked to define the problem of the case, diagnose the causes of that problem, search for and assess alternative ways to address the problem, decide upon a course of action, and finally reflect upon the likely outcomes of that action. Along the way, readers are asked to consider rationales for their responses. There is merit in applying such an approach to working with the stories in this book. At the same time, not all the stories lend themselves well. Sometimes such an approach fails to encourage personal or emotional engagement and reflection. Moreover, we recognize that school leaders often think quite differently about real-life problems and situations of practice and may employ other approaches effectively. With this in mind, we designed our questions to invite and support a wide range of mindsets and strategies to engage the stories.

Finally, we hope that you find these stories enjoyable to read, that you find them challenging, and that you find them reaffirming of the importance of caring in school leadership. We hope that you find them illuminating, instructive, and inspirational.

# Acknowledgments

This book is inspired by scores of practicing educators with whom we have worked in schools and in our classrooms. It is also inspired by the K–12 students who we see prosper in schools when they are both challenged and cared for.

We are deeply grateful to those practicing and retired educators and others who contributed stories to this book. We are indebted to the following persons, listed alphabetically, who shared their stories with us and gave us permission to share them with you:

Jacob Bellissimo, Renee Blahuta, Melissa Brock, Maya Bugg, Mary Bussman, Heather Byrd, Kristin Cantrell, Beth Cohen, Michael Cormack, TJ D'Agostino, Miah Daughtery, Lora Dever, Clinton Dowda, Vince Durnan, Jonathan Ellwanger, Andrea Evans, Abigail Felber-Smith, Kim Finch, Richard Frank, Ari Frede, Lauren Gage, Chris George, Nick Gesualdi, Joseph Goins, Andrew Goltermann, Cathey Goodgame, Heather Harris, William Hayes, Victoria Hollis, Robyn Huemmer, Jordan Hughes, Catherine Humphrey, Jeni Irwin, Avery Kenly, Kristyn Klei-Borrero, Debra Klein, Peggy Korellis, John Marshall, Matt Matthews, Cathy McGehee, Matt Miller, Alecia Mobley, Peter Monaghan, Monique Morris, Milton Nettles, Melinda Novotny, Emily Lilja Palmer, Julie Pavlini, Alice Phillips, Carolyn Probst, Renee Racette, Jake Rodgers, Ken Roumpos, Maisha Rounds, Matt Rush, Beatriz Salgado, Molly Sehring, Lisa Shalla, Julie Shively, Josh Simmons, Nicolle Smith, Chase Spong, Sonia Stewart, Nancy Strawbridge, Malia Turnbull, Jennifer Vest, Laura Vilines, Joan White, Ingrid Wilson, Jacquelyn Wilson, Tracy Wilson, Chris Winningham, Nancy Wong, Amy Woodson, Jim Woywod, Mary Yeboah, and Carol Young

We thank Lauren Gage, Avi Lessing, and Alicia Reese for their invaluable assistance to elicit student artwork for this book. We thank Anna Caldwell for editing and preparing many of these drawings for publication. Personal appreciation is extended to Sallie Smylie for her keen eye, critical perspective, patience and good humor, and sense of the whole puzzle we were trying to assemble as we were focused on individual pieces.

We thank Desirée Bartlett, Ariel Curry, Eliza Erickson, Janet Kiesel, Megan Markanich, and Corwin for help to bring this book to life. We are particularly grateful to Arnis Burvikovs for taking the chance on this project and for his steadfast support throughout.

Finally, we are ever so grateful to our families for their love, caring, and support.

## Publisher's Acknowledgments

*Corwin gratefully acknowledges the contributions of the following individuals:*

Elizabeth Alvarez, Chief of Schools
Chicago Public Schools
Chicago, IL

Neil MacNeil, Headmaster
Ellenbrook Independent Primary School
Ellenbrook, Western Australia

Angela Mosley, Principal
Essex High School
Tappahannock, VA

Catherine Sosnowski, Associate Professor, MAT program
Central Connecticut State University
New Britain, CT

Christian Zimmerman, Dean of Students
South Fort Myers High School
Fort Myers, FL

# About the Authors

**Mark A. Smylie** is professor of education emeritus in the Department of Educational Policy Studies at the University of Illinois at Chicago and visiting professor in the Department of Leadership, Policy, and Organizations at Peabody College, Vanderbilt University. Before his work in higher education, Smylie was a high school social studies teacher. Smylie served as secretary-treasurer of the National Society for the Study of Education and as a director of the Consortium on Chicago School Research at the University of Chicago. Smylie has worked with schools, school districts, and school administrator and teacher professional associations through joint projects, advising, and professional development activity. He has served on advisory boards of numerous regional and national professional and policy organizations concerned with education generally and leadership in particular. Smylie's research focuses on school organization, leadership, and change.

**Joseph F. Murphy** is the Frank W. Mayborn Chair in the Department of Leadership, Policy, and Organizations and associate dean at Peabody College of Education at Vanderbilt University. He has also been a faculty member at the University of Illinois at Urbana-Champaign and The Ohio State University, where he was William Ray Flesher Professor of Education. In the public schools, Murphy has served as an administrator at the school, district, and state levels, including an appointment as the executive assistant to the chief deputy superintendent of public instruction in California. He was the founding president of the Ohio Principals Leadership Academy. Murphy's work is in the area of school improvement with special emphasis on leadership and policy.

**Karen Seashore Louis** is Regents Professor and Robert H. Beck Chair of the Department of Organizational Leadership, Policy, and Development at the University of Minnesota. She has previously held positions at Tufts University; Abt Associates, Inc.; Harvard University; and the University of Massachusetts Boston. She has served in numerous administrative positions at the University of Minnesota, including director of the Center for Applied Research and Educational Improvement Department, chair of Educational Policy and Administration, and associate dean of the College of Education and Human Development. Louis's research investigates school improvement and effectiveness, leadership in school settings, and knowledge use in education. She enjoys collaborating with school administrators as they consider how their problems of practice become important questions that can be addressed with data.

**Smylie**, **Murphy**, and **Louis** are the authors of *Caring School Leadership* (2020; Corwin), the companion volume to this book.

Care Is Key. Kai Short, Grade 12

# Introduction
## Caring School Leadership[1]

We begin this book of stories by examining the concept of caring and why we should care about caring in schools. We examine key elements that make a person's actions and interactions caring. We also explore how caring works—that is, how it leads to particular outcomes for the ones cared for and the ones caring. We apply these ideas to school leadership, presenting a model of caring school leadership and discussing important considerations for its practice.

## Why Care About Caring in Schools?

There are four important reasons to care about caring in schools and to work to promote it (see Figure 0.1). First, caring is an intrinsic good, elemental of the human condition, and a worthy endeavor in its own right. According to education philosopher Nel Noddings,

> Natural caring [is] the condition that we ... perceive as "good." It is that condition toward which we long and strive, and it is our longing for caring—to be in that special relation—that provides the motivation for us to be moral.[2]

### Figure 0.1

**Why Care About Caring in Schools?**

| |
|---|
| 1. Caring is an intrinsic good |
| 2. Caring is crucial to the learning and development of children and youth and their success in school |
| 3. The alternatives to caring are unacceptable |
| 4. Caring is highly variable in schools today |

Similarly, philosopher Milton Mayeroff argues this:

> Through the caring of others, by serving them through caring, a [person] lives the meaning of his own life.... [H]e is at home not through dominating, or explaining, or appreciating, but through caring and being cared for.[3]

---

[1]This introduction is adapted from sections of the book *Caring School Leadership* (Smylie, Murphy, & Louis, 2020). We do not refer here to the substantial literature that we used in that book to develop and support our arguments. For specific citations, readers are asked to consult that volume.
[2]Noddings (2013, p. 5).
[3]Mayeroff (2017, pp. 2–3).

Such observations about caring can be found in literature and the arts, religion, and the human service professions. Author Langston Hughes writes through the character Jessie Simple in *Simply Heavenly*, "When peoples care for you and cry for you—and *love* you—they can straighten out your soul."[4] Nursing scholar Patricia Benner and medical researcher Judith Wrubel speak of caring as "the most basic human way of being in the world."[5]

A second reason to care about caring is because it is crucial to the learning and development of children and youth and to their success in school. It is, as Noddings puts it, the "bedrock of all successful education."[6] Research repeatedly emphasizes the importance that students place on caring in schools to their engagement, conduct, and academic success. Studies have linked caring relationships with adults and peers to healthy brain development and cognitive and social-emotional functioning. Research has shown relationships between caring and a number of positive psychological states, including self-concept, self-esteem, self-efficacy, safety, hope, and persistence. Caring is also associated with children's capacities for resilience, sense of belonging, social-emotional development, and prosocial behaviors, such as cooperation, communication, empathy, and responsibility. These, in turn, enable academic learning and performance. In addition, caring can lead to more caring. Children and youth who experience caring from adults and peers are more likely to act in caring ways themselves.

A third reason to care about caring is that the alternatives are unacceptable. Lack of caring or harmful uncaring can impede positive learning and development. Research, such as that by child psychiatrist Bruce Perry, indicates that lack of caring and support can negatively affect cognitive development and impede caring social behavior.[7] It can negatively affect children's ability to manage stress and form attachments with others. For students, lack of caring can lead to feelings of isolation, lack of attention, antisocial behavior, negative attitudes toward school, and poor academic engagement—all contributing to low academic achievement.

A fourth reason to care about caring in schools is that we cannot assume that caring is a present and unproblematic quality of schooling. There is a paradoxical notion that caring is present and strong in schools because caring is what schools are supposed to do. Health and social care expert Ann Brechin calls this an assumption of "spontaneously occurring caring"[8] that is not always borne out in student experience. Research shows that educators often see caring when students do not. Studies show that substantial portions of students do not see their schools as caring, encouraging environments. In fact, caring is highly variable in schools today, particularly for students of color, students of low socioeconomic backgrounds, low-performing students, and students placed at risk. Education researchers Maxine McKinney de Royston and her colleagues observe that positive teacher-student relationships are not the norm for African American male students.[9]

Ironically, the way in which most schools are organized makes caring problematic. Bureaucratic structures and hierarchical relationships, lack of resources, inconsistencies among programs and policies, and the stresses and strains these conditions impose restrict opportunity and create obstacles to meaningful, caring relationships in schools. Moreover, the approaches we have taken recently to improve schools, notably regimes of curricular specification, testing, and accountability, have made developing supportive caring relationships among adults and students all the more difficult.

---

[4]Sanders (2004, p. 201).
[5]Benner and Wrubel (1989, p. 368).
[6]Noddings (2005, p. 27).
[7]Perry (2002).
[8]Brechin (1998, p. 2).
[9]de Royston et al. (2017).

# What Do We Mean By Caring?

We use the word *caring* to represent qualities of relationships and of actions and interactions that exhibit concern, provide support, nurture, meet students' needs, and promote their success and well-being. We distinguish between *care* and *caring*. Care refers to an action provided on behalf of another. According to occupational sociologists Pamela Abbott and Liz Meerabeau, when associated with particular vocations, such acts are considered professional care or caregiving.[10] Acts of care are very important to address students' needs and concern. To us, however, caring involves more. Caring is not only what one does but also why and how one does it. Caring involves the matter, manner, and motivation of care as well as its competent provision. It is a particular way of being in relationship with others. Caring involves observing and assessing; identifying with; and responding to the situations, needs, interests, and concerns of others. It involves expressing particular positive virtues such as compassion, empathy, and respect. Caring is driven by motivation to achieve the betterment of others.

Caring is not simply *caring about*—that is, having concern or sentiment for someone or something. It is important to care about students and their success. However, it is another thing to be caring of them. According to Benner and journalist Suzanne Gordon, caring includes but goes beyond feelings of concern and sentiment to actions and interactions—practices—of being in relationship with others and achieving particular aims on their behalves.[11] Psychiatrist Arthur Kleinman observes that caring means both worrying and actively *doing something* about those worries.[12]

Caring is not defined by specific actions or interactions. Nor is it defined by a particular set of activities that are necessarily different from those in which one regularly engages. Caring is not necessarily another responsibility that adds to one's job description and workload. All actions and interactions—all activities—can be viewed through a lens of caring. Again, *caring*, as we define it, is a *quality* of a relationship—the matter, manner, and motivation of personal and professional action and interaction.

# What Makes Action and Interaction Caring?

From our study, we find three elements that together make actions and interactions caring: (1) the pursuit of particular aims, (2) the activation of positive virtues and mindsets, and (3) competent enactment (see Figure 0.2). These elements form a system of antecedents to caring. Each may have personal and professional dimensions. Moreover, the expression of these elements in caring action and interaction may be affected positively or negatively by a variety of interrelated contexts.

**Figure 0.2**

**What Makes Action and Interaction Caring?**

| |
|---|
| 1. Pursuit of the aims of caring |
| 2. Activation of positive virtues and mindsets |
| 3. Competent enactment |

---

[10] Abbott and Meerabeau (1998).
[11] Benner and Gordon (1996).
[12] Kleinman (2019).

# Aims of Caring

Caring is neither aimless nor agnostic in purpose. For actions and interactions to be caring, they must focus on achieving particular purposes. Caring aims to promote the functioning, general well-being, and success of others, as individuals and as groups. Caring addresses particular needs of others and promotes their interests. Caring aims to help others grow and flourish in their own right. Caring is sometimes framed as a response to pain, suffering, and trouble. But it can be proactive and an affirmative expression of joy and celebration. Caring can also be a worthwhile endeavor in itself.

Caring can aim to address particular needs, problems, and concerns. It can aim to achieve tangible benefits, the manner in which and the motivation by which they are provided being as important as the benefits themselves. These benefits can come from what we described earlier as care: particular services and provisions. Caring can aim to promote certain intangible benefits—social, psychological, emotional, and behavioral—that accrue from being in caring relationships and feeling cared for. Finally, caring can aim to promote further caring.

It is not difficult to think about particular aims of education that relate to caring. We consider the general purposes of schooling to provide for students' safety and nurturance; support their learning, development, independence, self-reliance, prosocial relationships, and ability to function in and contribute to community; promote academic success and general well-being; and prepare students for work, further education, and citizenship.

## Positive Virtues and Mindsets

A second element of caring consists of positive virtues and mindsets that are brought to the pursuit of the aims of caring. These virtues include compassion, empathy, patience, sympathy, and kindness. They include fairness and justice, authenticity, humility, and vulnerability. They also include prudence, transparency, honesty, trustworthiness, and respect for others and their integrity.

Four positive mindsets are particularly important to caring. The first is attentiveness to others. If caring is to address others' needs and interests, one must be attentive to understand, deeply and genuinely, who persons are and what their needs, concerns, interests, and situations might be. Another mindset is motivational orientation. If caring truly means acting on behalf of others, one must be motivated accordingly, and this orientation cannot be diminished by attention to one's own needs and self-interests. Attentiveness and motivational orientation toward others do not lead to permissiveness nor abdication of responsibility. Rather, they become a positive basis for the fulfillment of responsibility. As theologian Eugene Peterson argues with regard to the helping professions generally, "If we do not keep our assignment, we do not care."[13]

A third type of mindset consists of personal and professional identities related to caring. How persons see themselves as caring or uncaring human beings and as capable or incapable of caring will likely affect their efforts to be caring. Likewise, how persons see themselves in a professional role, what they perceive the norms of the profession to require of them, and what they perceive as others' expectations for them in their role may influence caring. A fourth mindset is playfulness. This mindset reminds us that caring is not a dour enterprise. Although difficult and taxing at times, it can be joyful and fulfilling. Moreover, playfulness is a way of knowing, seeing, and engaging with others that encourages creativity, inventive thinking, and flexibility. Playfulness can reveal the world

---

[13]Peterson (1994, p. 71).

through others' eyes—a view that is essential to understanding others, their situations, and ways to be caring of them.

## Competencies of Caring

In addition to aims and positive virtues and mindsets, to be caring requires competency. According to Benner and Gordon, professional practice "is always bound up in knowing and doing."[14] Effort and sincerity are important and may be appreciated, but particular actions and interactions may not be perceived as caring or very helpful if they are uninformed, inadequate, misguided, or poorly performed.

In caring, one important area of competency is knowledge and authentic understanding of others and their needs, problems, joys, concerns, and situations. If educators have inaccurate understanding of who students are and what they want and need, they may make well-meaning attempts to be caring but ultimately miss the mark as to what is caring and helpful in the eyes of students. Developing such understanding is related to one's ability to inquire, listen and hear, observe and see, assess and understand, and learn about others. Social-emotional intelligence is particularly important to caring and caring school leadership. Also important is understanding persons' and groups' races, classes, genders, sexual orientations, languages, cultures, religious beliefs, and relevant contexts. Education scholar Audrey Thompson argues that "the possibility of adequate responsiveness to others depends upon our being able to understand their situations in ways that do not simply reduce them to projections of our ... assumptions."[15] She continues that "[school] administrators need to understand the full picture of the worlds in which their students move."

A second area of competency concerns understanding the relative effectiveness of strategies to address the needs and concerns of others and to promote their interests. This includes knowledge and skills to engage these strategies successfully. Caring requires knowledge and skill to develop or select, adapt, and enact practices that pursue the aims of caring; that bring virtues of caring to life; and that align with the understanding of others, their situations, and their joys, needs, and concerns. Caring further requires the ability to wrestle with ethical and practical dilemmas posed by different and competing needs and considerations.

A third area of competency concerns knowledge of self and the ability to develop and deepen one's own capacity for caring. Knowledge of self involves understanding one's orientations and inclinations, strengths and limitations, and predispositions and prejudices. Recognizing the sources of one's fears and joys may be crucial in thinking and acting in a caring manner.

A fourth area of competency, especially important to school leaders, consists of knowledge and skills for developing caring among others and creating organizational contexts conducive to caring. This area includes understanding how to think about caring as a property of classroom and school organization, not only as a quality of interpersonal relationships. It includes knowledge and skill related to professional learning and development and organizational change. It encompasses knowledge and skill to create supportive structures and processes, to design work and social arrangements, and to develop organizational cultures imbued with the virtues and mindsets of caring.

---

[14]Benner & Gordon (1996, p. 50).
[15]Thompson (1998, pp. 541, 543).

# How Does Caring Work?

As we mentioned earlier, caring is associated with a number of positive outcomes for students. These outcomes can accrue from caring both big and little. By this we mean that caring can be expressed in major decisions and pivotal actions and interactions. Equally important and strongly influential are the small, routine ways that caring is expressed through everyday actions and interactions that nurture feelings of respect, trust, support, and dependability. Small gestures of caring can make big differences.

## Explanations of Outcomes

There are three general explanations for how and why caring may lead to these outcomes. The first focuses on psychological mechanisms triggered by caring. Attachment theory suggests that positive social relationships—in this case, caring relationships—promote feelings of safety, security, and comfort through the mediation of threat and stress. These emotional states are important preconditions for exploration, facing stress and uncertainly, risk-taking, and engagement in learning. Self-determination theory suggests that for persons—children and youth in our case—to become motivated, needs for relatedness, competency, and autonomy must be addressed. Adults can meet these needs through caring, providing clear rules and expectations, and giving children freedom to make their own choices. If these needs are met, children will be more confident and motivated to engage in learning activities. Consequently, they will learn more and achieve at a higher level.

A second explanation comes from logical arguments that link different factors related to caring found in theory and research. For example, care and support received by students have been found to be related to student affiliation and sense of belonging in schools and classrooms. Care and support have also been found to be related to students' sense of competency and self, notably academic self-concept and self-efficacy, among other positive psychological states. Care and support are also related to student motivation to learn and academic engagement. Through these intermediary outcomes, care and support—along with academic rigor, challenge, and press—promote social and academic learning. In short, caring social relationships power up certain psychological states of students, which deepen engagement—and that, in turn, fuels social and academic outcomes.

A third explanation is that caring may promote actions that provide tangible provisions and services to address the needs and interests of others. As such provisions and services are provided, benefits may accrue. For example, out of caring by a teacher or principal, a child may receive eyeglasses that help them see better in class, become more engaged in learning activities, and be more successful academically. Out of caring, a principal may initiate an antibullying program, which increases student physical and psychological safety and promotes engagement and learning.

Of course, these several explanations can be bound together to provide a robust understanding of how caring works. An important additional point is that the outcomes of caring are best understood in terms of the totality of caring—the systems of caring—that persons experience across settings, including family and friendship networks, schools, churches, and other institutions. Histories of caring or noncaring relationships and experiences are important also. Systems of caring are dynamic, and their elements likely influence each other. For example, while the close relationships students have with family, teachers, and close peers may affect them most, relationships with other adults in extended families, schools, and communities and with other peers will also have an effect. Elements of a system of caring relationships may be differentially strong, weak, or absent for different students.

Caring may be particularly strong for some students in family and community but weak or absent in school—or vice versa. The strength of caring in some relationships may compensate for weakness in others. Again, it is the totality of caring that is important.

Caring can have important benefits for the ones caring—in our case school leaders as well as teachers and other staff. It can lead to joy and personal and professional satisfaction and fulfillment. It can increase self-esteem, motivation, agency, persistence, and overall mental health. These positive outcomes can, in turn, enhance the prospects of ongoing and deeper caring. The experience of caring can lead to more caring as it satisfies a sense of personal and professional calling. It can propel a virtuous cycle of caring.

## Influence of Contexts

Several related contexts can affect caring and its outcomes positively or negatively (see Figure 0.3). Noddings observes that caring occurs in and through social relationships that constitute an interpersonal context.[16] Most conducive to caring are interpersonal contexts that are enduring; that are personally deep, open, honest, and revealing; that are characterized by trust; and in which attention is given both to the present and how the present relates to the past and the future. In interpersonal contexts that are shorter in duration, are more shallow, are lacking in transparency and honesty, grow from mistrust, or fail to acknowledge the past or consider the future, caring is less likely to form and grow.

**Figure 0.3**

**Contexts That Affect Caring**

| | |
|---|---|
| 1. | Interpersonal contexts |
| 2. | School organizational contexts |
| 3. | Contexts beyond the school (e.g., family; community; larger social, political, and economic forces) |

Organizational contexts can also enable or impede caring. Particularly relevant to caring in schools are structures that create opportunities for students, teachers, principals, and other staff to interact and learn about each other; to form long-term, deep, and trusting relationships; and to engage in caring action and interaction. These structures include the ordering of programs, goals, roles, responsibilities, and relationships. They include the organization of time and work, systems of social and academic support, as well as academic press—performance expectations and means of accountability. They also include incentives and rewards that can direct attention and action toward caring.

In addition to structural elements, school organizational climate and culture can affect caring. By climate we refer to the perceptions that students, teachers, and administrators have of each other, of their relationships, and of the school as a place for caring and learning. Particularly important to caring and other supportive behavior is how students and adults perceive the ethical climate of the school. A school's organizational culture—that is, its system of orientations, taken-for-granted assumptions, and values as well as the symbols, rituals, and routines by which they are communicated—sets expectations for caring and establishes a foundation for mutual accountability in caring. Other aspects of organizational context can be important for caring in schools. Power and authority relationships and processes of school decision-making create conditions that can support

---

[16]Noddings (2013).

or impede caring. How a school balances collective and individual interests and how it engages in competitive and adversarial or consensual and constructive politics can be important to caring. Also relevant is how a school may rely on consolidated or expansive and inclusive distribution of power and influence.

Beyond the school are extraorganizational contexts that can affect systems of caring. These contexts include families, communities, and broad policy and social-historical-cultural environments. Notable are social resources in families and communities and characteristics of the broader environment. Norms and values that emphasize the individual, such as independence, self-sufficiency, competition, and individual success, are less supportive of caring than those that emphasize community, such as interdependence, cooperation, and collective responsibility and accountability. In communities, resources for caring include social-emotional support from peers and from nonparent adults, such as relatives, family friends, and neighbors. Opportunities for caring and support can also come through community organizations and the resources and services they can provide. These include civic organizations, recreational and youth development programs, health care and social support services, religious congregations, businesses, and local government. Economic and political forces, crime and violence, racism and other forms of oppression, and population instability can mitigate these community resources and caring generally.

## Problems and Pitfalls

Caring does not always function in a straightforward or positive manner, even when it is enacted with the best intentions. Boundaries must be negotiated. Relationships need to be monitored and managed. Caring can cause embarrassment and make persons feel vulnerable. If not careful, caring can evoke a sense of obligation that is inappropriate or impossible to fulfill. Caring can also lead to objectification—people can be seen as inanimate problems to solve and relationships can become contrived.

Moreover, acting on particular virtues can create dilemmas as one virtue may bump up against another. According to education ethics scholars Joan Shapiro and Jacqueline Stefkovich, such dilemmas present ethical choices to be managed.[17] For example, caring can create tension between acting in the best interests of an individual student and abiding by the rules and policies of the school or district. Acting in the best interests of individuals and groups can create tensions with the interests of the whole and with values of fairness and equal treatment of all.

Some virtues that drive caring can bring both benefits and unexpected problems at the same time. For example, psychologist Paul Bloom observes that empathy can be a positive force on how we act and interact with others by making it possible to resonate with their positive and negative feelings.[18] At the same time, empathy can be superficial and biased. It can set a cognitive trap by which presumptions can be reinforced to the detriment of another person. Neuroscientists Tania Singer and Olga Klimecki contend that through empathy we feel happy when we vicariously share the joys of others and we feel pain when we share the suffering of others.[19] Shared feelings of pain and suffering can be difficult, sometimes leading to stress and distress, which then can lead to negative feelings, withdrawal, antisocial behavior, blame, and burnout. To guard against this prospect, empathy must be linked with compassion—that is, to feelings of warmth, concern and care for another, and motiva-

---

[17]Shapiro and Stefkovich (2010).
[18]Bloom (2018).
[19]Singer and Klimecki (2014).

tion to improve the other's well-being. Compassion directs empathic thinking toward positive action and helps avoid empathy's pitfalls and problems.

Caring can lead to unintended and potentially harmful consequences. For the ones caring, it can be extremely demanding and psychologically, emotionally, and physical stressful. Caring can result in what communications scholars Katherine Kinnick, Dean Krugman, and Glen Cameron call *compassion fatigue*, the emotional overload that occurs when one gets overinvolved, overextended, and overwhelmed by the emotional demands imposed by others.[20] Finally, caring can spawn unintended harmful consequences for the ones cared for. Caring relationships can develop inappropriate dependencies, codependencies, and transference. They can result in unwarranted control, subjugation, and infringement of privacy, autonomy, and rights. In the worst instance, the interpersonal closeness of caring can create opportunities for abuse and victimization. Without careful attention, without mindfulness and self-regulation, and without the monitoring and watchful support of others, the risk of negative consequences can emerge.

# A Model of Caring School Leadership

Applying this discussion of caring, we define *caring school leadership* as leadership that is itself caring, which proceeds from the aims of caring, positive virtues and mindsets related to caring, and competencies for the expression of caring in action and interaction. We believe that caring is not a specific domain of leadership, nor is it a discrete set of leadership strategies. While its practice may vary depending on the people involved, interpersonal and organizational contexts, and the environments surrounding the school, it is a quality or property of leadership generally.

School leaders certainly care deeply and passionately about many things—children's learning, development, and success in school being paramount. Caring about children and their success is good but insufficient. We can care strongly about important things but act in ways that do not measure up. School leaders must go farther and be caring in their actions and interactions regarding that which they care about.

As a quality of relationship, as a quality of action and interaction, caring can permeate almost everything that a school leader says and does. It can cross the span of school leadership work. Any aspect of leadership can be caring, noncaring, or even uncaring. What matters is that a school leader brings the aims, virtues, and mindsets of caring to life through competent action and interaction. As organization and management scholars Peter Frost, Jane Dutton, Monica Worline, and Annette Wilson remind us, care and compassion are not antithetical to or outside of normal work: "They are a natural and living representation of people's humanity in the workplace."[21]

The relational aspects of leadership—the trusting interpersonal relationships that leaders form with students, teachers, and parents—lie at the heart of caring school leadership. Yet caring leadership is not confined there. Caring can be infused in developing and promoting a school's mission, vision, and core values. It can be integrated into expectations for teaching and student learning. Caring can be a driving force of academic program development and implementation, of instructional leadership, of providing services for groups of students, and of allocating resources to support teaching and learning. Caring can shape the nature of academic demand and support, testing and accountability,

---

[20]Kinnick, Krugman, and Cameron (1996).
[21]Frost, Dutton, Worline, and Wilson (2000, p. 25).

student discipline, and administrative decision-making. Caring can guide programs of outreach to families and the school's community.

## Our Model

Following the main points of our discussion, we present a model of caring school leadership in Figure 0.4. This model contains three major components: (1) foundational elements for caring leadership; (2) arenas of caring school leadership practice; and (3) student outcomes. Reflecting how caring works, our model traces with arrows relationships among these components and how each relates to others. Our model does not focus on every aspect of school leadership or how the totality of school leadership work might be performed in a caring manner. Rather, it focuses on three key arenas of practice particularly associated with caring for students: (1) caring in interpersonal relationships with students; (2) cultivating schools as caring communities; and (3) fostering caring in families and communities beyond the school. While caring for teachers, staff members, parents, and families is critically important, our model focuses on students because their learning and development, their academic success, and their overall well-being are the primary responsibility of school leadership.

Our model shows caring school leadership proceeding from the aims, positive virtues and mindsets, and competencies of caring. It suggests that the presence and strength of these elements enable and shape the character and impact of caring leadership practice. At the center of the model lie three arenas of practice particularly associated with caring for students. The first arena involves school

**Figure 0.4**

**A Model of Caring School Leadership**

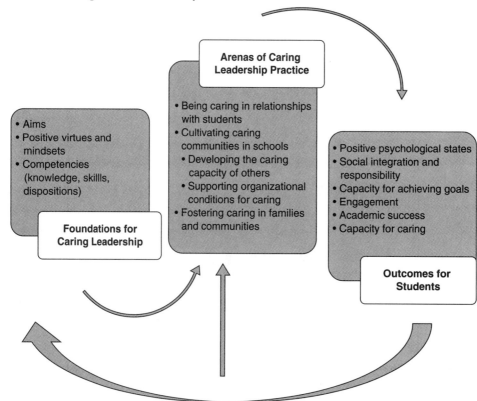

leader caring in interpersonal relationships with students. The second arena, cultivating schools as caring communities for students, involves developing the capacity and context for caring within the school. This arena encompasses work to develop caring learning environments in classrooms and in student-teacher and student-peer relationships. It also involves work to develop organizational conditions that support the development and enactment of caring throughout the school. The third arena of caring school leadership practice focuses on fostering caring for students beyond the school in families and in the community at large. Bridging the gaps between schools and families and communities is a crucial part of school leaders' work for which many leaders feel ill-prepared. It is work to which most principals devote little time. Nevertheless, we know that school leaders can play an important role in developing the broader systems of caring that students experience and that contribute to their growth, success, and well-being.

In the lived work of school leaders, these arenas of practice are often intertwined, but our model does not presume that they are. A school leader may be particularly attentive to interpersonal caring with students but not to developing the school as a caring community—or vice versa. A leader may be strong in working outside the school with civic leaders and community organizations on behalf of students and their families but weak in interpersonal caring of students and developing caring within the school. Our model allows for the possibility of one arena of caring school leadership practice compensating for another.

We would expect principals to act in caring ways and provide caring support to students with whom they are able to form trusting interpersonal relationships. At the same time, to ensure that every student receives caring support, principals can promote teacher and staff caring so that each student experiences caring relationships with a number of adults in the school. By doing this and in fostering caring in families and communities, principals need not take on all the work themselves. Principals will be much more effective if they develop the capacity of others, work in partnership with others, and guide and support others to step up and be better at caring.

The right side of the model shows the student outcomes that we expect from caring school leadership. The model identifies several types of outcomes important to students that we discussed earlier, including positive psychological states, social integration and responsibility, capacity for achieving goals, engagement, academic success, and capacity for caring. The model indicates that the stronger the practices of caring school leadership, the more likely caring's benefits to students will accrue. We recall that students benefit most when the totality of caring they experience is strong and positive.

The major parts of the model are laid out in linear order, indicating with one-way arrows that the foundational elements of caring shape caring leadership practice and, in turn, promote student outcomes. The model indicates with feedback arrows that student outcomes can shape the nature of caring leadership practice and the three foundational elements of caring. For example, students' responses to positive experiences of caring may motivate leaders to continue those practices. When students ignore or resist particular actions or interactions intended as caring, attentive leaders may seek more information, reflect, and perhaps alter what they are doing. While it does not depict them, our model recognizes the importance of dynamic and interrelated interpersonal, organizational, and extraorganizational contexts. These contexts and the importance of developing and managing them are emphasized by our framing of the three arenas of caring leadership practice. While the arrows in the model suggest a sequential order of elements, the reality of leadership generally and caring school leadership in particular is more nonlinear and dynamic.

Finally, we recognize that there may be crucial differences between our model's application to a caring leader's relationship with an individual student and its application to a leader's relationship with a whole student body, with adults in a school, or with families and community. We also recognize there may be differences between the caring of an individual school leader and the caring that emanates from a schoolwide community. The latter may hold additional meaning and exert greater influence than the sum of individual interpersonal caring therein.

## Considerations for Practice

As we move to the collections of stories that illustrate how caring school leadership can be practiced, we take a moment to explore several important considerations (see Figure 0.5). The first is that the practice of caring school leadership is framed and guided by the profession of school leadership. While not inseparable, there is a distinction between personal caring as part of being human and caring as part of one's professional role and responsibility. The profession of school leadership defines the purpose, foci, and scope of caring school leadership work and pairs it with professional knowledge, orientations, and skills. The profession also defines critical boundaries that distinguish personal from professional caring and that distinguish caring school leadership from caring work in other human service professions.

**Figure 0.5**

**Considerations for the Practice of Caring School Leadership**

| 1. | Framed and guided by the profession of school leadership |
|---|---|
| 2. | The subjects of caring—for whom and for what should school leaders be caring |
| 3. | Caring as principled practice |
| 4. | Caring as a way of promoting educational equity |

School leadership focuses primarily on organizational leadership and management of schools to promote the learning, development, and well-being of students. According to the National Policy Board for Educational Administration Professional Standards for Educational Leaders 2015 (PSEL), school leadership in all its forms and functions is to be guided by professional norms of integrity, fairness, transparency, trust, collaboration, perseverance, learning, and continuous improvement. School leaders are to place children at the center of education and accept responsibility for each student's academic success and well-being. School leaders are to safeguard and promote the values of democracy, individual freedom and responsibility, equity, social justice, community, and diversity. They are to lead with interpersonal and communication skill, social-emotional intelligence and insight, and understanding of all students' and staff members' background and cultures. In addition, school leaders are to provide moral direction for the school and promote ethical and professional behavior among faculty and staff.

A second consideration concerns the subjects of caring—that is, for whom and for what school leaders should be caring. The PSEL make clear that in all areas of their work, school leaders should care for and be caring of students, their academic success, and their overall well-being. Caring school leadership should have concurrent concern for individual and groups of students as well as teachers and professional staff. This concern centers on the school as an organization and how it supports a caring community for students, teachers, and staff. Caring school leadership also concerns others outside of school who affect students' lives in school and in general. Most immediately, this includes families and helping families be caring of students. It involves enacting caring work in communities, being an advocate on behalf of children and families, promoting conditions that support children, and improving conditions that impede their learning and development. Caring school leadership applies to caring for the institution of schooling and for education in democratic society. Finally, caring school leadership encompasses caring for the profession and its ability to serve children, families, and communities well.

A third consideration is viewing the enactment of caring school leadership as principled practice. By this we mean that the practice of caring school leadership is propelled by principles of purpose, positive virtues and mindsets, and norms that orient the nature of one's relationships with others—particularly meeting the needs and concerns of others, promoting the betterment of others, and helping others fulfill their human potential. The practice of caring school leadership is also principled as a moral and ethical endeavor that resides within the norms, expectations, and boundaries of the profession. The practice of caring school leadership evokes orientations toward others as human beings and how we see ourselves in professional roles working on behalf of fellow human beings, living and working in community, and being responsible for one another.

The practice of caring school leadership can also be viewed as principled in recognition of the situational and dynamic nature of leadership. Situational perspectives emphasize that effective leadership requires fashioning specific actions and interactions to fit particular objectives, tasks, situations, persons, and contexts. Inasmuch as these considerations are also continually changing, leadership practice must also continually change. It is therefore very difficult and not appropriate to consider leadership practice as a uniform set of discrete, immutable strategies or behaviors. Leadership practices that are similarly effective in different situations and settings can look very different. This recognizes the importance of thoughtfully and strategically aligning practices to situations and adapting those practices as situations change. Such alignment requires that norms and principles guide action choices. What makes caring school leadership principled practice is consistency with the aims of caring, the virtues and mindsets that orient and drive the pursuit of those aims, and the competencies that translate intention into actions and outcomes.

A critical consideration for practice is educational equity. We believe that caring school leadership is an essential means of promoting educational equity in schools. We have woven equity into the design and fabric of our model. We see every aspect of the model contributing to it. To be genuinely caring of students, a school leader would be caring of each and every student, especially those students who have been marginalized, who struggle to fit in and achieve in school, who have not received support, and who have not been provided high-quality opportunities to learn. To be caring calls on school leaders to work on behalf of each student, address their needs and concerns, help them achieve their interests, move forward on their life projects, and promote their well-being and human potential.

To be caring is to be driven by virtues that require a school leader to value and be empathetic and compassionate to each student, to be kind and fair, honest and authentic, patient, trustworthy, and respectful. To be caring demands that leaders be attentive and understand each student for who they are as individual learners and persons. This involves understanding them as members of groups; of races, ethnicities, religions, and cultures; and of different socioeconomic situations, each with historical and social and political dynamics. To be caring is to be motivated to support each and every student's success and well-being and to act in ways consistent with the knowledge and understanding derived from caring's attentiveness. The foundational elements of caring pull school leaders away from unproductive, deficit ways of thinking about some students and direct leaders toward more positive ways of thinking about and acting toward all students—ways that are socially, racially, and culturally responsive, equitable, and efficacious. Caring does not mean lowering expectations. Education leadership scholar Muhammad Khalifa argues the following:

> Principals must both take the lead ... [as] "warm demanders" and maintain relationships directly with students. These relationships will allow leaders to encourage students to succeed academically in ways that students will interpret through the lens of love and care.[22]

It is difficult to imagine any other pathway. Caring leads toward equity of opportunity for every student. Moreover, it is difficult to imagine credible school leadership for educational equity that does not place caring at its core.

We now turn to our three collections of stories of different ways in which caring school leadership is practiced. Each collection represents one arena of practice shown in our model of caring school leadership.

---

22   Khalifa (2018, p. 158).

# Stories of
## Being Caring
## in Relationships
## With Students

# Introduction

This collection of stories illustrates the first arena of caring school leadership practice: how principals and other school leaders can be caring in their relationships with students. These stories focus primarily on the interpersonal aspects of leadership. They show how principals and other school leaders can develop caring relationships with their students. They also show what principals and other school leaders can do so that these caring relationships become more trusting, helpful, and durable. Many of these stories illustrate the benefits to students and school leaders when caring relationships form and flourish.

Each story in this collection makes visible in one way or another the aims, positive virtues and mindsets, and competencies of caring. Like stories in the other collections, not all of these stories are positive. You may find some ambiguous and even troublesome. Some you might consider *negative* examples, revealing problems that may arise out of the best of intentions.

The stories in this collection are grouped by level of school. Otherwise, they are not presented in any particular order. Nor do they represent the full extent of ways that principals and other school leaders might be caring in their relationships with students. You may begin by reading stories from the level of school in which you are most interested, but we *strongly* encourage you to read stories from the other level for the insights and lessons they provide. An example of caring in a high school

**Hug? Andrew Dominic Bachmann, Grade 2**

or middle school may be very helpful in an elementary school and vice versa. Across the stories in this collection, pay attention to the importance of knowing and understanding students both as persons and as learners. Consider the role of context and how principals' and other school leaders' knowledge, skills, assumptions, biases, and sense of professional role function in their relationships with students.

A number of the stories in this collection illustrate accessibility and presence in developing caring relationships with students. It is difficult to imagine principals being able to know students, understand their needs and interests, and be caring of them if they are not accessible and present. Presence is both physical and mental, the latter meaning that principals must be continually mindful of students to be caring of them. Many stories illustrate different ways that principals and other school leaders can be attentive to students to know and understand them so as to be caring of them. Some of these stories show practices of observing and noticing and how leaders can inquire to increase their knowledge and understanding of students. Most of these stories also illustrate how principals and other school leaders not only listen but hear what students have to say. Several stories demonstrate the importance to some students of persistence and longevity in caring relationships—even what can happen when caring relationships end.

Most of the stories in this collection portray different ways in which principals and other school leaders can act or give care on behalf of students to address their needs and help them learn and grow. Some illustrate ways in which principals and other school leaders discern the needs and interests of individual and groups of students to provide meaningful help and assistance, doing so in a caring manner. Several stories tell how school leaders engage others on behalf of students. Sometimes acting in the best interests of students means making difficult decisions, perhaps engaging in what René Antrop-González and Anthony De Jesús call *hard caring*. Several stories illustrate hard caring, and some tell of decisions and actions with which you may not agree. Last but not least, several stories show how acting on behalf of students can conflict with district rules and how principals bend these rules toward the students rather than bend students toward the rules.

Figure 1.1 shows the stories in this collection, by number, in which examples of such caring school leadership practices can be found. You may use this figure to navigate your way through the collection.

# Questions for Reflection and Discussion

## General Questions

1. How does each story reflect the three foundational elements of caring school leadership described in Introduction: Caring School Leadership in the beginning of this book? (a) The aims of caring? (b) Positive virtues and mindsets of caring? and (c) Competencies of caring? In what ways might these three elements be strong or weak in the story? How might these strengths or weaknesses shape the actions and interactions of the school leader and any outcomes apparent in the story? How might caring in the story be seen as a part of everyday work rather than as something *extra* that school leaders do? How can the caring demonstrated by school leaders in these stories help others in their schools to be more caring?

2. How might the school leader's assumptions, understandings, and biases affect the way each story unfolds and the outcomes apparent or that might be expected? How might different contexts affect the story? The qualities and characteristics of interpersonal relationships? The organizational context of the school? The environment beyond the school?

Figure 1.1

**Caring School Leadership Practices Represented in Collection I Stories**

| Practices | Story Numbers |
|---|---|
| Being accessible and present | 1, 2, 5, 6, 8, 9, 10, 12, 14, 15, 17, 19, 20, 23, 24, 26, 31, 32, 33, 35, 36, 40 |
| Observing and noticing | 1, 2, 3, 5, 6, 7, 9, 13, 14, 16, 17, 18, 23, 24, 26, 27, 30, 31, 32, 36 |
| Inquiring to learn about students | 2, 3, 5, 7, 9, 10, 11, 13, 14, 15, 16, 17, 20, 23, 24, 26, 30, 31, 32, 36, 40, 42, 43 |
| Listening and hearing | 1, 2, 5, 6, 7, 9, 10, 11, 14, 15, 16, 18, 19, 24, 25, 26, 31, 40, 42 |
| Being persistent | 2, 4, 10, 15, 16, 18, 22, 26 |
| Discerning students' needs and interests | 1, 2, 3, 4, 5, 6, 7, 12, 13, 14, 16, 17, 25, 26, 27, 28, 30, 31, 32, 34, 39, 41 |
| Providing help and assistance | 1, 2, 3, 5, 7, 8, 10, 12, 13, 15, 16, 17, 18, 26, 27, 28, 29, 30, 32, 37, 38, 41, 43, 44 |
| Engaging others on behalf of students | 2, 3, 8, 16, 17, 27, 41, 42, 43, 44 |
| Hard caring | 22, 34, 41 |
| Bending rules toward students | 4, 9, 13, 15, 21, 29, 30, 39 |

3. What do you see as the main lesson or lessons of each story? If you were to write a moral for each story, what would the moral be?

4. What is your personal reaction to each story? Why do you react this way? What might be influencing your thinking?

5. Imagine that the school leader in the story met you and asked, "What do you think about what I said and what I did?" Looking through the eyes of the different people in the story, how would you respond? What advice would you give to this school leader?

# Collection-Specific Questions

1. Think about how the professional responsibilities of school leadership might shape the nature of caring interpersonal relationships that principals and other school leaders form with their students. Where are the appropriate professional boundaries? Where are the ambiguities and dilemmas? How do these considerations appear in the stories and, where they do, how well do school leaders attend them?

2. What professional and personal ethical issues do these stories raise? What legal issues? Where such issues are apparent, what advice would you give the school leader to address them?

3. In what ways are knowledge and understanding of students as persons and as learners important to the actions and interactions of school leaders in these stories? In what ways do

school leaders' efforts to further their knowledge and understanding of students contribute to their ability to be caring? In what ways do insufficient or incorrect knowledge and understanding make caring more difficult and less effective?

4. How do these stories illuminate the importance of the ordinary, everyday things in developing and deepening caring relationships with students?

5. How do these stories help you better understand the types of assistance that might be helpful to students? How do these stories help you better understand the ways in which the caring motivation and manner of rendering assistance influence how assistance is received by students and how assistance actually helps them?

## Application Questions

1. How might your own assumptions, preconceptions, and points of view influence how you read and make meaning of these stories? Consider your understanding of yourself as a caring person and a caring school leader, including your strengths and weaknesses in being caring of others. Consider your understanding of what the professional role of a school leader requires of you; what your situation calls on you to do; and what your students, your staff, and your community expect of you. How does your thinking and sense of self affect how you practice caring in this arena of leadership?

2. Put yourself in the position of the school leader who is the focus of each story. Would you think and act in the same way in the situation described in the story? Why or why not? In what ways might you think and act differently? Why?

3. For each story, recall a similar, actual situation in your school. How would you retell the story for your own setting, with yourself as the focal school leader? In what ways would your story be similar? In what ways would your story be different? Why?

**Holding My Hand. Hadley Green, Grade 2**

4. Consider the positive ways that school leaders in these stories form, maintain, and deepen caring relationships with students. How might you adopt and adapt these positive practices in your own setting with your own students? What factors—personal, professional, and contextual—might support or impede your effort? How might you address impediments to make your effort more successful?

5. Consider the difficult aspects of being caring of students that are revealed in these stories. Do you see similar difficulties with some of your students? Are there other difficulties? How might you address these difficulties? How do you think about being caring when the student or the situation is difficult as opposed to when the student or the situation is easy? What do you do in such situations to become more caring? How do you think about being caring when you have to make tough and unpopular decisions about a student or a group of students? When you must administer hard caring? When your decisions may be consistent with your understanding of the best interests of students but may not be understood or received that way?

6. What other leadership practices and strategies, beyond those illustrated in these stories, might be effective to strengthen caring in your interpersonal relationships with individual students and groups of students in your school? Explain why you think these practices and strategies might be effective in your situation. Explain the groundwork that might need to be done to increase the likelihood of their success.

# Stories From PreK and Elementary Schools

## 1. Walk You to School?

—Told by the principal of a suburban elementary school
*Adapted from Stevens (2019).*

It was the last day of the school year. The bell had just rung for students to head to their classrooms. I was out and about on the playground helping latecomers into the building and made my way up to the third floor when I saw the mother of one of our students, Mati, and his resource teacher on the phone. Mati is a first grader. He is on the autism spectrum, and changes, like the end of the school year, can be challenging and frightening for him.

The teacher and mom were talking with Mati. The teacher had seen the mom walk Mati's twin brother to school but did not see Mati. She asked about him. The mom said that Mati was still at home, and he was refusing to come to school. Too daunting, the mom explained. Mati had dug in. "I am not going to school," the mom said,

repeating Mati's words. "It's the last day, and I am not going. Period." "Perhaps we can FaceTime him," the mom said to the teacher. "Maybe if he sees you, he'll feel better and be willing to come."

So they dialed Mati. From the doorway I heard both of them use all their tools and tricks to get him to agree to come, but he wasn't budging. I stepped in and asked if I could join in the call. When he saw me with his teacher and mother, Mati lit up. He said, "Mr. E, why are you on the phone? You're calling my house?" I asked Mati if he'd like to know what was on the lunch menu that day. I asked if he'd like to come join us for the last day of school. And then I said, "Well, buddy, would it help if I just walk over to your house and pick you up to go to school? I've never been to your house!" Mati replied,

**Be Nice. Bronwyn Massey, Grade 2**

"Yeah! Yeah, that would work! Daddy, is that OK?" It was OK. I asked Mati if he knew his address and he did. I said that I'd be right over.

A few minutes later I was at Mati's door ready to escort him to his final day in the first grade. Once we were on our way, it was just the two of us talking, just shooting the breeze. We talked about what he'd be doing this summer. We talked about what we're going to be having for lunch. We talked about our days. When we arrived at school, I walked him to his classroom. Mati was no longer anxious, and he had a good last day in the first grade.

I know that often a little grease for the wheels is all that somebody needs, a little change of pace.

A new face. I just offered to get Mati unstuck, and in this instance a little bit of grease is what was needed. Mati's just one of our Bryan School Bobcats. Every principal I know would have done what I did. Every teacher here would have certainly done the same thing if they had the freedom and time to go walk down the block. For all of us, little things are big things. If we put ourselves in places where we can really get to know our students, see their needs, hear about opportunities to help, and ultimately offer to accompany our students, we can help them to help themselves. This was a little thing, but it's what we do and what we are trying to be about as a school.

---

# 2. Terry

—Told by the assistant principal of a small-town elementary school

Terry was in a downward spiral of behavior choices and grades. He was increasingly lashing out at his third-grade teachers, saying things like "This is stupid! You're dumb, and I hate you!" He even told his math teacher to shut up! He began throwing objects, hitting his fist on desks, and engaging in other disruptive behavior.

Just prior to this increase in behavioral outbursts, Terry had broken his hand severely during a bike wreck. He was in pain and was undergoing therapy to regain use of his hand. This meant that he was missing class time. His teachers tried different strategies in the classroom, such as allowing Terry to take naps because he was noticeably tired. They tried to watch for triggers and were becoming increasingly frustrated themselves. They began sending Terry to my office.

At first, I did some of the same things as the teachers. I gave him a place to rest and calm down. But as his behaviors continued to increase, I recognized nothing we tried was working. There was discussion among the teachers, the principal, the guidance counselor, and me about what new steps we could take. We did a day of in-school suspension (ISS), then another. His behavior continued. I went to the principal and

shared that the suspensions weren't working. "There's something going on. Perhaps it's the hand or something more." I suggested giving Terry a mentor within our building, an adult he would feel comfortable around and looked up to. I had learned over the course of those few weeks that Terry had some turmoil going on at home—no dad in the picture and mom was in and out. I talked with Terry about who he might like to check in and check out with each day. Knowing he liked to draw, I suggested our new art teacher. His eyes lit up! They started meeting every morning and afternoon to discuss his day.

We had a calm period for several days, but then once again an outburst occurred. During the calm time, I had been discussing Terry with a behavior specialist, and she shared some suggestions to give the check-ins and check-outs more meat. So, when Terry came to my office this time, I gave him time to calm down, and then we talked through what his body was feeling and what he was thinking so he would begin to recognize warning signs within himself. We then talked through what to do and develop a plan of what he could do when he knows he is getting angry and frustrated. Terry opened up and shared personal feelings at this point, and we came up with a plan that was personal to him. He liked the calm spots but wanted to have his fidget spinner with him to help. It was special to him because his mamaw gave it to him. He said he liked to have tight hugs too—they always made him feel better.

I shared the plan with his teachers, the art teacher, and our counselor with Terry in the room so he knew we were all on board. I created visual reminders because he liked the idea of having them. Has it been absolutely perfect? No, but he is using his strategies more, and he is better verbalizing his feelings instead of *exploding*, as he called it.

I have made it a point to check in on Terry during breakfast time. I also check in with him a few days a week to see how his strategies are working. The team is fully on board and is providing the supports to help Terry have more success. Around the time of the last *exploding* behavior, the team reached out to mamaw to support her and provide resources Terry might need to deal with some of the issues affecting him when he is home.

# 3. Ana

—Told by a former head of a Catholic preschool

Ana had a terrible fear of separation from her parents that began when she was about one and a half. By preschool, she had made some progress, but leaving her mom, in particular, remained just as challenging as it was when she was a toddler. Ana would become extremely upset as they drove to school and would cry, scream, refuse to leave the car, throw herself down on the floor in the entry hall, and grab at her mom's legs and ankles to stop her from leaving. Ana *loved* school, but the moment of saying goodbye absolutely terrified her. It was not a rational fear, but young children often have irrational fears. And those fears are just as big and real as any other. Ana is extremely bright and highly verbal and in need of some help.

I saw what was happening and how stressful it was on Ana's mom, her teachers, and Ana herself! We had tried some on-the-spot interventions but knew it was time for a plan. At some schools, staff might leave parents to figure out issues like this on their own, but we valued family and community. Ana's fears and her mom's struggles were ours too. We had to support them.

We created a safe, soothing entry routine and designated some grown-ups on standby to help as necessary. We knew we had to have some flexibility and a few layers. Some days, a ride up in the elevator with my administrative assistant was enough to facilitate the transition. Other days, time in the soft spot—a rocking chair in a semi-private corner, with stuffed animals and small and engaging toys—would do the trick. On more difficult days, we had a nook set up in a nearby storage closet. It might sound odd at first, but we decked out this little space like a bedroom for Ana and filled it with things that she loved: a giant teddy bear, some toys, a small chair, and soft blankets. It was a bit like a pillow fort, and it was just for Ana. This snug, secure, and private space allowed her to have her big feelings, to calm down, and then to rejoin the class. A team of three or four teachers took turns, using the same routine and language with Ana, quickly decreasing the time she needed in the nook before she could join the class.

We gave Ana a lot of positive affirmation. "We care so much about you, and we're so glad you are in school today. I'm here, and I'll just sit and do a little work while you take some time and let me know when you are ready to go. Why don't you set five minutes on the timer and see how you're feeling then?"

Sometimes, recognizing what a child needs and finding a way to provide it is all it takes. After a few weeks, most days, Ana transitioned without visiting the nook. And even when she used the nook, it was typically for less time than even the timer allowed. We gave Ana space to have her feelings and gave her support as she learned to *regulate* them. She can now enter class and have a successful day—loved, seen, and cared for.

# 4. I Don't Have a Knife

**—Told by a turnaround leader of an urban elementary school**

"I don't have a knife," said Jasmine.

It was hard to believe her after the report I had heard the day before, but the benefit of the doubt should still have some credence, right? All kids in my school deserve the right to be taken at their word, but the reality of the principalship means that *in loco parentis* extends beyond a single student.

Knowing Jasmine for the last couple of years, it was easy to imagine that Johnny's report of her having a knife was true. I just didn't want it to be the case. Jasmine's parents were divorced, her mom lived itinerantly in a local motel with her five siblings, and Jasmine lived with her disabled dad in their one-bedroom apartment (in a not-too-savory part of town), so the idea of her coming to school with a knife was not too far-fetched. "Jasmine, we've come a long way together. While I want to believe you, I have to look a little deeper to make sure that you're being safe." Jasmine, knowing that our relationship was rooted in the experiences of her brother, Johnny, who was taken from their home last year, decided to parlay a question: "There's nothing there. But . . . what would happen if you found something?"

After talking with Jasmine's dad and looking through her locker, the one-and-a-half inch knife was in my hand, and I was left with a choice: Do I *zero-tolerance* her, or do I approach it from a position of understanding and find a solution that keeps the ultimate outcome in view? Bringing any kind of weapon to a school is a nonstarter that must be met with a swift and strong response. But why is this student carrying a knife? What is her motivation? Is she a threat?

Jasmine and I spent the next three days together as she served the in-school suspension (ISS) that I meted out to her for her infraction. While it certainly was not the most severe of punishments, the consequence supported her growth as a student and development as a young lady. In the fallout of this situation, Jasmine's attendance improved significantly, she was more open with her counselor about her challenging life, and school continued to be the one consistency in her life of turmoil. Hardliners would likely be disinterested in my approach, but the ultimate outcome for Jasmine is one that honors her value as a person and promotes the notion that her quality extends beyond this unfortunate situation.

A long-standing relationship with Jasmine's reality provided the context to allow for a more nuanced and specific approach to a challenging situation. Leveraging that relationship and reminding Jasmine of my steady involvement in her difficult home life allowed her to lower her defenses and open herself to trust. I'm excited to see where Jasmine ends up as I know that her innate ability and caliber as a person will take her far. I'm glad that a situation in elementary school will not irreparably harm her going forward.

# 5. Opening Up

**—Told by the principal of a small city elementary school**

A bus driver came into my office. She needed to see me. She said, "I am sorry to take up your time, but I have dealt with this all year and I can't do it anymore!" I said to please come in and sit down. She sat down and said that she had a student on her bus who only rode the bus for eight minutes. She said, "This student yells and is very disrespectful. He dares me to take him to the principal's office. Basically, he is a big distraction while I am driving!"

I knew who the student was without her saying his name. He was a sixth grader with a rough home life. I asked if it was the student that I was thinking of. She said it was. I told her that I would talk to him. I would put him at the silent lunch table. I would give him a chance to improve his behavior, but if he could not, I would suspend him off of the bus. She thanked me and left.

I asked my secretary to call the student down to my office. He came down, and I invited him in. I started the conversation with "Do you know why I have asked you to come in to my office today?" He replied, "No." I told him about the bus. I told him that his behavior was dangerous because the bus driver was distracted and that could harm everyone if the bus driver wrecked. He told me that he felt that the bus driver disrespected him.

We continued our conversation. Before I knew what was happening, he told me that his mom and her boyfriend sold drugs. He told me that he listens to classmates talk about how good their life is. He said he has nice things, but he doesn't like his life. He said he wants to have adults who care about him. He said that his mom and dad fought a lot when he was younger. His dad now lives with a new woman and her children. He wants to be with his dad. He told me that he had seen his dad get tased and arrested. He told me how scared he was. He told me that people are constantly coming in and out of his house to buy drugs. He said he doesn't get sleep at night sometimes because his mom and her boyfriend play loud music and get drunk. He said that his teachers think that he is sleepy because he plays games all night. He told

me he doesn't play video games! He told me that two years ago a man hung himself on his front porch. He told me he could see his feet dangling from his window. The man had hung himself with the kid's dog's leash. He said that family services had been to his house. He said that they had called and told his mom that they were coming by. He said that his mom cleaned up the house and got rid of all of the drugs. He said that family services didn't do anything. He said that he has asthma from them smoking in the house. He told me he sounds like a goose when he runs!

The boy was crying at this point. He had been through more than anyone should ever have to go through. He didn't feel cared about or loved. I told him that he shouldn't have had to go through any of that. I told him that I was sorry. I told him that I cared for him. I told him that I would help him. I told him that education was his golden ticket to anywhere and anything. He told me he had anger issues. I told him that I could help. I told him that anytime he needed to talk I would be there. I told him that if he was about to get into trouble to come find me. I would tell him how to handle the situation and what to say.

Instead of silent lunch, I invited him to have lunch with me. He went and got a taco from the lunchroom, and I heated up my pasta. We sat together eating and chatting. We talked about how well he does in science and how he placed in the science fair. When he left my office, I felt that we really had a plan going forward. We truly connected, and he knows that I will do everything that I can for him. Moments like that are what it is all about. I may not be able to get him out of the situation, but I can be a listening ear and an adult who cares. I can help him sort through situations and give him guidance on how to cope.

## 6. Had It Gone a Different Way
—Told by the president of a nonprofit education advocacy organization
*Adapted from TED Radio Hour (2019).*

Sixth grade is difficult for a lot of kids. I know it was hard for me. I remember a fight I got into and how frustrated I felt. The boy was taller and stronger and had been taunting me for

**Are You OK? Reese Mehr, Grade 2**

weeks. That day, he stepped on my new shoes. I demanded that he apologize, and he refused. That unleased a force in me that I could not control. Looking back, that fight was less about that boy and my shoes than about many other things that were going on in my life at the time. I was so filled with anger about so many things that I grabbed him and threw him to the ground.

The fight lasted less than two minutes, but it released the fury that was building inside of me as a young survivor of sexual assault and as a girl who was grappling with abandonment and exposure to violence in other aspects of my life. I was fighting him, but I was also fighting the men and boys who had assaulted my body. I was fighting the culture that told me I had to be silent about it.

A teacher broke up the fight, and my principal called me in her office. We sat down, but she didn't say, "Monique, what's wrong with you?" She gave me a moment to take a few deep breaths and then asked, "What happened?" My principal approached me with empathy. She knew me. She knew I loved to read and to draw. She knew I adored Prince. She used this knowledge to help me understand why my actions and those of the boy were disruptive to the learning community she was leading. I was not suspended. She did not call the police. My fight didn't keep me out of school the next day. It didn't keep me from graduating. It didn't keep me from eventually becoming a teacher.

I think about that incident as a critical moment in my life. It was certainly one of those events that, had it gone a different way, there could have been a radically different outcome, not just for me at that moment but certainly for other things that happened later in my life.

# 7. Three Musketeers

**—Told by a former teacher and principal of a rural elementary school**

I recall a story from the time I was a first-grade teacher in a poor, rural school in the southeastern United States. This incident, this boy, made a profound difference in the way I thought about my work as a teacher and later my work as a school principal. Indeed, it shaped the way I have thought about my work in higher education to prepare school leaders.

I had this tough little boy named Benjamin for a student. He and his parents lived in a trailer park on the edge of town. His mom and dad worked several part-time jobs for very little money. They got by. One day, Benjamin appeared at the classroom door crying. "Someone stole my Three Musketeers bar," he sniffled.

"Come on in, Benjamin. Relax. It will be OK." I walked over to him, put my arm around his shoulder, and helped him into the room. "I'll get you another candy bar by lunchtime." This is easy, I thought. A candy bar was missing. I replace it. Benjamin is happy. Problem solved. I did not see it coming. "But my father gave me that Three Musketeers." And Benjamin began to cry again inconsolably.

I had completely missed it. I was looking at the problem through my own eyes, my own assumptions, my own understanding of what had happened and what was wrong. To me it was a missing candy bar. But to Benjamin, it

was a symbol of his father's love, his father's treat, his father's sacrifice to buy him that bar. "But my father gave me that Three Musketeers." In those few words, Benjamin had summed up the meaning of this rare gift given to him by his dad.

To try to connect with what mattered most to Benjamin, I spoke to the whole class. I explained what the loss of the candy bar really meant to Benjamin. We talked about *hurt* and how *we*, together as a class, had the ability to help Benjamin be happy again. When we returned to class after lunch and playtime, the candy bar was back in Benjamin's cubby.

Benjamin had taught me an invaluable lesson: if you don't understand a problem from the student's point of view, you are not likely to be able to address it productively.

---

# 8. Fever Free and Smiling
### —Told by the assistant principal of an urban elementary school

Six hours had now passed, and little Freda was still sitting in the front office with a 102-degree fever. The office staff had not been able to reach her mother or any other known family member. It was now time for dismissal, and little Freda had begun to break out in small hives. She had no choice but to board the bus with her brother and sister and head home sick and tired. Dr. Fields, the assistant principal, and Dr. Roy, the school guidance counselor, got in Dr. Fields's car and journeyed ahead of the bus to meet little Freda and her siblings at home and ensure that she got the medical attention that she needed.

The children arrived at the trailer park and got off the bus. Dr. Fields and Dr. Roy were standing to greet them and walk them from the street to their home. When they arrived at the front door of a tattered mobile home, Freda's older sister was afraid to let them in. "Where's your mother?" asked Dr. Fields. "She's on her way home, but we can just lock the door," Freda's sister replied.

Dr. Fields explained that he and Dr. Roy could not leave until an adult was present to receive them. After all Freda was only five, her older brother was seven, and her older sister was nine.

The older sister went to get a neighbor who barely spoke English. "Cual es telephono de madre de los niños?" asked Dr. Fields. The neighbor was able to contact the mother and provide the phone number to Dr. Fields. She agreed to stay with the children until the mother arrived. Dr. Fields knew that Freda was still very sick and that none of the children had eaten since lunch. He went to a nearby pharmacy, bought some children's Motrin for Freda, and stopped by a nearby Kentucky Fried Chicken to pick up a late afternoon meal for the children. When Dr. Fields and Dr. Roy returned to the home with the medicine and food, the mother had arrived.

Little Freda returned to school the next day fever-free and smiling.

# 9. Now What Do I Do?

—Told by the principal of a suburban elementary school

I quickly learned that most of the things I needed to know to be a principal were not taught in graduate school. There was no coursework on directing early morning traffic, mediating between fighting neighbors, organizing a Halloween parade in a thunderstorm, or what to do when a friendly but impulsive fourth-grade boy decides to bring a box cutter to school. These were just some of the moments that I stopped and asked myself, "Now what do I do?"

I had been a principal for only about seven months when several students came into the office and asked to speak with me. I'd spent most of the summer memorizing student names by using the yearbook from the previous year and quizzing myself before bed each night. My goal from Day 1 was to build relationships with students. I did a variety of things, like eat lunch with them, start a Student Council, and greet them by name whenever I saw them. Consequently, there was a group of fifth graders who felt comfortable enough to come and share their concerns.

I knew right away they were troubled by something. As their story came pouring out, my mind began to spin. One of their classmates *brought a weapon to school*! I knew the district policy on weapons, and I also knew this was going to be the topic of conversation throughout the building. If I didn't handle this appropriately, I would also have a public relations problem on my hands.

After retrieving the box cutter from the student's backpack, which was hanging on his hook in the hall outside his classroom, I walked out to recess. I found the boy, and I asked him to come with me to my office. As we slowly made our way into the building, I said to him, "I have something pretty serious to talk with you about. Would you happen to know what it is?" Immediately his head dropped lower, and he nodded. We walked into my office, and we sat at a table next to each other. In a quiet voice I asked, "Why

do you think I needed to see you?" He raised his eyes, which were now brimming with tears, and told me he brought a box cutter to school.

He told me where he found it at home and that he wanted to show his friends. It didn't cross his mind that his peers would find it scary. He never considered what would happen if he was caught. He just thought it was thrilling to bring something to school that he snuck from home.

I reached over to my bookcase and pulled down a large, heavy binder. It was our district board–approved policy book. I showed him that I had a rule book I needed to follow to make sure our school was safe. I softly and seriously explained that the rule book stated that in this situation a student could be suspended from school. Now the tears came freely. He knew he had made a big mistake.

At this point I told him that I never keep secrets from parents, so I needed to call them. It was important that his classmates noticed that he didn't return for the afternoon. I wanted them to know that they were safe and that the situation was handled. Therefore, I had the child stay in my office for the remainder of the day. I went to his classroom and collected lessons for him to do. Then with trepidation I lifted the phone receiver and called his parents.

I reached his father first. After his initial surprise, he explained that he and his wife had been doing work on the house, and he probably left the box cutter out with the other tools. He was dismayed and disappointed in his son's choices. I told him that sometimes children make poor impulsive decisions that seem completely out of character, but that didn't mean his son was bad. I told him I was glad he could learn from this mistake now, rather than in middle school. I said that I believed his son was truly remorseful and that it would never happen again. As a consequence, though, I was going to give him a one day in-school suspension (ISS). "What are your thoughts on that?" I asked. He gave a sigh of relief and told me he agreed and was grateful.

Later in the week, both parents stopped by school to say thank you. They were so kind and appreciative on how the situation was handled. They felt that we managed to protect their son's integrity yet still delivered him a serious message. I was grateful to collaborate effectively with parents who believed in being partners. Luckily, I had enough of a relationship with and understanding of these students to be able to make these choices. I was able to think with both my head and my heart. When I ask myself "What do I do now?," I remember to consider the whole child before responding to their actions.

# 10. Sheila

### —Told by the principal of an urban elementary school

Sheila came to us to begin the second grade from a Title I inner-city school with an enrollment that was majority minority. She came here—a well-resourced, predominantly white suburban school. It was difficult for her to leave a school where she was known and loved by many and come into a place where she knew no one and where few were like her.

Sheila was excited and eager to make new friends. A naturally social kid, she reached out to other kids to make friends the same way she had at her previous school—by being her precocious, outgoing, humorous self. But cultures clashed. She was not very well received by her peers or adults in the school. Every day of her second-grade year, her innocent, well-intentioned attempts to engage classmates through jokes, pokes, puns, fun, and games were resisted by other students and reprimanded by teachers. She was sentenced to lunch and recess detention nearly every day that school year, depriving her of much-needed opportunities to build positive peer relationships.

Teachers also didn't recognize Sheila's intellectual prowess. She completed every assignment accurately and often finished her work early. She aced every test and quiz, and despite a 99 percent average in every subject on her report card and requests for more challenging work, Sheila's need for advanced work and enrichment went unmet. So Sheila sought to meet that need herself. She quietly entertained herself at her desk with her school supplies. She was told to put them away. When she didn't, her teacher often took them away, annoyed at what she perceived as Sheila's refusal to follow directions. A happy-go-lucky kid, Sheila was confused by her teacher's apparent frustration with her. But Sheila never let that get her down. Refusing to let boredom get the better of her, Sheila tried to play with her classmates, but they were too busy trying to finish the assignments she had already completed.

One day, Sheila figured out a way to get her class partner to lighten up by engaging him in play. She noticed he had a really cool eraser on his desk, so she grabbed it and waited for him to respond. Much to her chagrin, he didn't. She put it back and tried again, but he still didn't seem to notice. On her third try, she snagged the eraser, then waited and waited. Surely he would notice, right? She waited and waited longer. Finally, she tapped him on the shoulder, held up the eraser, and smiled, hoping he'd smile and join the game. He didn't and yelled, "Hey, I'm telling you stole my eraser!" Shocked by his accusation, Sheila immediately returned his eraser to its resting place on his desk. "No, I didn't," she said. "I just wanted to play with you." He insisted that she stole his eraser and marched off to tell the teacher, who promptly sent Sheila to the office with a yellow office referral slip in hand.

Seated in the principal's office, Sheila read and reread the yellow slip that named her a thief, wondering how she ended up here. She had never been in this much trouble before. She had been the star student at her old school and the first-grade spelling bee champion. The trophy sat proudly atop the mantelpiece over her fireplace at home. But now, she was a thief.

Sheila's heart sank as she entered the principal's office. Not knowing what to expect, her eyes lowered to the floor. "Have a seat." She stared at her feet and sheepishly took a seat, her heart pounding in her chest, nearly ready to explode. What would happen? Would she be sent to the behavior improvement room? Suspended? Expelled? What would her parents say?

"Sheila," the principal spoke. It was a familiar voice. Sheila slowly raised her eyes and came to focus on someone she knew. In this sea of strangers, a familiar face. "Ms. Jones!" Sheila exclaimed. Her new principal had been the vice principal at her old school and knew Sheila to be a stellar student. "What are you doing here?" "I should be asking you the same thing," Ms. Jones smiled and said. "I was offered the opportunity to become principal here, and it was a tough choice. I didn't want to leave our old school because I'd miss everyone there. But seeing you walk into my office just made my day! I am so happy to see you, though not quite under these circumstances. Looks like we're both new here and still adjusting. Can you tell me about how things are going for you?"

Sheila opened up to Ms. Jones and shared her experiences, every detail, from her failed attempts to make friends and the frequent lunch detentions, down to the eraser incident. "Sounds like it's been a bit of a rocky transition for you, would you say?" Ms. Jones said. Sheila nodded. Ms. Jones asked, "May I please see your yellow slip?" Embarrassed and reluctant, Sheila handed Ms. Jones the yellow slip. Ms. Jones read it, then gingerly dropped it into the garbage can beside her desk. This simple act of kindness showed Sheila that someone at this school really knew her and actually cared about her.

"I know this isn't who you are," Ms. Jones affirmed. "You're an amazing student who's

trying to make new friends and adjust to a new school. That can be really hard. I'll tell you what. I'll give your parents a call to let them know that we talked about this, and I'll let your teacher know that we talked. But you don't deserve a yellow slip, detention, or anything like that. Just make wise choices from now on. Taking another student's belongings is not the best way to make friends. Try talking to them during lunch and recess. And I would love for you to drop by and visit me sometimes. But I don't want any more yellow slips. Think we can do that?"

Sheila nodded, grateful for the grace shown by her principal during this caring conversation. Determined to fulfill her pledge and rise to her principal's expectations, Sheila did everything in her power to keep her hands to herself. She returned to her classroom and was eyed suspiciously by her teacher, who seemed surprised by her return. Sheila received extra scrutiny after this office visit. She began to think that her teacher did not seem to care for her very much because everything Sheila did seemed to get her into trouble, although not yellow slip trouble. When Sheila asked questions, her teacher would say, "You should have been listening, Sheila!" When she answered questions, her teacher would say, "Stop calling out, Sheila!" When she finished her work early, her teacher would say, "Go back and check your work, Sheila." And when playing with other kids, her teacher would say, "Not so rough, Sheila!" "Keep your hands to yourself, Sheila. "Don't do that, Sheila." "Don't say that, Sheila." And when she tried to explain herself, her teacher would say, "Stop being disrespectful, Sheila." Sheila decided not to say or do anything in class that could spark the ire of her teacher or rejection by her peers. The vibrant, bubbly little seven-year-old began to withdraw.

By third grade, Sheila had become much quieter and resolute, promising herself she would not get in trouble this year. Noticing her change in behavior, Ms. Jones began doing regular check-ins with Sheila just to talk about her school life. These check-ins became the highlight of Sheila's third-grade year. Sheila was able to share her successes and challenges. Ms. Jones supported Sheila in navigating tricky social terrains. There was someone in this building who knew her and cared about her well-being.

This made all the difference when Sheila began being bullied at the bus stop and on the school bus. Sheila was much smaller than the other third graders and, in fact, smaller than many of the second graders. Older kids and bigger kids teased her, called her names, mocked the way she talked. "You talk so white!" they would say. Once, some kids threw rocks at her at the bus stop. After the rock-throwing incident, Sheila didn't know who to tell. It didn't happen at school. It didn't happen at home. And even if she knew who to tell, she was afraid to. It was already hard enough making friends. It would be even harder if kids believed she was a snitch.

One afternoon during the bus ride home, a second grader, Marilyn, who was twice Sheila's size and had repeated first grade, grabbed one of Sheila's long, braided ponytails and pulled hard. Sheila screamed in pain and begged her to stop. Marilyn laughed and pulled harder. The bus driver couldn't see what was happening. Sheila fought back tears, refusing to cry in front of everyone. "Stop!" Sheila screamed again. Marilyn yanked harder still and held on relentlessly. For nearly fifteen minutes, Marilyn tugged, pulled, and laughed, ignoring Sheila's pleas until the bus stopped at Sheila's destination. Marilyn promptly released Sheila's braid so the bus driver wouldn't see as he looked up into the rearview mirror at students. Sheila grabbed her backpack and ran off the bus in tears, kids' laughter spilling from the bus windows. Sheila burst into her grandmother's house and recounted the whole ordeal. Grandma checked Sheila's reddened scalp and loosened braid with grave concern. She called the school immediately and reported the incident to the principal.

The next morning, Ms. Jones called Sheila into her office to find out what happened. "I'm so sorry that happened to you, and it's not OK. Would you mind if I called Marilyn into my office right now to apologize to you?" Ms. Jones asked. Sheila consented. When Marilyn arrived, Ms. Jones asked what happened. Marilyn confessed to everything and apologized to Sheila. Ms. Jones asserted in the presence of both girls, "If you put your hands on Sheila or bother her in any way again, you will be suspended. Do you understand me?" Marilyn solemnly nodded and hurried back to class. Ms. Jones hugged Sheila and encouraged, "If anyone else bothers you or does anything to you, please let me know immediately. OK?" Sheila hugged Ms. Jones again. She felt loved and protected. Things began turning around for Sheila after that.

Such caring transformed Sheila's life. She was on the road to becoming disengaged and a discipline problem in a school system where the odds were stacked against her. Caring empowered Sheila to strive to overcome, knowing she had an ally in her corner. By the end of her third-grade year, the kids in her class had warmed up to Sheila, and she had formed a few really close connections. Some of her classmates had begun to ask Sheila for help when they struggled with math, reading, and writing. Her third-grade teacher noticed her intellect and quick wit, recommending her for gifted and talented testing in the fourth grade. Sheila was admitted into the gifted and talented program in the fifth grade. She blossomed academically and socially. She won numerous awards and was recognized for scholastic achievement.

Sheila eventually graduated from high school with honors, attended a university on a full academic scholarship, and majored in education. She taught for sixteen years trying to provide the same caring for her students who had changed her life. Sheila later graduated with high honors and a second master's degree in school leadership at the top of her class at Harvard. Committed to caring leadership and paying it forward, Sheila is currently working on her doctorate in educational leadership at Vanderbilt University. Sheila has dedicated her life to affecting systemic change to support the needs of marginalized, disenfranchised, and diverse learners like herself.

I am Sheila.

Can I Help You? Caroline Semier, Grade 2

## 11. Pizza and a Football

**—Told by the assistant principal of a small-town elementary school**

At one of the schools where I work, we have an emotionally disturbed child who has endured more than a ten-year-old should have to endure. One of our school case workers/therapists had approached me and our school resource officer about mentoring this student. We are his third school this year, and each of his previous stops resulted in a negative experience.

On the Saturday after his first week at school, the school resource officer and I went to the child's house with a football and a pizza. We invited the student, his mom, and sister to have lunch with us and allow the student to throw the football with us. It was a great time for us to get to know each other. The child smiled nonstop all day, and his experience at our school has been great ever since.

The most touching part of our outing was a card his mother sent just last week, thanking us for taking an interest in her son. She said that before, every time a school had called or visited, it was because her son was in trouble. She was thankful for the gesture of kindness and support.

## 12. Connecting

**—Told by a visitor to a suburban elementary school**

I found an empty parking space right in front of the school, as if it was reserved for me. Entering the school's vestibule, I was greeted by brightly colored walls and carpet. Student art adorned the walls and filled the display cases. Entering the front office, I was welcomed warmly by the school secretary and was offered a cup of coffee or bottled water. I was a few minutes early for my 10:00 appointment with Diane. I had spoken with her several times on the telephone but had never visited her school. I had no agenda but to meet Diane in person and see her in her element. From the waiting area, I could hear through her open office door that she was on the phone—perhaps with a parent or the central office.

Diane was off the phone at 10:00 sharp and came out of her office to greet me, apologizing for making me wait. We went into her office where, again, I was offered coffee or bottled water. Diane's office was warm and inviting. Natural sunlight poured in through the windows. The only other light in the room came from the calming yellow of incandescent desk and table lamps. No bright, sterile white of fluorescent lighting here. The colors on the walls and furniture were bright but not jarring. The prominent furniture in the office was not Diane's desk but a small table and chairs for close conversation and an upholstered reading chair. It was clear that the desk was in use, but it was tidy.

On the walls, Diane had hung photographs of her spouse, children, and parents. These photos showed Diane's family, with Diane among them, in travel and at play. These photos invited questions. Who are you with? Where were you when these pictures were taken? What are you all doing? These photos were a subtle way for Diane to reveal herself personally to students, parents, teachers, and others who might come into her office. They were a way to break the ice, begin conversations, and make connections. There were bookshelves behind Diane's desk with binders and professional books that one might expect to see in a principal's office. But across the top shelf and down the ends of each lower shelf, Diane displayed a whimsical collection of vintage children's toys and books. There were dolls and clowns, a red toy wagon, a model of an old wooden school desk, a few airplanes, automobiles, trucks, and brightly colored blocks and balls. And there was an old Remington manual typewriter. I asked how her students liked the toys. She said that they loved them, that

they asked her about them all the time. "Where did you get that?" "Was that your toy?" "May I hold that doll?" What about the photos, I asked? "Oh, yes. I get questions and comments about them all the time too."

We left Diane's office for a walk around the school. In each classroom we visited, students stopped what they were doing, delighted to see her: "Ms. Clune! Ms. Clune!" Some got out of their seats and ran up to her. The teachers did not seem to mind this at all. Diane greeted each of the students by name. "What are you working on? How cool! Well, get on with it! You'll have to tell me more later." She introduced each of them to me by name, noting something they had done of which they seemed particularly proud. Some of the boys looked embarrassed by the attention, but it was clear that each was pleased.

Coming out of one classroom, we met a fourth-grade girl in the hall, pack on her back, note in hand. It was 10:30, and she was just arriving to school. "Hi, Ms. Clune!" "Hi, Ellie! Are you just getting to school?" "Yeah. I was tired, and my mom let me sleep in." "OK. But *I* need you in school for the full day. Can you do that?" "Yes, ma'am!" "OK, get to class." As Ellie ran off to her classroom, Ms. Clune called after her. "Your hair looks great this morning!" "Thanks, Ms. Clune!" Ellie said, looking back over her shoulder. "Like my nails too?" she asked, flashing them and a bright smile without breaking stride. "Nice!" As Ellie turned the corner, Ms. Clune whispered, "I'll be calling her mom this afternoon."

We returned to Diane's office after touring the school. We sat at the table, and as we began our conversation, the school secretary entered, handed Diane a note, and whispered something in her ear. Diane calmly said, "Sorry. I've got to go." And she dashed out of the office. I gathered my things. As I was leaving, I heard the school secretary on the telephone with the police. Another staff member was talking on a walkie-talkie. A parent volunteer was in the office awaiting instructions.

The next day, I received an apologetic e-mail from Diane. "I'm so sorry to have bolted out on you yesterday. What a day!" She told me about the special education student who, in one of those very rare brief moments when no one was looking, took off from the playground and went running down the street. The teacher, afraid to leave the rest of her students with only her aide, called the office. While the police were being notified, Diane and a teacher on break jumped into Diane's car to find the student. She said that it was her personal responsibility to do so. She found him a few blocks away, hugged and comforted him, and brought him back to school safely. Diane said she was the one who called his parents to explain what happened and to reassure them. And Diane said that she and the faculty and staff would meet to discuss the incident, see what went wrong, and discuss what could be done to prevent something like this from happening again. Diane continued that later that day, another student had a severe asthma attack. Diane had stayed with the student to comfort her as medical care was provided and until her parents could come to take her home. What a day indeed! Diane invited me back to continue our conversation. We scheduled a return visit in several weeks.

# 13. Two Yearbooks

### —Told by a teacher at an urban elementary school

I have two sixth-grade yearbooks. They stand side by side on the shelf that holds all my yearbooks. Elementary school. Junior high school. High school. College. Each yearbook represents a period of my educational life. Each contributes to the narrative of my journey from student to teacher to soon-to-be-principal. The most coveted of these yearbooks are the two I received at the end of the sixth grade.

Elementary school in my town in the mid-1980s included students from kindergarten through sixth grade. Before the launch of middle schools in the late 1980s, sixth grade was the culminating year of elementary school. It was the year of the boy-girl dance. It was the year that included a formal graduation ceremony (sans cap and gown). Above all else, sixth grade was the year that students received yearbooks for the first time.

Having been raised by immigrant Chinese parents who arrived in America in the spring of 1980, I grew accustomed to the ritual of explaining public school traditions and conventions to them. Back to School Night. Parent-teacher conferences. Report cards. These customs became more familiar as we navigated our way through my elementary years. Then came sixth grade.

Then came the yearbook. Then came the culture clash with my parents over a thin book with pictures.

I pleaded over dinner, "But why can't I?"

"It's a formal book. We don't write in books."

I pleaded again, "But all the other kids will be signing each other's books!"

"I said no."

I remember dreading the ride to school the next day. We were going to get our yearbooks in class, and our teachers were providing extra time at the end of the day for sixth graders to sign each other's yearbooks. I knew I wasn't allowed to have anyone sign my yearbook. I just didn't know how I was going to manage the awkward moment when a classmate asked me for my yearbook, and I'd have to explain why they couldn't sign it.

It has been nearly thirty years since that day. I can barely remember the chaos in the sixth-grade hallway as students from each of the three classes scrambled to sign yearbooks before dismissal. What I do remember clearly is the moment I went back into my classroom, sat down at my desk on the far right side, and thumbed through my yearbook, noting its clean pages without the ink-stained scrawl of twelve-year-olds. I clearly remember Mrs. Anson, my assistant principal, walking by my classroom, seeing me, and asking why I wasn't running around with the others. I remember explaining to her that my parents didn't want my classmates to sign my yearbook because it would ruin the book. Most vividly of all, I remember the moment she returned to my classroom, walked over to me, and quietly handed me another yearbook for my classmates to sign.

I have two sixth-grade yearbooks. I have two yearbooks because someone saw two sides of me. I have two yearbooks to remind me that we can profoundly change the lives of students in a brief moment.

# 14. The Lunchroom
### —Told by the principal of a suburban elementary school

Beyond the opening days, it is our youngest students who are most in need of continued support. For the first six to eight weeks of school, I encourage as many staff members who are able to do so to work the lunch shift of the kindergartners. I would make sure that I was free the entire hour to support students while they navigate the lunchroom as well as the playground. Everything from opening packets of condiments to reassuring an anxious or homesick student happens during the lunch hour. The kindergarten teachers were very generous with their time too, but eventually they needed to take advantage of a break in their day to recharge for the afternoons. It is remarkable what you can learn about a child from tying a shoe, offering a tissue, helping him find a classmate, or reassuring her that she will be reunited with her parent or teacher in some small amount of time. This time was very well spent as I learned much about all of the students new to kindergarten—and before too many weeks passed, all of the names of this new class of children. Parents, and sometimes staff members, often marveled that I knew each child's name, but it was an easy return on an important investment of time. As we moved further into the school year, it remained important for me to be present during as many portions of as many lunch hours as possible, but the beginning of the school year was when the investment in the children was most crucial.

Once I was able to make a connection with students on an individual basis, it was possible to more easily see when someone was in need of assistance—whether accident or illness, loneliness, hurt feelings, or misbehavior was the underlying cause. I was always able to honor that classroom teachers know their students at a much more intimate level than I ever could, but in those times when students were among the entire school population, it was good to know that I was able to be an advocate for their emotional well-being so they could resume being learners as their day continued.

# Stories From Secondary Schools

## 15. Minister of Presence
### —Told by a university faculty member

Affable and a little prone to ramble, he interjected early in our conversation: "They say that Mr. Anderson's the sports principal, that I like sports." Seemingly aware that this was likely not a compliment and eager to justify his approach, Mr. Anderson shared, "But what people don't realize is you've got that extra hook in a kid, you've got another adult in their life, if not three or four. And they've got to keep their grades up, their attendance has got to be good. So to me, it's that extra hook." He proceeded to describe his veritable *ministry of presence* as the principal of a large, urban high school serving a population of low-income white and black students.

> You've got to be present. I've got to be visible in the building. I'm out in the hallways, in the classrooms. So, you've got to be visible, your teachers have got to see you, the students have got to see you. So it's just been this way over the years. I'm involved with the community. You've just, you've got to be visible, go to the ball games. It takes a lot of time. This job is almost 24/7, 365.

His approach was one of showing equal attention to all manner of clubs and sports and activities of all students. For Mr. Anderson, it was a way to communicate care and build relationships with students. I think he liked it too. He was probably into the sports, but the philosophy was deeper, and it was rooted deeply in an ethic of care.

You've got to treat everybody, from the custodians to cafeteria workers to your teaching staff . . . you've got to treat them right. Always try to stop by, talk with people, see how they're doing. If there's a death, I'm at the funeral home. So it's, you just gotta let them know that you *care* about them. I think that the key is *that* culture and climate. And let the kids know you care about them, you know.... They see you at the wrestling matches, like this Saturday, we've got regional cheer competition here, I'll be here. I'll be at our wrestling match over at Doss.

More than the sports principal, perhaps we should call Mr. Anderson the care principal. For at its root, that was what his philosophy and approach as a school leader was all about. He summarized this best when he said, "I think kids care more. If you show kids that you care about them, they'll reciprocate."

Mr. Anderson has an intuitive sense that caring for kids by showing up, honoring them, being part of their lives, recognizing how they are investing their time, and taking your own time to do so will foster their deeper engagement in the school. It will hook them. They, in turn, will care more about school and also about you and one another. Mr. Anderson, perhaps in large part through his presence everywhere, was a witness to and a cultivator of an ethic of care.

## 16. Sue Knows She Is Loved
### —Told by the assistant principal of a rural middle school

Sue came to a rural town from a behavior management school in an urban setting. She had been adopted along with two older biological brothers (who had already left home). She

**At the Heart, Hannah Metric, Grade 11**

returned to the area to be closer to aging grandparents whose health was declining.

She adjusted well to a resource room setting where she benefited from the small-group interaction. But as her grandmother's health declined, she and her father moved into the family home, and Sue changed schools once again. She enrolled in a small school that did not offer a resource setting, and her classes consisted of approximately twenty-five students. Sue did not adjust well. She felt out of place. She became withdrawn and defiant to teachers and administrators. She had suffered abuse in the past and struggled to overcome her emotions and feelings. Sue refused to complete assignments, participate in activities, or interact with classmates except for Sally. Their friendship was unstable and lacked consistency. If they had a day of bitterness and controversy, we all knew what lay ahead: a day of turmoil and demands to go home. She made threats to harm herself to her family and to school faculty and staff.

I struggled to connect with Sue. She was extremely creative and possessed artistic abilities. So the first thing I did was purchase some art supplies that she could use during acts of defiance or breakdowns. Continually, I sought opportunities to reach out to Sue, to her father, and to other professionals to help Sue. My heart broke for Sue, a girl who had experienced such trauma and disappointment in her first twelve years of life. Being present and listening to her concerns, fears, and needs did not fix Sue, but she did know someone truly cared for her and wanted to be there for her.

Sue eventually learned coping skills and found comfort in my office where she often stopped for visits on her way to class. Sue still has her days, and a team works together to help her at school and at home. Sue knows she is loved.

# 17. What's Going on With Renee?

*—Told by a teacher at an urban high school*

Renee was a vibrant young lady with a creative mind. Ms. Morse, then principal of the middle school, enjoyed seeing her each day as she purposefully walked by her classroom just to make sure she had the chance to say hello. Ms. Morse had the opportunity to get to know Renee when she was a student in the eighth grade. Ms. Morse was impressed with Renee's writing and ability to ask questions that seemingly were beyond her years.

Ms. Morse moved to become principal of the high school, *graduating* there from middle school with Renee. Both were excited to tackle the challenge of high school. After the first quarter of the semester, Ms. Morse noticed she would see Renee less and less. She assumed Renee was just too enthralled with the demands of being a high schooler. When Ms. Morse did run into Renee, their encounters were rushed, hurried, as if Renee didn't want Ms. Morse to read the worry on her face and in her eyes.

One day Ms. Morse saw a few of Renee's friends. After they exchanged pleasantries and jokes about new boyfriends and which teachers they hated, Ms. Morse changed the tone of their conversation. "Hey. On a more serious note, what's going on with Renee? She seems off lately." The girls looked down and around in that suspicious way that teenagers do when they are trying to hide something from adults who care. "Well, we really can't say, Ms. Morse. You'll have to talk to her about it—." "She's pregnant, Ms. Morse!" blurted out one of the girls as the others shot her a sharp look but also a relieved one. They were glad to finally have told an adult who might be able to provide Renee more support than they ever could as newly minted high schoolers.

Once Ms. Morse was able to get ahold of her later that week, Renee finally broke down and told Ms. Morse her story. She had been carrying the burden of this secret because she did not want to disappoint one of the main people at the school who she knew cared for her deeply. Without judgment, Ms. Morse proceeded to talk through a plan with Renee, starting with how she could tell her parents. Ms. Morse made it clear that Renee could always come to her no matter what the situation. Her role as a mentor was not to judge but to provide a safe space where students like Renee could feel loved and cared for at school—no matter what.

# 18. Promise

**—Told by the principal of an urban alternative high school**

The long-planned alternative school was finally scheduled to open in January. Ms. Conner, a chemistry teacher at one of the high schools, would serve as the new principal—her first leadership position since entering the teaching profession. Now it was up to her and her three newly hired teachers to screen the applications to determine which students would be part of the inaugural class of Promise Alternative High School.

The school had the capacity for thirty-five students, and with over one hundred recommendations from the district's social workers and counselors, the staff had no problem getting thirty-five students. Soon after the selection process, Ms. Conner received a call from the assistant superintendent.

"Ms. Conner, I've got a student I would like for you to consider for the alternative school." "Dr. Thomas, we have an application and screening process, and we just completed it. Are we abandoning that process already?" "No, no. But this young lady met with the superintendent today, and he called and asked that we consider her for Promise."

Michelle was a seventeen-year-old African American who was in the second year of a two-year expulsion from one of the district's high schools. She lived in a nearby suburb with her aunt who had taken her in after her dad went to jail and her mom struggled with drug addiction. Upon first glance, Ms. Conner felt that Michelle didn't look the part of a bad girl.

"How did you end up in the superintendent's office?" Ms. Conner asked. "I felt that I had been out of school too long and went to make an appeal to him to let me back in. I told him that I can't be out of school this long and that I needed to get back in." "Why were you expelled?" Ms. Conner asked. "Well, I was part of a fight in the cafeteria with a bunch of girls, and they considered it mob action. They thought it was some kind of gang fight. I knew the girls, but I'm not in a gang. Anyway, the dean, who told me that one day he was going to get me, stood over me after the fight, pointed down at me cuz I was on the floor, and said, 'I finally got you.' He always wanted me expelled."

Ms. Conner took a look at her transcript and saw that Michelle had been an average or better student for the first two and a half years of her high school career.

"I'm no dummy," Michelle said. "I need to get in school. I have to make something of myself, and I can't do it sitting at home. I need to get into this school. The superintendent told me you are opening a new alternative school." Upon the recommendation of the new principal, the staff admitted Michelle and told her to show up the next day for the first day of class at the new school.

The alternative school curriculum included self-paced computer-aided instruction for most academic courses; a writer's workshop, which would serve as an English course; and a life skills course. In addition, students were required to complete ninety hours of community service by the time they completed their academic coursework.

In the first few months of the new school, everyone, teachers included, struggled to get a handle on the computer courses. Ms. Conner noticed Michelle working diligently each day to quickly complete each lesson so that she could proceed to the next one. She came early and stayed late and finished chapters, sections, and tests faster than everyone. It soon became clear to the teachers and to the other students that Michelle was the most serious, if not the best, student at the school.

It took very little time for Ms. Conner to realize that many of the students were actually fairly good students and that their major downfall that landed them at the alternative school was the fact that they missed a lot of school. Some students, seventeen or eighteen years old, had only nine or ten credits. Yet it became obvious to Ms. Conner and the teachers that many of the students had the capacity to do better than their past academic record showed. For this reason, Ms. Conner set up an ACT prep course at the school, during the after-school hours, for those who wanted to try college. Michelle signed up immediately. Ms. Conner, a former science teacher with a biology degree, taught the science prep part of the ACT prep course and found that the students caught on well to the type of analysis that would be expected of them on the ACT.

By April, a number of students signed up to take the ACT. The teachers expected a wide range of scores, but they were excited that they were able to encourage the students to give it a shot. When the scores were returned, Michelle earned one of the better scores—a 17. Considering that she had been out of school for eighteen months prior, Ms. Conner and the teachers were thrilled at the outcome. The other amazing thing was that every student at the alternative school scored a 19 or better in science, a source of pride for Ms. Conner, the former science teacher. Michelle, who got a 22 on the science section, felt particularly excited and encouraged and decided to take the test again to try to improve her score. She did, and her composite score improved by a point.

By the summer, Michelle had become Ms. Conner's favorite student and her personal project. Michelle, who sometimes talked about her horrible circumstances, confided in Ms. Conner about her family life and how she felt she would be unable to attend college.

"Michelle, I think you can get into some schools with that score. You should try State U. You can start working on your essays this summer and put your applications in this fall." "What am I supposed to write with this summer? I don't have a computer. I don't have money for application fees. Where will I get all of that?" "Don't worry about the application fees. You can probably get some fees waived and the ones you don't, I'll pay. And I've got a laptop to give you."

A couple of days later, Ms. Conner pulled up outside of Michelle's house and honked the horn so that she could come out. Ms. Conner handed a laptop out of the window. "Keep it—it's yours. Get the essays done, and send them to me."

By August, Ms. Conner and the other teachers felt the energy that Michelle brought to school each day and knew the example she set for the other students. Yet in private, Michelle had doubts and fear that she just was not good enough to compete with other students to get into a four-year college. She would be the first in her family to attend college. Ms. Conner felt that Michelle had a compelling story, showed grit and resilience, and had the persistence to work through challenging college courses. What Michelle lacked in confidence, Ms. Conner made up for and tried to spread it to Michelle.

Michelle started dragging her feet, not feeling confident, not completing the application, not taking care of all that she needed in order to apply. "I'll just go to Town Junior College," she said. "You are not going to Town Junior College. You're going to State U," Ms. Conner replied.

As the application deadline approached, Ms. Conner began to feel that perhaps this might not happen. If Michelle didn't feel she could do it, how could Ms. Conner force her? With one day left before the deadline, Michelle brought all of her materials in, ready to mail. It was already late in the day, and the mail had already been picked up. Ms. Conner said, "I will drive down there and hand deliver your application." And that's what she did.

Michelle got accepted at State U! Ms. Conner spread the word across the district, to the assistant superintendent, and to the school dean who saw Michelle as nothing but a thug gang girl. However, she would have to attend the summer bridge program. By this time, Ms. Conner began to contemplate her future and soon decided that she would leave her current role and pursue other positions and a PhD. Michelle attended summer bridge, received B and C grades that summer, and never returned to State U. Ms. Conner left the alternative high school the next year, and she and Michelle fell out of touch.

Fast-forward ten years. Ms. Conner received an e-mail message from someone named Michelle. "Could this be Micky?" It was the nickname she began calling Michelle once they became close. It was. She left a phone number and asked Ms. Conner to call.

"Michelle? Oh my god! How are you?" "I'm doing well, real well, Ms. Conner." "Excellent! How's the family? And you can call me Angela. You're an adult now!" "They are fine. My mom is fine. I have a daughter now. She's four." Micky is a mom! Oh wow! "What are you doing these days?" "Well, I wanted you to know that after I left State U, I worked for a year, then enrolled at Robinson University. And I graduated. With a degree in biology. Just like you!

Ms. Conner laughed out loud with such joy as tears of pride rolled down her face. "And I still have the computer you gave me back in high school. It lasted me through college."

Right after college, Michelle worked as a paint chemist at a major paint company. The next time they spoke, about eight years later, Michelle was making a six-figure salary at that same company. It was not bad for a thug gang girl who went to an alternative high school and for her principal, who saw her potential, removed the real and imagined barriers, and showed her the pathway to success.

# 19. Red Sneakers

## —Told by the former principal of an urban middle school

Lloyd Middle School was one of the three largest middle schools in the city, with diverse and high immigrant populations. The student body represented twenty-six nations with twenty different languages spoken at home. Around 70 percent of the students qualified for the federal free and reduced lunch program. Halls were brightly lit, clean and shined. Student work was displayed throughout the halls, classrooms, and office. The trophy case in the lobby was full of athletic awards, plaques, and trophies.

I was the principal at Lloyd from 2004 to 2007. Being an immigrant, I wanted to lead Lloyd to become an academically high-performing school. The majority of my time was spent in the classrooms observing, monitoring student learning and instruction, and walking in the hallways. My attire was the same as the student uniform, with just an added blazer and a pair of sneakers, which I needed for the long hours on my feet. Students and teachers expected to see me in their classrooms every day.

One day, I was in Ms. Reese's eighth-grade class wearing my sneakers. A student asked me, "Mrs. Gold, do you know the Air Force 1?" I replied "Of course, it's the president's airplane." The entire class laughed and said, "No, it's Nike shoes." Ms. Reese gave me a look and told me that I needed to be in tune with student fashion.

A few months later, an office staff member told me that Ms. Reese wanted me to stop by her classroom. The students and Ms. Reese had been waiting for me anxiously when I entered.

She said, "Our class has something for you." Then she presented me with a gift bag. I took out a box from the gift bag and found a pair of red-and-white Nike sneakers and socks with pom poms. Ms. Reese said, "My students saved their lunch change for weeks and bought these

Nike Air Force 1 sneakers for you, Mrs. Gold. You can walk around the school in your own Air Force 1s." I was truly touched by their generosity, thoughtfulness, and attention to what I was trying to achieve for school. Together, we were building the culture of high expectations for teaching and learning and of care. We achieved all A grades in the core subjects on the state assessment my second and third year at Lloyd.

From that day on, I wore my red Air Force 1s every day visiting classrooms, and the red sneakers became a historical artifact of Lloyd Middle School. Red sneakers were the visible symbol of my commitment to quality instruction and care for all students. The eighth graders moved on to Greenwood High School, and the new fifth graders came the following fall. A fifth grader saw me in my red sneakers during my classroom visit and asked me, "Are those the Air Force 1s that the eighth graders gave you? My cousin told me about the sneakers." He had proudly told his classmates.

After I left Lloyd, I became the principal at Hudson High School, an inner-city high school, and continued to wear my red sneakers. One of the assistant principals at Hudson worked at Greenwood High School as the summer school principal. She told me later that some students at the summer school asked her whether I still wore their red sneakers.

A few years later, I left the school district and became a college professor teaching education majors. On my first day of teaching, a wide-eyed undergrad student in my class blurted out, "Mrs. Gold, what are you doing here?" She was a student at Lloyd Middle School when I was the principal there. Erin grew up in a trailer park and became the first one in her family who went to college. She was majoring in English and wanted to become a teacher because of the teachers at

Lloyd Middle School who inspired her. Then she asked, "Do you still have those red sneakers?" She told her undergraduate classmates, "Dr. Gold visited classrooms every day and wore the red sneakers." Then she turned to me and asked, "Can you wear the red sneakers to class sometime?" "Of course, I would love to wear them to class again," I replied.

# 20. Nate

### —Told by the assistant principal of a small-town middle school

Nate has been a student in my care for two years now, in my role as assistant principal. In my time of knowing Nate, he has needed several academic and behavioral supports provided through our school. A fully capable student, Nate has struggled having consistent care and support in his home. As a result, his academic performance and behavior show themselves in negative ways. As an attention-starved eighth grader, Nate has learned through experience that gaining attention through academic struggles and negative behaviors is better than gaining no attention at all. As Nate and I have worked through some of his behaviors, he and I have developed an honest and open relationship with each other. There are frequent times where he will have to serve out a punishment. I see, interact, and speak with Nate as if he is my own son.

**I Am Here! Mick Sankowski, Grade 12**

One week, Nate made a serious mistake that resulted in an out-of-school suspension, per district policy. As heartbroken as I was to have to hand down the punishment, he looked at me with tears in his eyes and apologized, saying that he had "let me down." He also let me know that I was "one of the two people in the building who had really gotten to know him and cared about him." The other was our academic support teacher. He told me that when he came back to school after the suspension, he would do whatever it took to make things right. The conference ended with him giving me a hug and him telling me that he loved me.

It was at that moment that I realized that for many students in our schools like Nate, you have to put the emphasis on the care of the students before they will buy into the other aspects of school. We have to do our due diligence to develop relationships with students who are the hardest to reach and the hardest to teach. I often worry about what Nate's life journey will look like, but by getting to know and work with him, I will be a better support to all the Nates who walk through the doors of my school.

# 21. Patrick

### —Told by the principal of a small-town high school

A caring and passionate educator named Bruce is the principal of the Farnsworth Institute of Technology, a high school in West Virginia. Bruce believes that all children should have a future that engages them in the career of their choice. Farnsworth believes it provides a continuum of education to its students, which allows them to acquire advanced technical training in high school but ultimately provides them with the skills needed to be successful beyond high school. The mission of Farnsworth is to assist individuals in preparing for, becoming employed in, and advancing the skills required for their career choice. According to Bruce, "The changing economy and the explosion of technology demand that Farnsworth provides cross-training and the effective use of this technology. Technical training at Farnsworth is available on an open-door basis to all those who meet the basic education requirements. We are accessible and flexible so that the greatest number of students can benefit from our services. We strive to recognize the individual differences of our students and foster their success."

Two weeks before his freshman year in high school, Patrick got into trouble and was assigned to a juvenile program, a lockdown facility. This was a mandatory program for thirty-six days, and it was not his first time as a visitor. Patrick was sent there two years earlier. In his own words, Patrick says there was nothing for him to strive for in school. He saw no point in high school and was completely lost until he had his first experience with Farnsworth. For Patrick, the idea of a *goal* was one that left him at a loss. His experiences had neither a relationship nor relevance to what he perceived as his future. To him, he had already been cast away by a system that saw him as troublesome and uncommitted to schooling.

Once he was released from the juvenile facility, Bruce took an interest in Patrick and invited him to take a tour of the facility at Farnsworth. Here, Bruce showed him how he could work with his hands and how the *high-tech* skills he could learn were in demand by professional businesses every day. Patrick was immediately engaged for the first time in his school years. He slowly began to see a future—one not so daunting but filled with possibilities and opportunities. One problem remained. Patrick was not allowed to come to school that year as the district had suspended him. Bruce nonetheless enrolled him in Farnsworth and allowed him to come to school every day despite the policy forbidding him on a school's campus. Bruce turned his eye away as Patrick was at the school each day striving to become a certified welder in his chosen career field.

Bruce saw potential in Patrick and engaged him at an emotional level. He showed value and created an environment where Patrick could succeed, so much so that Patrick was assigned to work on a significant new project at a nearby national park. A project commissioned by the state, it was one where Patrick would have his name engraved as a contributor for all to see for years to come. Patrick began to excel in school and is now graduating at the top of his class as a certified welder. In his own words, Patrick says,

"If you know why you need to learn something, then it gives you more drive to learn. It opens my eyes to learning and makes me think before I act and what my consequences are going to be later on in life and in my job and my occupation. This school does not have to have you here. If it hadn't been for Farnsworth, I don't think that project would have taken me on, and I would have been right back at that facility."

# 22. Four Years With That Student

### —Told by the principal of an urban charter high school

He is the one who told me on the first day of school to fuck off.

He is the one who told me four years later that no one before had ever given a damn about him.

He is the one who walked out of school. This uniform is bogus, he screamed at me.

He is the one who wore his cap and gown with a milewide smile.

He is the one who told me that people always let him down, and he doesn't trust a soul.

He is the one who confided in and trusted me.

Four years of "Good morning, how are you doing today?"

Four years of "Nice work on that science lab. Your teacher told me it was great."

Four years of "Today you made a poor choice, but it doesn't define you. What can you do next time differently?"

Four years of "I'm proud of you, no matter what."

He is the one who sobbed through muffled tears that he'd never amount to anything.

He is the one who cried onto his mom's shoulder after walking the stage.

He is the one who complained that I never let him get away with anything.

He is the one who told me thanks for never letting him get away with anything.

He is the one who said it was the worst decision he ever made to come to our school.

He is the one who wrote his college essay about how our school changed his life.

Four years of "I'm sorry. I made a mistake."

Four years of "I'm sorry. I made a mistake too."

Four years of "I'll try not to let you down again."

Four years of "I'll try not to let you down again either."

He is the one who needed hope when he was down.

He is the one who gives me hope when I am down.

**I Understand You, I've Got You. Jules Marshall-Seinitz, Grade 12**

# 23. On the Bus Ramp

### —Told by the assistant principal of a small-town middle school

Every morning at 7:30 a.m., Mrs. Jolly makes her way to the bus ramp to greet the middle and high school students as they are getting off their school buses. She smiles at all of the students when they get off the bus, making sure that the first thing they see is a happy face. Mrs. Jolly is often cold or hot or is dodging raindrops from the holes in the covered walkway. But she still stands out there every day making sure that the stress or frustration she may be feeling is never shown to the students. She watches the students carefully and especially takes notice of the student who doesn't smile, looks tired, or who she knows has had some trouble the day or night before. She doesn't just smile at those students. She calls them by name and tells them good morning.

Often, Mrs. Jolly is swamped with paperwork, phone calls, and unanswered e-mails, but when she hears that 3:00 p.m. bell, she knows it is time to head back out to the bus ramp to tell her students goodbye. Out on the bus ramp, there are always two brothers standing all alone. These boys face so much heartache and emotional issues that Mrs. Jolly always spends a few minutes to ask them about their day and to remind them just how much she cares.

Mrs. Jolly is an assistant principal who could be spending her mornings and afternoons working in her office. However, she knows that she must be visible. Her compassion and joy are sometimes the only compassion and joy that her students may experience that day.

---

# 24. Giving and Taking the Chance
—Told by the assistant principal of an urban charter high school

I stood at the graduation podium giving my speech. The moment was full of joy and pride in the year's graduating class. I had made a point that I would mention every senior by name in some special way, recalling fond memories, acknowledging growth, and sending well wishes for their future. I paused as I got to the next name in my speech. While I did not say it, this student had proven to have the greatest impact on my career up until that moment and still to this day.

My first encounter with her was in a hallway of the school, breaking up a fight she was in with another young lady. I knew her vaguely as one of the younger students, a student with a bit of an attitude, and, at that moment, the center of an uproar in the middle of the hallway. In those few minutes, I judged her, and I assumed that she would be a problem next year when she got to the class I taught as one of my duties at the school. I assumed that she was another unmotivated, hard-to-reach troublemaker. The worst part was that I hadn't realized the degree to which I had negatively judged her in one instance until she came to my class the following year. She entered my room, and in our early conversations, I told her that I remembered she was the girl who got into that fight the previous year and that I hoped she didn't plan on bringing any of *that* into my classroom. In those few words, I created a wall of judgment. I never gave the girl a chance. And I couldn't have been more wrong about her.

The kid who entered my class looked the same and sounded the same as the year before, but the fact that I was now her teacher gave me the chance to get to know her. Her answers to questions were insightful, and her work habits were impeccable. She was driven, and I was compelled to do my part to make up for the wrong I had done and for all who had prejudged her before me. That year was full of ups and downs. I watched her conquer family challenges, the loss of friends, and the burden of providing for her family. But she continued to persevere and kept college on the forefront of her mind. I encouraged her and saw the hard shell she presented to the world begin to disappear. She became like a niece to me, and classroom lessons became infused with life lessons about being your best self and not giving up despite growing up in difficult circumstances. She laughed, she cried, and she got angry, and I promised her that if she did her part, she would find her place in college. She trusted me enough to tell me her dreams of one day being successful for her family, and she shared her fears that she would never achieve her dreams. I challenged her even harder, expected even more, and supported her every step of the way.

As I stood at the podium on that graduation day, I paused and then spoke her name. I announced to the audience of students, family members, and friends that I simply wanted to apologize. I wanted to apologize for not seeing the amazing student that she was, and I thanked her for giving me the opportunity to be a part of her journey. I thanked her for being a constant reminder that the future is what you make of it, and greatness comes in all types of packages. I closed by congratulating her on the full scholarship she had received to attend a selective East Coast college. My own biases had almost hindered me from committing to and expressing the level of care necessary to see this student through to the finish.

I was reminded how important it is to care for our students when I received the following Facebook message from this former student five years later:

I just want to thank you for everything you have taught me and your seriousness when it came to being an educator. Many of the things you told me still stick with me today. Like "you might have to work 10x harder to get where some other people are at and you have to do what you have to do." Although I knew I was going to college, I'm not sure if I would be where I am today without your influence. Thank you. PS: I will never forget the fact that you really thought I was a hood rat because of that fight. LOL!

# 25. You Just Gotta Be Calm
—Told by the director of an urban education foundation

Ms. Morris is the academy coordinator at Wooddale High School, which serves a predominantly African American and low-income student population. One day while walking alongside her in the hall, we came across a student who was running out of a classroom, shouting curse words. Ms. Morris made a face at him and motioned him toward her with her finger. He came to her and she put her arm around him, and he lowered his head.

She talked softly to him, asking, "What are you so upset about?" He responded that the teacher took away his cell phone for using it in class. She asked him if he thought his behavior was appropriate as they walked off into a corner out of earshot from me. They continued to discuss the incident in hushed tones. When it was over, she patted him on the back and said, "I love you, baby" and watched him walk down the hall. She came back over to me shaking her head, saying, "Sometimes they have a hard time handling their emotions. You just gotta be calm with them and bring 'em back down."

# 26. Not Giving Up
—Told by the principal of a small-town high school

I returned from Christmas break last year to find one of our senior girls, Amanda, not coming to school. I spoke with her mother who said that she moved out of the house, and they had not heard from her since. They believed that she moved in with her boyfriend.

I began to investigate, calling friends of hers into my office to figure out why she wasn't coming to school. They gave me a new cell number, and I began to call, leaving messages sometimes twice a day. I even showed up to her place of work to discover that she had recently quit. Days were passing, and I felt her diploma quickly slipping away. I started investigating the boyfriend she might have been living with. I found his telephone number and began to call. After leaving many messages, I showed up to his place of work and voiced my concern with him. Amanda lacked two credits for graduation. Where was she, and why was she not coming to school!??

Amanda *finally* got wind that I wasn't giving up on her and called to set up an appointment to go over a plan to graduate. I was thrilled. Now I began to plot and plan with our guidance department where and how she would graduate after being gone from school for months. Our school houses a program called the Star Fish Program where students have their own cubicle space and finish courses online. Attendance is strict, and there are many rules and guidelines to follow. Amanda interviewed and got a spot in the program.

I thought my job was finished. She would graduate. However, weeks later, she was missing again and not coming to school. I began to plead with her. It was April, and graduation was in May. She wasn't thrilled with the program and wasn't feeling supported by the math teacher there.

I began to tutor Amanda in math myself, shutting her in my office daily as she was finishing. The Star Fish Program was *not* happy with me. I only saw the chance to save a senior who wouldn't have graduated. I apologized numerous times to her academic supervisor, but we made a new plan that supported her math needs in a different way. We involved a new counselor within the program who took her under her wing as her mother and held her hand until the end. Once she completed her online courses, Amanda, another teacher, and I celebrated with cake, balloons, and conversation. We discussed Amanda's career goals and plans.

Amanda later moved out of her boyfriend's house and back in with her parents. She had greater hopes and dreams for herself after accomplishing her goal of graduation. Amanda held her head higher and believed more in herself.

# 27. The Last Leg

—Told by an instructional facilitator at a suburban high school

Though small, Matthew was a lot to handle. He repeatedly got kicked out of class and cursed at his teachers and administrators; he was on his last leg. Here at the alternative middle school, there is a strict policy that if you get more than five (it seems like a lot) administrative referrals, you must serve another semester or face expulsion from the district. Matthew was on referral number four. Sensing that there was potential in this young man given he was academically a good student, I saw that he needed someone to take an intense interest in him. Sitting on his fourth referral, Matthew was again sent to my office. After repeated attempts, I finally reached his mother on the speakerphone, and in a voice that Matthew and I could hear, she said that she had had enough and didn't care what we did with him. Looking into his eyes, I could see his spirit dwindle.

Instead of writing the referral, I asked Matthew to walk with me.

The district organized this school according to two programs. The first serves students who have been removed from their home school for disciplinary reasons. The second serves older students behind in credits, seeking to catch up in hopes of graduating. Walking down the hallway, I decided to take Matthew to the part of the school where the second program was located to see some of the opportunities offered to those students. Our first stop was to see Mr. Waring, who taught automotive technology. Matthew was awestruck observing students incessantly focused on working on cars. I could see a spark immediately. Our next stop was the audiovisual room, where students were filming a commercial. Matthew was sold at this point. After taking our tour, we returned to my office, where I suggested we make a deal. I told Matthew I would allow him to take an elective of his choice if he eliminated his outbursts and inappropriate behavior. This was a big ask, but he seemed up for the challenge and readily accepted the deal.

For the next two months, Matthew was a remarkably changed student. He did not receive one referral during this period, and his teachers named him student of the month. After congratulating Matthew, I set him down and let him know how proud I was of his progress. Beaming from ear to ear, I remarked that I had some news as well. I told Matthew that I would be leaving the next week, as I got a promotion to the district level office. His spirit vanished. I obviously missed the mark, as I thought he would be happy. Matthew stated, "That's great." Then he quickly walked out of my office.

It was two months after I went to the district office when I got the call that Matthew had been arrested. I returned to the school to speak with the principal, and he indicated that after I left, Matthew began a downward spiral. I asked to speak to Matthew, and he obliged. Sitting there, I could see a change in Matthew as he entered the office. He looked despondent and angry. Asking how he had been, knowing about some of the issues he'd had since I left, Matthew simply said, "You left me like everyone else does." It threw me for a loop. I didn't realize the effect my absence would have on his life. I tried to maintain a connection with Matthew after that, but it was too late; his mother had decided to move out of the district a few weeks later. Matthew made me understand the power of care but more importantly the need for consistency when one is immersed in chaos.

## 28. I've Got Your Back
—Told by the principal of an urban high school

Fifteen minutes to go until first period on Monday, and Luis quietly knocked on Principal McCory's office door as he entered. "Good morning! *Buenos dias*! How are you, Luis? *Como estas?*" asked McCory. "*Bien*. And thanks," replied Luis, head bowed, as he handed a small laundry bag to McCory. "Have a great day! I'll see you after school," said McCory.

Luis headed off to class, and after the halls cleared for class, Principal McCory tucked the laundry bag under her arm and headed to the laundry room in the athletics department, taking a back hall where few students and teachers would see her. Once there, she worked quickly to start the load of Luis's dirty clothes. She would return an hour later to put them in the dryer and an hour after that to fold and return them to the laundry bag with a couple of travel tubes of toothpaste and sticks of deodorant for Luis to pick up from her office at the end of the day.

It had been almost eight months since Luis had become homeless. With this quiet arrangement, the teasing and ridicule meted out by other students about Luis's personal hygiene had all but stopped. He was feeling better about being a freshman in high school and glad to have an adult like Principal McCory looking out for him.

## 29. Toss and Turn
—Told by the head of a small-town independent girls high school

Good school leaders know that holding high expectations and following up with clear consequences consistently creates a positive school culture. At our independent girls school, our student-run judicial council hears violations of major school rules and recommends consequences to me. I can accept, reject, or modify their recommendations. Rarely do I change their recommendations in any material way because the student leaders, elected by their peers, have been thoughtful in their deliberations, and I want them to have ownership of the process and our school values, one of which is integrity. But sometimes I know more about a student's situation outside of school and understand that the standard consequences would be detrimental to the student even if I have to take some flack for being inconsistent. That's where the caring comes in.

One of our first semester seniors had made several appearances before the judicial council for plagiarism and for violations of our acceptable internet use policy for posting inappropriate photos. Since coming to our school as a sophomore, she had been suspended and had been on warning. When she appeared in my office near the end of the semester for yet another violation of our acceptable-use policy, she had used up all her chits, and the recommendation from the judicial council was for expulsion. Still, I felt this was a girl who wasn't getting the lesson from the standard penalties. Her parents were quite critical of her, often selling her short. At the same time, they got angry at the school or bailed her out, sending her incredibly mixed messages. She seemed desperate for affirmation from her peers. It had been two-and-a-half difficult years with her.

I always toss and turn the night before I meet with a student who needs to be separated from the school. I ask myself whether we, as a school, have done everything we can for the student. In this case, I knew that the teachers and other students were fed up with the girl and didn't hold much sympathy for her. She had been given second and third chances but never seemed to learn. Still, I felt there was one thing I had never been successful in getting her parents to allow: counseling. So when I met with the parents and their daughter, I put forward a proposal of suspension for the rest of the semester, and if she got regular counseling twice a month, I would consider allowing her to complete her degree. She would not be allowed to participate in extracurricular activities or board at the school (she lived locally), but she could earn a diploma. And she would have to report this change in status to colleges to which she had applied.

What I didn't know was that this student had recently received news from her family that had shaken her very sense of self. She learned that she had been adopted and that a family member wasn't who she thought she was. The requirement of counseling was exactly what she needed, and she was transformed through the process. She made it through the end of the year and received her diploma. She also was accepted to a college she was excited to attend. She left high school with tools and resources for self-care and with a stronger sense of confidence. She still has some growing up to do, but I feel she's on her way.

# 30. Authentic Care

**—Told by the director of special services at a suburban school district**

The word *care* has myriad meanings in education. To me, care viewed through an equity lens translates to high expectations and authentic relationships. I have seen numerous instances in which *nice* teachers expected less of their students of color, believing that by refusing to place the same rigorous demands on them as they do on white students they are being caring of them. They were making accommodations for the students' difficult home life, poverty, or lack of English-language proficiency, but such *accommodations* for the students' difficulties may unintentionally send the message that they are incapable of learning.

I have also seen many examples of authentic care that have shaped my own relationships with students. For example, for Desmond, care was manifested in questions to determine why he was always late to school or class. A special education administrator learned that Desmond, a teenager, was taking care of his younger siblings with little support and had made a choice to stay home or come late when needed. His relationship with his principal opened the door for us to make a home visit and assist in providing supports that led to more consistent attendance.

For Paul, care was wondering how a static and outdated behavior contract would support his academic success in school. Paul, a wise and sociable fourteen-year-old, signed a behavior contract that stated any further mess-ups would yield a long-term suspension and perhaps expulsion. A caring administrator intervened and advocated on Paul's behalf to have the contract revoked. A contract of that sort was never again used at the school. Supports instead of ultimatums were used instead.

For Stephen, care was reiterating that access to the school environment was a civil right. Stephen was given access to school after completing restorative practices and learned that one mistake does not determine his destiny, a lesson we adults try to share with our students every single day.

And for Terrance, care was making sure that the school-to-prison pipeline was not actualized by what clothes he chose to wear on a particular school day. Terrance was handcuffed after kicking a trash can during the school day. My inquiry led to the understanding that he was told he was going to be charged with indecent exposure if he was caught sagging his pants again in the hallway. After looking around and seeing several of his peers doing the same thing and feeling targeted, he took out his frustration on the trash can. After making calls, and having several courageous conversations, the principal made sure that this incident did not bring a charge against him.

In all of these examples, these students were in line to be suspended, expelled, or coached out of schools. It was the care of courageous administrators and leaders that led to a different successful outcome for these scholars. These stories illustrate some of the situations our students have to navigate daily. They illuminate what personal care for each student can look like. This care is grounded in restorative practices and high expectations. Authentic care is what students crave, seek, and are willing to do just about anything to get. Being nice is not enough.

# 31. Jason

## —Told by the head of a suburban independent PK–12 school

Jason came to our school as a shaggy-haired, overweight, lost middle school boy. With lower entrance exam scores and even lower self-esteem, he was destined for failure in a private school. Or was he?

Inevitably, Jason and I ended up spending time together in my office talking about his grades. Twice that first year, he teetered on the edge of academic probation, the last step before being asked to leave. We spoke about motivation, and we discussed strategies. I tried to break through both the metaphorical wall he had constructed as well as the hair that literally covered his eyes. I told him I believed in him and wanted to help and that together we could make his private school journey continue and be successful.

Periodically, I would say hello in the halls and give him a guy head nod, or a fist bump. As weeks passed, he began to want to talk regularly. In January of that year, the wall Jason built around himself began to crumble. He shared with me his battle with dyslexia and "not really liking to read that much." We talked about sports and about his family life. He began to share what was really meaningful to him. We moved past the brief perfunctory interchanges between administrator and student.

Later that year, Jason asked me if we could talk sometime soon. We scheduled a time. When he came in, he shared that he was feeling really conflicted about a big decision. Not knowing what he was going to spill, I was relieved when he told me that he was having a hard time deciding between playing football or playing soccer the next fall. Seeing his level of angst, I listened to him spell out how he wanted to try something new. He felt that eighth grade was probably his last chance to try a new sport. At the same time, he felt he would be letting down friends and the coach if he didn't continue to play football. My advice was simply what anyone who knows and loves adolescents would say: Do what you feel most strongly about and your friends and coaches will support you. And he did.

On the first day of school the next fall, Jason showed up with a crew cut, a bright orange polo shirt, khaki shorts, and an amazing smile. While his academic struggles did not completely disappear during his last year of middle school, his work ethic and self-esteem were drastically improved. Like clockwork, he would e-mail me to meet every month, wanting "just thirty to forty minutes of my time" to bounce ideas off me, seek advice, and talk about hunting—a new passion that he had developed with his uncles.

In early May, we met, and he shared his dreams of going to West Point, how that would work, and what he wanted to do for the next twenty years as an army officer. I wish I could have videotaped him to show his parents, teachers, and other students what maturity in an eighth grader looks like. This was the true Jason.

After our eighth-grade graduation ceremony, as the crowds began to exit the building, a few parents lingered to share their thanks with me. I stood on the stage taking it all in. From my right, a sharply dressed, clean-cut, smiling, and confident young man approaching me. Extending his right hand and looking at me with wet eyes, his words will be indelibly etched in my memory. "Thank you for everything you've done for me."

By no means does it turn out this way for every student I have met. I know that my influence was only a part among countless other factors in Jason's life. However, I truly believed in this young man from the minute I met him in the hallway during an admissions visit. Perhaps as the faculty and I began to believe in him, he took the risk of starting to believe in himself.

I often speak to students about risk-taking. I contend that in order to know oneself better, risk is required. For adolescents, they need to know that either jumping off a roof or playing in traffic is not what I am talking about. But if I were unwilling to live by my own advice, my core would be as empty as a donut box in the faculty lounge. Maybe Jason was a risk—he certainly was on paper. And while things turned out well for Jason, I know that it does not always end this way. I have learned, however, that students—all students—need an advocate, a cheerleader, and someone to truly believe in them. I believe this is true for faculty as well. In my career as a teacher, division head, and head of school, there have been students who I failed to reach. With every one of them, I questioned myself, cursed myself, and surprised myself with what I learned from them. For me, the ultimate goal is to successfully engage and involve everyone in the school to support our students and help them learn.

As an administrator, the opportunity to have meaningful interaction with students is always constrained by time. Nevertheless, I see my role as identifying their potential, encouraging them, and supporting them through the blessings that are skinned knees. A former university president once said, "The potential possibilities of any child are the most intriguing and stimulating in all creation." Children encourage us to dream, wonder, and continue to grow ourselves. Jason's words at his middle school graduation are the ultimate gift for any educator and are the fuel for our incredibly demanding work. Students are the ones who make us think, cause us to grow and learn, and provide the reason why there will always be great hope and possibility in education.

# 32. Let Me Work on That

—Told by the principal of an urban high school

A veteran educator in the school district and nearing retirement, I was appointed the second principal of a high school newly constructed in a largely Mexican American community adjacent to a highly segregated low-income African American community. The school was built as the result of a long-fought, highly charged political battle between the Mexican American community and a cash-strapped school district that has substantial capital improvement needs. The majority of students are Mexican American with a relatively small minority of African American students.

In the story of its founding and in its art and architecture, the school boasted the culture and heritage of Mexico and celebrated the Mexican American struggle. It was named for the Mexican American community in which it was built. The first principal, a Mexican American male without previous school administrative experience, left the post two years after the school opened to take a principalship elsewhere. I am an African American woman, fluent in Spanish, assigned to the school from an associate principal position at a predominantly African American school across town.

Toward the end of my first month at the school, I learned that one of my African American students was planning to transfer to another school. He was doing well academically and gave no outward cause for concern. I made a point to run into him between periods as he made his way to study hall. "DeShawn," I said, "would you walk with me for a minute?"

"I wanted to talk with you because I'm concerned about why you are transferring to another school." I waited awhile for a response.

"I am not really happy here," he replied respectfully. "Why? What's going on?" He mumbled something, but he was avoiding my questions. After walking a bit farther in silence I asked, "So, help me understand something. How are you treated as an African American student on this campus?" I will never forget his answer. "I wasn't treated badly. I just wasn't treated at all." I put my arm around his shoulders and gave him a little squeeze. "Let me work on that," I told him. "Give me a chance to help."

DeShawn did not transfer. During the next few weeks, I made a point of taking strolls with him and other African American students and asking them how they were doing. Although on the surface they seemed OK, some complained that they were not being treated fairly because "this is really a Mexican school." Most told me they were lonely and felt a sense of disenfranchisement in school.

I began meeting with the faculty and staff to think of ways that we could promote unity, inclusion, and respect for both our Mexican American and African American students. I encouraged the faculty to listen more intentionally and carefully to their students, particularly their African American students.

I encouraged them to ask regularly "How are you?" as a serious question, not a rhetorical one. My assistant principal and I set up listening sessions for African American students to speak to me, my fellow administrators, and teachers. I worked with teachers to develop their understanding of both African American and Mexican American students and to develop their ability to listen and communicate effectively with them.

We took other steps that first year to promote a sense of community and respect for all students in the school. In addition to the art and symbols

I See You, Hear You. Jasper Nord, Grade 12

of Mexican American culture and heritage, we displayed more art and symbols of African American culture and heritage. I encouraged the faculty to develop a new yearlong history course that devoted one semester to African American history and one semester to Latin and Mexican American history. This course became a requirement for all eleventh-grade students in the school. I also worked with teachers to help students develop more sensitive and respectful ways for communicating with each other. We looked for ways to help Mexican American and African American students better understand each other. We looked for ways for them to deepen their knowledge of their respective languages and cultures while increasing expectations for respectful discourse and consequences for ethnic slurs. For Martin Luther King's birthday, the administration and I organized a march of six hundred students, faculty, and staff to promote cultural understanding and unity—a march that made its way through both the Mexican American and African American communities that the school served. Last but not least, the administration and faculty petitioned the school district to change the name of the school, and all its signage, to reflect the names of both communities it served. While the petition was not granted that first year, the administration and faculty decided to use the more inclusive name inside the school.

# 33. The Business Card

### —Told by the assistant principal of an urban high school

It's three days before graduation. The last of the final exams are being graded, and the building is starting to feel quiet. Tomorrow, the class of 2016 will celebrate at the prom, and then on Friday they'll cross the stage at graduation. I look up from piles of end-of-the-year tasks to see Michael standing in the doorway of my office. He looks down as he rubs his well-worn sneakers together. "Mrs. Roberts? Do you have a minute?" I smile. "For you? As many minutes as you need. What's up?"

I immediately run through options in my mind. We took care of Michael's prom ticket, right? Yes, I know we did. Maybe he needs a ride to get his tuxedo. We took care of the tuxedo, didn't we? Yes. Yes, we did.

Michael places an old and somewhat dirty business card on my desk. I immediately recognize the card, which reads "Shirley Covington, School Counselor." My name and title have since changed, which means this business card is at least three years old. I also recognize my handwriting on the back of the card: "I want you to attend MY school—Westtown High School— phone: 555-0812."

Michael is one of seven children. When it became clear that Michael's family was going to lose their house, I wrote that information on my business card and told him to use that phone number whenever he needed. I felt strongly about Michael and his siblings staying in our school and wanted to ensure that they were not pressured to transfer to whatever school was closest to the shelter or shelters they ended up in. Michael was no stranger to neglect and abuse. In his short life, becoming homeless was not the worst thing to happen to him.

But on that June day, Michael stood in my office about to graduate from high school with a spot waiting for him in college. He had earned a scholarship through the university to cover his tuition, and he had secured enough community scholarship money to pay his room and board. As Michael placed the business card on my desk he said, "I carried this in my wallet for years. Three shelters, a foster placement, and a group home. This school's been my home. I figured it's time I give it back." I slid the card back across my desk to him. "Why don't you keep it? School's ending, but we'll always be here."

Since he graduated almost four years ago, Michael sends me updates on what is going on in his life. He seems to be doing really well.

# 34. Not All Who Wander Are Lost

—Told by the principal of an urban Catholic high school

I got my first copy of *The Hobbit* in a principal's office. Technically, he was the dean of students, but this distinction didn't mean much to me as a seventh grader. I simply knew I was in trouble and that I was serving my in-school suspension (ISS) with Mr. Henry. Like all seventh graders at my school, I knew that Mr. Henry was in charge of discipline.

Shortly after I checked in, I was surprised when he handed me a book. His instructions to me for the next two days were to spend the time reading because we were going to talk about it when I was done. This was long before the Peter Jackson movies came out and, although I had heard the name J. R. R. Tolkien before, I didn't know what to expect. I wasn't much of a reader either. Despite that, I found that I couldn't put this book down. In fact, after the ISS was over, I went on to read all of them in the series in a span of a few weeks (to the neglect of my homework!). I might not have had the words for it yet, but I was immersed in the idea that an author could create an entire world, replete with language and mythology, and that I could visit this place through the mystery of imagination and language.

More than twenty years have passed. As I reflect on my career as an English teacher, a dean/disciplinarian, and now a principal, I can't help but see that ISS as transformational. I keep a quote in my office from Tolkien, "Not all who wander are lost." It reminds me that every child is on a journey and that consequences, in a context of care and support, should meet them on that journey, wherever they are.

Recently, a teacher colleague shared a story of a senior who had earned a write-up in his class. Rather than punting this to the school disciplinarian, he gave the young man the option to join him over lunch for a book club for three weeks in a row. This particular student was notorious for behavioral issues in and out of class. For whatever reason, the student agreed to the terms. He joined the book club, and he and my colleague called their meetings lunch detentions. Afterward, the student said something profound: "I've been in trouble a lot in school. This is the first time I've ever been given a punishment that aimed to make me a better person." I offer these anecdotes only to remember that we might do well to envision a world in which justice is relational and that we might create this world in the school cultures we create.

# 35. Not Too Tired to Be Caring

—Told by an assistant principal of an urban high school

Last week was a very busy week. We had several deadlines to meet and a basketball game. When I got home Friday evening, I was exhausted both physically and mentally. On Monday, as I walked into the building, I saw one of the other assistant principals. I asked her how her weekend was—just making small talk. She said it was good. Then she told me that she and her husband went down to juvenile hall to look for one of her students. I know the student she was talking about. He is constantly in trouble—skipping class and usually being disrespectful and very rude. I know she was very tired after work on Friday, and she had to pick up her husband from the airport late that evening. I look at her with an even deeper sense of respect.

# 36. Swimming Upstream

—Told by the principal of a small-town middle school

Hey, Anna! Your science teacher says that your project is fantastic. I'm coming to your class to check it out soon!" "Joe, how's play rehearsal going?" "LaShonda, how's your sister? Is she feeling better?" "Shemika, great sweatshirt! Is that where you're going to college?" "Josh, lose the hat! Great to see your mom at the grocery store this last weekend." "Jeremy and Sharon, enough of that. A little separation, please. Better hurry to get to your next class." "James! Sean! How's it going?" "Eva, Elizabeth, and Morgan! Stick it to 'em at your lacrosse game this afternoon!" "Brittany, I hear your brother is coming home on leave. Wonderful news! Have a great time with him!" And so it goes three times a day every day as Principal Jones walks the halls of the middle school during passing periods, swimming upstream in the crowd, connecting with her students.

# 37. Try This

—Told by the principal of a small-town high school

Kevin had a recurring problem with tardiness. He is a great kid, and he always worked hard at school. He has a part-time job in the evenings to help support his family. He is exhausted and simply has a hard time getting up in the morning. And Kevin doesn't have much support at home to help him. His mother has a job that requires her to leave the house very early in the morning, and he gets no help from his siblings, whose school has a later start time. If Kevin misses the city bus, he misses most of the first period. His tardies were starting to pile up and hurt him, putting him at risk of failing his first period class.

After arriving late (again), Kevin's first period teacher sent him to me. We began to talk, and Kevin came right out and told me that he's tired and that he tries as hard as he can to get up and get to school on time. He has no alarm clock and no one to wake him. I understood and nodded to him. I reached down behind my desk chair to unplug a clock radio that is sitting on my shelf. It has an alarm built into it. "Try this," I say, handing the clock radio to him. "Maybe this will help you. Keep it as long as you would like. Now, get back to class. Check in with me some mornings, and let me know whether it's working for you. If not, I may have to come over and wake you up myself!"

Kevin smiled and returned to class. From that day on, he was rarely late to school.

---

# 38. The Tux

## —Told by an instructional facilitator at a suburban high school

Antoine was an outstanding well-rounded student, but he did not take any advanced placement courses, nor was he in the top 10 percent of his class. To some, he would be considered an above average student, but masking his positive dispositions and academic prowess were daily struggles that the average person would find difficult to bear. Antoine came from a poverty-stricken environment. He lived in a one-bedroom apartment with six other siblings. In conversations, he would tell me about his regrets of not having known his father. He often wore the same clothes to school every day—blue jeans, a gray polo shirt, and white Nike shoes. Not one to ask for help, he often sat with me at lunch, and I would offer him some of my food.

As his senior year approached, Antoine felt the pressure, as many seniors did, of how to pay his senior dues and find money for the prom. Knowing his background, the $320 assessment would not be something his mother could handle. While I offered to pay his fee, Antoine was a proud young man and asked me to help him get a job instead. After about a month of job searching, Antoine was able to secure a position at the neighborhood grocery store. In no time, he paid his senior dues with his own money. After working during the fall, Antoine's mother fell sick and needed him to stay home to help monitor his brothers and sisters, so he left his first job reluctantly. As the year went by, Antoine continued to handle all of the pressures of school and family.

It was a month before the prom when I overheard some of the office aides talking about Antoine and his prom situation and how they wished they could do something to help him. He wanted to go to prom, and though he had a ticket paid for through his senior dues, he didn't have the money for a tuxedo. Realizing this, I took it upon myself to rent him a tuxedo so that he could enjoy everything that he worked so hard for. I also found sponsors to provide transportation to and from the prom as well as to pay for a trip to the barber. I called him into my office and told him that everything will be taken care of free of charge, and he started crying.

Two weeks later, I would be the one crying as Antoine walked into my office and announced that he had been awarded a Gates Millennium Scholarship. Though he did not necessarily fully recognize the significance of this award, I knew it would be life changing for him and his family. I was right. I received a text last year with a picture of a badge. Four years earlier, Antoine had gone on to attend a highly selective university to study political science. The text was a picture of the badge he received during his employee orientation at the US Department of Agriculture in Washington, DC. He sent a note thanking me for helping him get his first suit and that now he needs a few more. Smiling, I knew someday he would.

# 39. Breaking the Law

—Told by the principal of an urban high school

*Adapted from Stewart (2018).*

This is a story about a time when I broke the law. I could say that this is the only time I broke the law as a principal in a situation like this one, and that may or may not be true.

Darryl started with us his freshman year. He was smart, quiet, and brilliant at flying just under the radar. He was socially powerful and street savvy, even at fourteen years old. He finished his freshman year and then disappeared. Darryl returned during the last week of school two years later wanting to reenroll. He communicated that he had been locked up for a year and was trying to get back on track. With final exams underway, I recommended that he demonstrate his commitment to getting caught up by enrolling in summer school and earning a minimum of two credits. He succeeded.

During that summer, I got to know Darryl. He shared where his choices and lifestyle had led him—and his commitment to do better. Darryl just had a way about him—a soft smile, insightful thoughts, and a sincerity that simply made me want to believe him. As we worked through his senior year, I could see the war raging inside Darryl—the war between street life and an unknown future. Darryl had lots of people in his corner—teachers, friends, administrators, our school resource officers, and myself. All of us were grasping on to who we knew Darryl could be.

Working with young people is a glorious challenge. One of the harder parts for me is watching potential wasted. I see students every day in our classrooms and hallways not yet able to be fully invested in their futures and take hold of their true potential. In education, many of us struggle with the root causes of that disregard and work desperately to remove barriers and plant seeds in our students that enable them to aspire for more. We want more than aspiration, however; we want the skills and knowledge to make aspiration a reality.

One day during the spring of Darryl's senior year, we caught Darryl in possession of marijuana. This was his second offense and required that he be expelled for a full calendar year based on state law. In that moment, all that I know to be true about the future outcomes of students, particularly African American males, who are expelled and who do not graduate from high school confronted me. There have been endless studies on the cradle-to-prison pipeline, but when a decision before me can so clearly alter the future course of a child, I did, and will always do, all that I can to disrupt that pipeline. I refuse to knowingly contribute to outcomes that are staggeringly bleak. I simply cannot do it. So I didn't.

We moved Darryl into our Choice Academy, in lieu of expulsion, and he proudly walked the stage with his graduating class. After graduation, one of our school resource officers contacted a friend who offered Darryl an apprenticeship to become an electrician. Just six months later, Darryl graduated with his electrician's license and is gainfully employed today.

I suppose some laws may just be meant to be broken.

---

# 40. No Pity, Just Care

—Told by the assistant principal of a small-town middle school

When John came to school, he always said, "Yes sir, no sir" and "Yes ma'am, no ma'am." He was always respectful when adults were around. He always gave me a hug when he left my office or when he saw me in the hallway. But when he was unsupervised, he caused many problems with other students—fighting on the bus, fighting in the hallway, saying rude or mean things to other students. The list goes on and on. All the sixth-grade teachers wanted me to send him to alternative school, which might have been the best place for him. I wasn't willing to give up on him at all. I saw something in this kid, and what I saw was that he had a heart of gold.

One day I had him in my office, and I just started asking him questions. He eventually came to tell me about his home life. He wasn't using it as a crutch; he just happened to start talking about it. He lived with his grandmother. His dad was in jail for drugs. His mother had left when he was a little boy and had not seen him since. However, he did know his mother was also in and out of jail for drugs. His uncle was also in and out of jail for the same issues. The grandmother who was raising John looked like she had been through multiple wars in her own house, which, listening to her stories, turned out to be true. John had witnessed all of this. He had been in multiple schools with no luck, getting kicked out of most all of them. I did a home visit one day, and while I was there, the resource officer of our school found out another person who was living in the house had a warrant out. So John got to see, yet

again, someone else get arrested and taken away from his home in handcuffs.

I come from a loving family with two educated parents. My brother and sister both have a college education. When I was growing up, the cops never once came to our house for any reason. My mom and dad rarely fought. At one point, I am sitting in my office talking to teachers about John, and I realize that his teachers (from what I know) had the same upbringing as myself. Not one of us could empathize with what John was going through, yet we all had the answer to his problem. Every teacher had a solution to a problem John was going through yet had no idea about the actual problem he was going through.

John eventually did something severe enough to get sent to alternative school. I hated it. When he went, it hurt. He had something in him that was just screaming to get out. He had good in him that could have done so much for the people around him. I cared for him where he was. I still visit him at alternative school monthly. I make a trip to the school just to see him. I will never know if the care I gave to him made any difference, but I do know I cared for him. I encouraged other teachers to do the same. I didn't want them to pity John; I just wanted them to care.

---

# 41. It's Because My School Family Loves Me
## —Told by the principal of an urban charter middle school

Ben and I started talking regularly about his academic progress about halfway through his sixth-grade year. Ben has struggled in school since the early elementary grades and was retained in third grade. Each time we talked, he had all of the *right* answers. He would start trying harder, start doing homework, and start paying attention in class as soon as he left my office. He never kept these promises, and by the end of sixth grade he wasn't academically ready to move on to seventh grade. It didn't seem like he would benefit from retention either.

After much conversation and soul-searching, we decided to promote Ben to the seventh grade with the agreement that if we didn't see significant improvement, he would be retained at the end of the next year. By the end of the seventh grade, nothing looked different for Ben, so he was retained. It was one of the most difficult decisions I have ever been a part of. I have never taken retention lightly. It can be disastrous for a student. But promoting Ben to the eighth grade would have likely set him up for even more failure. To make matters more difficult, Ben was the only student in the school who was retained that year—a young, black man who had already been retained once and now a second time. We had to figure out how to reach him. His odds for dropping out of high school down the road were increasing by the day, and we had to reach him somehow.

During his retention conference, we talked about Ben's grades and expectations for the next year. We also talked about how much he was loved by his school family. Yes, we talk about love at our school, and we really use the term *school family*. We let him pick his adviser and a few teachers he trusted so he could feel safe and loved. We talked about how hard the first couple of weeks of the new school year were going to be, and we reminded him again that he was loved by his school family. When he left the conference, we weren't sure that we would ever see him again.

On the day before the first day of school each year, the students come to pick up their schedules and meet their teachers. I looked out the front door more times than I could count that day and, finally, there he was. Ben was walking up the sidewalk, heading for the building. He had his hoodie pulled over his head and was looking down the whole time, but he was here. We all knew he wanted to stay at home, but he came to school that day and the next day, the first day of school, and every day after. He did everything he possibly could do to be around his friends in the eighth grade, and we did everything we could to help him find his place in his new class. Most importantly, we reminded him early and often that he was loved.

The beginning of the school year was rough, to say the least, and we questioned our decision to retain Ben almost every day. But slowly Ben started to connect. He wandered the halls less, hid in bathrooms less, and found fewer reasons to *coincidentally* be in the cafeteria when the eighth graders came to lunch or went to recess. We knew we had turned the corner when his advisory team lost in a schoolwide freeze flag tournament but another seventh-grade

team won. He thumped his chest, smiled, and shouted, "It's OK that my team lost because seventh grade won!" Not long after that, Ben found out that some eighth-grade boys were messing up the bathrooms, and he asked to speak to the school community about it. You could have heard a pin drop when he stood up in front of his school family and spoke to us about responsibility. Things were definitely changing for Ben.

Ben worked harder this year than ever before. We greeted each other almost every day with a hug, and sometimes I wondered to which of us that hug meant more, to Ben or to me. When we sat down to talk about his progress after the midyear reports, Ben was passing about half of his classes. When we checked in just before spring break, he was passing six of eight and had a solid plan of how he would pass his seventh class. With one month left in the school year, he was passing seven of his eight classes. He continued to struggle with math and hadn't made a passing score in that class in almost two years. Math was the one class where Ben didn't feel confident. He said it was just too hard, and he didn't understand no matter how hard he tried. He seemed defeated. But unbeknownst to me, he had set one more plan in motion.

Ben knew he couldn't stay after school to get help, so he asked his math teacher to have lunch with him a couple of times a week so he could get the help he needed. They had been eating lunch together and talking about math for weeks. When he walked up to me last week, he put his arm around my shoulder and said, "Check out your boy's math grades." I wasn't sure what to expect. It had seemed hopeless a few weeks before, but surely it had to be good news. As we walked to my office, I asked, "Will I be proud?" He said, "I know you will." As I opened my laptop and looked at his grades, I saw the first passing grade he's had in math all year. We hugged, and I told him how proud I was. He smiled and said, "It's because my school family loves me." Then he turned around and headed off to class.

# 42. Natalie

—Told by an assistant principal of an urban middle school

Two days before Natalie ended up in my office for flipping over and breaking a desk during math class, I ran into her and our in-school suspension (ISS) supervisor walking through the cafeteria. He had found her roaming the halls, skipping her computer class. "Oh my god, I don't want to go!" she yelled defiantly. This was not the first time she had been caught skipping computer class. She had recently served a day in ISS for skipping and talking back disrespectfully to her teacher. The dean of students handled both skipping incidents, but she ended up in my office when she flipped the desk.

I knew Natalie from last year, when she was in seventh grade and I was in my first year as assistant principal at the middle school. I went almost that whole year without knowing her name. She was quiet in class, never got in trouble, and was never mentioned by her teachers. At the very end of seventh grade, I met her when I was investigating a fight. I found out she knew it was going to happen and didn't tell anyone. I was frustrated, called her home, and asked her mother to talk with her about her decision not to tell an adult. I should have seen the lack of connection with any adults in the building as a red flag, but my attention was focused on the fight.

Natalie had a rocky start to eighth grade. She either flew under the radar with some teachers or was disruptive and skipping with others. When she flipped the desk, I was concerned about the escalation of her behavior. When I asked her what she was thinking when she did it, she didn't answer and scowled at me. I'm sure frustration was evident in my voice. I told her she would have to spend the day downstairs in ISS the next day as a consequence, but I also had a realization that I had to change my tune. "Natalie," I said, "I have no illusion that spending the day in ISS is actually going to do anything to change your behavior or make things better.

It is just a consequence. But I am really worried about you. I don't know what it is, but I see a different student than I did last year. Who is your adult in the building? Who do you trust to go and talk to?"

"Ms. Nelson," she said. Ms. Nelson was our school counselor. I was both surprised and relieved that she named Ms. Nelson. I wondered if she was going to name anyone at all. "That's great. I'm so happy to hear that. When was the last time you checked in with Ms. Nelson?" I asked. "Two days ago." "Good. Well, you will spend the day in ISS tomorrow, but I want you to continue to check in with Ms. Nelson and talk about whatever is bothering you."

The next day I saw Ms. Nelson, I mentioned to her that Natalie named her as her *trusted adult*. She was also surprised but understood the importance of that honor. We briefly discussed Natalie's recent behaviors, and Ms. Nelson made note of a few next steps.

I then went to talk with Ms. Matthews, our eighth-grade team lead and Natalie's English teacher. Students often name Ms. Matthews as their trusted adult, so I wanted to discuss the situation with her. Ms. Matthews admitted that Natalie was so quiet and compliant in her class that she often overlooked her when other behavior issues or more needy students took her attention. She promised to do a better job *seeing* Natalie, talking with her, and engaging her outside of the lesson.

This is still a work in progress, but two weeks later, Natalie had not skipped any classes, nor had she had any other office referrals. When she saw me in the hallway the other day, she came over to me and confided that she had been to see Ms. Nelson earlier that morning. "That's great," I said smiling. "We're all here for you." "Thanks," she said and walked off.

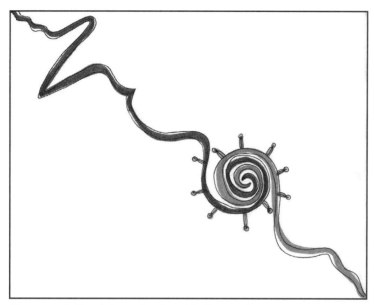

**Connected. Dominique Sandoval Delanoe, Grade 12**

I think it took something as simple as remembering that her behaviors were symptoms, signals for help. As soon as I saw her as a young person who was really struggling, everything changed. This is an ongoing case for our teachers, our counselor, and myself as an administrator working together to see a student and asking ourselves what we can do to connect, help, and support her. And it took me remembering to set aside a punitive mindset and ask very simple questions to show some caring.

# 43. Our Collective Responsibility

### —Told by the assistant principal of a small-town high school

Mid-February, in the midst of flu season, the attendance office was tracking flu numbers and calling absent students daily. I phoned Michael, a senior who started missing a great deal of school lately, to see if he was one of the many students afflicted by influenza. Upon answering my call, Mike explained that his parents took him to get a tattoo to honor his eighteenth birthday. Upon his return to school, Mike showed me his tattoo—a compass rose reminding him of his *true north* on the inside of his forearm. He explained that he had turned eighteen and that his parents were relocating out of state because of his dad's job. They gave Mike the choice to stay or go. With three months until graduation, a lead in the school play, a top seed on the tennis team, two AP classes in process, Mike decided he could not leave our school. The tattoo was a reminder of his parents and of their love for him.

Mike quickly became the school's child— penniless, alone, and in need of support. Having small-town connections, a young couple agreed to house Mike. Several faculty members and the administrative team transported Mike to his part-time job, gave him spending money, sponsored him and his date to the prom, cheered uproariously for him at the school play, paid for his AP exam fees, and gave him a gift shower for his college dorm room. The guidance team worked tirelessly to help him with scholarship applications and got him a full ride, including housing and a meal plan at a state university. Mike graduated loved, with numerous surrogate parents who welled up with tears at graduation.

Mike had become *our* collective responsibility, teaching us what we can do as a community to support *all* students in our building.

---

# 44. Bicycle Built for Two

**—Told by an administrator of a small-town independent boys high school**

Pieter applied to our school from a boarding school in the United Kingdom where he had been the recipient of aggressive bullying. He hails from the Netherlands. He is African by ethnicity. He is autistic, and as a by-product, his speech pattern is slowed. He was born albino, and as a result, his complexion is unique. He is legally blind and can see only indistinctive blobs of color unless a text or image is held three inches from his eyes. He is also brilliant, motivated, and genuinely curious.

Pieter dominated the academic curriculum with relative ease, but he yearned for success outside of the classroom on the sports field. After spending significant time contemplating various ways in which a legally blind student could safely participate in sports, a faculty member who is our mountain biking coach and I found a way that Pieter could join the mountain biking team—a tandem bicycle. Our coach could pilot the bike, and Pieter could pedal for both of them in competitive races. We all knew, and so did he, that he was unlikely to win a race. But that didn't matter. Hearing him talk proudly of his place on the team and the fantastic smile he wore on his face as he whizzed down the trail were enough for him and for us. At the conclusion of his first competitive race, the team flocked to Pieter to celebrate his great personal victory—the first time in his life that he had ever competed in an interscholastic sport. Pieter was the first athlete in the country to ride a tandem bike in league competition. At the end of his senior season he was awarded the Extraordinary Courage Award from the National Cycling Association.

During our graduation ceremonies, Pieter was visibly moved when he was presented with our mountain biking award. He graduated as school valedictorian and matriculated to a highly selective university in the Northeast. In his valedictory address, he remarked at the incredible feat that *we* had accomplished together and about how truly grateful he was that we provided him an opportunity to experience this success.

# Stories of
## Cultivating
## Schools as Caring
## Communities

# Introduction

The stories in this collection illustrate the second arena of caring school leadership practice: how principals and other school leaders can cultivate their schools as caring communities for students. These stories focus on two primary aspects of this work. The first concerns ways in which principals and other school leaders can help develop the knowledge, skills, and motivations of teachers, staff, and students to be more caring for one another and to guide the school to become a caring community. The second aspect concerns ways in which principals and other school leaders can create organizational conditions in their schools that are conducive for developing caring capacity, for enacting caring behavior, and for caring community to emerge and thrive. Of particular interest is what leaders might do to develop their schools' cultures, structures, and authority relationships and governance.

An important part of this work is how principals and other school leaders engage teachers, staff, students, and parents in developing schools as caring communities. Central to this engagement are the ways in which principals and other school leaders are caring of them. While being caring of teachers, staff, and parents is good in itself, it is crucial for promoting caring for students and for developing schools as caring communities. It is difficult to imagine the full investment of teachers, staff, and parents in cultivating a caring community for students if they do not feel cared for themselves.

Each story in this collection makes visible in one way or another the aims, positive virtues and mindsets, and competencies of caring. Some stories illustrate several practices at once. Also, like stories in the other collections, not all of these stories are positive examples. Some you may consider problematic, even negative examples.

The stories in this collection are grouped by level of school. Otherwise, they are not presented in any particular order. Nor do they represent the full extent of ways that principals and other school leaders might cultivate their schools as caring communities. For example, there are few stories of directly teaching students or teachers how to be more caring of others. As you read these stories,

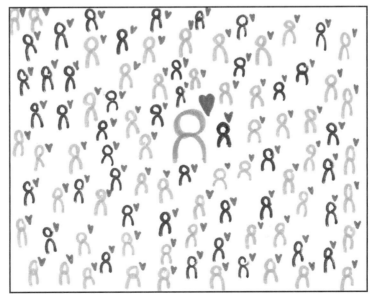

**Surrounded by Care. Nicholas Fogg, Grade 12**

pay attention to the importance of caring relationships in fostering community. Consider the role of context and how principals' and other school leaders' knowledge, skills, assumptions, and sense of professional role function in this caring leadership work. You may begin by reading stories from the level of school in which you are most interested, but we *strongly* encourage you to read stories from other levels for the insights and lessons they provide.

A number of stories in this collection illustrate different approaches to developing the capacity for caring among teachers and school staff. These approaches include leader modeling and experiential learning from being cared for by principals and other school staff both in everyday work and under exceptional circumstances. They also include leader coaching and teacher professional development. Some stories tell of what principals and other school leaders do to foster student capacity for caring and caring community. These efforts range from encouraging instructional changes at the classroom level to making changes in classroom learning environments so that they are more conducive to student caring. Several stories reveal approaches that principals and other school leaders can take to promote positive student conduct, positive conflict resolution for both students and teachers, and students' physical and psychological safety.

This collection also contains stories of principals and other school leaders working to support the development and expression of caring community. Some stories illustrate how principals and other school leaders integrate the values of caring and community into the lived experiences of their schools. A good number of stories show how leaders can promote a culture of caring community in their schools. Other stories give examples of what principals and other school leaders can do to strengthen structural supports for caring community, such as creating opportunities for interaction and forming caring relationships, and providing services and resources important to that effort. Additional stories tell of how principals and other school leaders reshape authority and influence relationships within their schools to foster caring, notably how they open opportunities for student and teacher voice and influence.

Finally, this collection contains stories of engaging parents and families in ways that are themselves caring and that may contribute to caring within the school community. These stories differ from stories in Collection III, which are focused on ways that principals and other school leaders can be caring of families and communities beyond the school. Several stories in Collection II recount ways that principals and other school leaders are welcoming and express caring for parents and families in their engagement with school. This includes how principals and other school leaders engage in positive and supportive communication with parents and families, bringing them into the work of schools and helping them contribute to a caring school community. Several other stories illustrate ways for parents to express their voice and help build school community.

Figure 2.1 shows the stories in this collection, by number, in which examples of these caring school leadership practices can be found. You may use this figure to navigate your way through the collection.

# Questions for Reflection and Discussion

## General Questions

1. How does each story reflect the three foundational elements of caring school leadership described in Introduction: Caring School Leadership in the beginning of this book? (a) The aims of caring? (b) Positive virtues and mindsets of caring? and (c) Competencies of caring? In what ways might these three elements be strong or weak in the story? How

Figure 2.1

**Caring School Leadership Practices Represented in Collection II Stories**

| Practices | Story Numbers |
|---|---|
| Modeling | 45, 50, 51, 53, 54, 56, 58, 59, 60, 61, 62, 64, 66, 67, 70, 73, 74, 80, 82, 84 |
| Being caring of teachers—experiential learning | 50, 51, 52, 53, 54, 56, 59, 60, 64, 74 |
| Coaching and professional development | 48, 51, 52, 53, 56, 59, 63, 69, 76, 80, 81 |
| Supporting instructional and environmental changes in classrooms | 49, 51, 52, 56, 59, 63, 65, 79, 81 |
| Promoting positive conduct, conflict resolution, and safety | 46, 48, 53, 54, 61, 66, 79, 83 |
| Cultivating a culture of caring | 45, 47, 48, 49, 50, 54, 55, 57, 58, 59, 60, 61, 62, 63, 64, 66, 67, 68, 69, 71, 72, 73, 74, 75, 78, 79, 81, 82, 83, 84, 85 |
| Creating opportunities for interaction and forming caring relationships | 48, 49, 54, 55, 57, 59, 61, 62, 64, 67, 68, 69, 71, 73, 75, 79, 81, 82 |
| Providing services and resources | 50, 55, 59, 66, 68, 73, 75, 81, 82, 84, 85 |
| Providing opportunities for student voice and influence | 45, 48, 57, 59, 61, 63, 65, 66, 67, 70, 73, 75, 76, 79, 83, 84 |
| Providing opportunities for teacher voice and influence | 46, 55, 59, 63, 68, 70, 75, 81, 83 |
| Being welcoming and expressing caring for parents and families | 46, 47, 48, 54, 55, 59, 62, 76, 77, 78, 85 |
| Providing opportunities for parent voice and participation | 47, 48, 54, 55, 70, 76, 77, 85 |

might these strengths or weaknesses shape the actions and interactions of the school leader and any outcomes apparent in the story? How might caring in the story be seen as a part of the everyday work of school leaders or as something extra that they do? How can the caring demonstrated by school leaders in these stories help others to be more caring in their schools?

2. How might the school leader's assumptions, understandings, and biases affect the way each story unfolds and the outcomes that are apparent? How might different contexts affect the story? The qualities and characteristics of interpersonal relationships? The organizational context of the school? The environment beyond the school?

3. What do you see as the main lesson or lessons of each story? If you were to write a moral for each story, what would the moral be?

4. What is your personal reaction to each story? Why do you react this way? What might be influencing your thinking?

5. Imagine that the school leader in the story met you and asked, "What do you think about what I said and what I did?" Looking through the eyes of the different people in the story, how would you respond? What advice would you give this school leader?

## Collection-Specific Questions

1. How can each story be interpreted as one of how principals and other school leaders model caring to others and how modeling can develop or discourage caring on the part of others? Think about modeling as an intentional strategy, and think of it as an unintentional influence. Consider also how the lessons of modeling might need to be expanded upon or reinforced with other developmental strategies.

2. How do these stories illustrate the importance of time and opportunity for teachers, staff members, students, and parents to be together, to interact, and to develop understanding of each other in order to foster deeper, more caring relationships? What are different ways that principals and other school leaders can create more time and opportunity for such relationships to form? Think about ways suggested by the stories. Think of other ways too.

3. We assume that teachers and staff members care about their students and are motivated to becoming even more caring of them. We also assume that teachers and staff members possess some knowledge and skill to be caring of their students and to develop caring classroom environments to support their students' learning and development. In what ways do these stories suggest how principals and other school leaders can build upon the competencies that teachers and staff members have to be even more caring of their students? How might teachers and staff members become more skilled at being attentive to and inquisitive of students and their needs and interests? How might they become more knowledgeable about their students as persons and learners, more reflective of how their caring actions and support are perceived and received by students, and better able to adjust their actions to be more caring? What might be done to help teachers and staff members stay motivated, especially as caring becomes difficult and stressful?

4. Think of the ways that different aspects of school organization can affect the development and expression of caring among students, teachers, and staff. Consider the structural elements of school organization; school culture; and authority, voice, and power in the school. What role might different elements of school organization play in these stories, with regard to developing capacity for caring and bringing that capacity to life in caring action and interaction? How might these elements support or impede efforts to strengthen caring? Step back and think about what school leaders in these stories might do to address more fully organizational impediments to their efforts.

5. In these stories, how might school leaders' caring of students and their caring of teachers and parents contribute to their respective ability and motivation to be more caring of one another? How might school leaders' caring of others foster the development of caring community in their schools? Consider in each story circumstances in which school leader caring might beget more caring on the part of others and contribute to the development of caring community.

# Application Questions

1. How might your own assumptions, preconceptions, and points of view influence how you read and make meaning of these stories? Consider your understanding of yourself as a caring person and a caring school leader, including your strengths and weaknesses in being caring of others. Consider your understanding of what the professional role of a school leader requires of you; what your situation calls on you to do; and what your students, your staff, and your community expect of you. How does your thinking and sense of self affect how you practice caring in this arena of leadership?

2. Put yourself in the position of the school leader who is the focus of each story. Would you think and act in the same way in the situation described in the story? Why or why not? In what ways might you think and act differently? Why?

3. For each story, recall a similar, actual situation in your school. How would you retell the story for your own setting, with yourself as the focal school leader? In what ways would your story be similar? In what ways would your story be different? Why?

4. Consider the positive ways that school leaders in these stories work to develop and promote caring and community in their schools. Consider ways that school leaders may develop capacity for caring and aspects of school organization that enable the development and enactment of caring. How might you adopt and adapt these positive practices in your own setting with your own students? What factors—personal, professional, and contextual—might support or impede your effort? How might you address impediments to make your effort more successful?

5. Consider the difficult aspects of caring in this arena of leadership practice that are revealed in these stories. Do you see similar difficulties in your school, with your teachers, staff, students, parents, and families? Are there other difficulties? How might you address these difficulties? How do you think about being caring when the situation is difficult as opposed

**On the Playground. Kenzie Mulron, Grade 3**

to when it is easy? What do you do in such situations to become more caring in your work with teachers, staff, parents, and families in fostering caring and caring community in your school?

6. What other leadership practices and strategies, beyond those illustrated in these stories, might be effective to cultivate your school as a caring community? To develop the capacity of teachers, staff, and students in your school for caring? To create the organizational conditions conducive to this development and to bringing caring community to life? Explain why you think these practices and strategies might be effective in your situation. Explain the groundwork that might need to be done to increase the likelihood of their success.

# Stories From Elementary Schools

## 45. We Like the Egg Chairs

—Told by the principal of an urban elementary school

We constantly sought to increase student voice and choice throughout our school community. We focused on doing this in instructional and noninstructional settings. For example, in the instructional setting, we offered students the opportunity to choose the order in which they completed center work or to choose how they would show their learning. In other settings, we offered them the opportunity to organize school events and to co-construct hallway routines and expectations.

One concerted effort to increase student choice and voice involved redesigning classroom and schoolwide spaces to better serve student needs and preferences. Using both formal methods (e.g., surveys) and informal methods (e.g., conversation), we asked students to tell us what worked best and worst about existing spaces and to articulate their preferences about spaces where they learn best. By asking students these questions, we adults received very specific, actionable feedback that sometimes challenged our own notions of student preference and needs. For example, students frequently expressed the need for both individual and group work spaces that were tailored to task, when adults consistently believed students would only prefer social

or group work spaces. Many also indicated that they wanted the option to work at traditional furniture some of the time. Our second-grade students clearly articulated the need for *zones* that were delineated by how loud or interactive students were to be in them and then told us that the zone 1 silent areas needed to be positioned on opposite ends of the room from the zone 4 group work areas.

With this information and funds from a small grant in hand, we purchased and borrowed furniture and other materials that students said they wanted and reconfigured two classrooms and one schoolwide space, the school auditorium where all grades had music class, into prototype student-centered classrooms. Students were delighted and consistently took great care of their new rooms given their understanding of the logical consequences that would follow if they didn't (e.g., furniture would be wrecked and have to be replaced with the regular school furniture because we had no additional funds to replace furniture that wasn't impacted by just regular wear and tear). Students were more productive! With ongoing explicit guidance and reflection, they largely worked when and where they could do their best work.

## 46. Hear My Message, Not My Tone

—Told by the principal of an urban elementary school

I was an experienced principal but new to a turnaround school in a large West Coast city. The beginning of the school year had been rocky, but things were finally settling in. I knew

all five hundred-plus students by name. Teachers had found their pacing and were starting to find their confidence with students who were several grade levels behind academically. Because most of our teachers lived outside the neighborhood, I had hired the majority of our support staff from the community. I made sure that they had a voice in meetings so we could do our best to understand and serve our children and families.

While most mornings were not dull, this particular one started off with Ms. Jones—one of our teachers—screaming at Ms. Tallie, another one of our teachers, in the hallway. Screaming is a polite term for what was taking place. Visibly shaken, Ms. Tallie was almost in tears as I quickly approached. Not able to make out most of her words, I stood close to Ms. Jones, and in a low but stern voice, I told her to make her way to my office immediately as this display was not appropriate for the children to witness.

I made sure another teacher attended to Ms. Tallie and quickly made my way to the office where Ms. Jones was now yelling at our secretary and office manager. I stood at the door to my office, didn't say a word, and pointed in with a wink. While still yelling, Ms. Jones made her way into my office.

I asked her to have a seat. It was a minute or so before she finally sat down. I asked her to calm her voice so I could better understand her and her frustration. I got a bottle of water from my small refrigerator and gave it to her, asked her to sip it, and take a deep breath. While she drank the water, I sat next to her and assured her of two things. I am always here to support you. And if you become so upset that you can't control your anger, the only person you can yell at is me. The latter lent a bit of levity to the moment that allowed for pause and for her to catch her breath. While describing the incident that she was so upset about, I took notes, made eye contact, and assured her I would investigate the situation and get back to her before the students were dismissed that day. She confirmed that she would come to my office before dismissal so we could review my findings.

According to Ms. Jones, her son, Jawan, had been fighting on the playground with another student, and Ms. Tallie had not addressed the boys in class or after school. Ms. Jones was upset because she had not been notified, and her son said that it all started because he was being made fun of on the bus on the way to school that morning.

As I investigated what had happened, I quickly learned that Jawan's aunt, who was one of the educational assistants at the school, had broken up the two boys who were *play fighting* and had handled it on the playground, never making Ms. Tallie aware of the incident. While it was true that kids were ridiculing Jawan, which was the problem that really needed to be dealt with, many of the other details Jawan shared were slightly off.

When we met again before dismissal, Ms. Jones apologized for having lost her temper. I asked her why she felt so deeply about this. In the end, what had happened with Jawan and the other student was relatively easy to address, but there had to be a reason it angered her so much. She shared stories about how no one ever stood up for her when she was a student in school and how scared she was that Jawan would "be expelled for his behaviors like he was at every other school." She had been afraid.

I thanked Ms. Jones for sharing. I promised her—one I never broke—that I would always hear her and support her understanding of any situation.

I also thanked Ms. Jones. I thanked her because she trusted me enough to share her fears with me. Her vulnerability would allow the two of us to work together to ensure that Jawan had a successful academic career at our school. I also reassured her that I didn't believe in expulsion, so he could settle in and become a part of our community.

In the end, Ms. Jones gave me a hug. What a difference seven hours makes! When she apologized again, I told her that no apology was needed for me but that I would like for her to connect with Ms. Tallie and apologize to her. She graciously did and later that year shared some of the stories with Ms. Tallie that she had shared with me. In the end, Ms. Tallie became a strong advocate for Jawan throughout his time at our school.

Following this incident with Ms. Jones, I began to recognize how so many of the families must feel as they approached our school because of their previous experiences as students. As a team, we set a goal to make sure every family member felt respected and heard by approaching each situation with open inquiry and doing our best to welcome families into our school, our classrooms, and our offices.

# 47. Family Connect Time
### —Told by the principal of a suburban elementary school

We changed our parent-teacher conferences into a more deliberate way to build stronger, more caring relationships with parents and families. We began to refer to them as "family connect time."

In the fall, family connect time is all about the family, all about developing the relationship. It's about me—all of us—understanding what "family" means to our students, parents, and guardians. It's about how we're going to communicate throughout the year. In the spring, teachers reach out to parents and guardians with invitations to identify things that *they* want to cover during their time together, going beyond what the teachers want to talk about.

Grade-level teacher leaders and I created a monitoring system where teachers could flexibly connect with families at times that were mutually convenient for them rather than only on the three nights of conferences at school in the spring. Teachers were responsible for recording sixteen hours of contact time, which could be at school, at a coffee shop, in parents' homes, or over the phone.

We literally blew up an old structure. How did that impact the child? I truly believe that our students received a much better experience in the classroom because our relationship with the family is so much stronger.

# 48. Our Transformation
### —Told by the principal of a suburban elementary school

I reflected on the transformative shift in perspectives that occurred in my school as a result of my district's prolonged immersion in conversations about racial equity and how these discussions have led to a stronger sense of caring throughout the school. Our district not only engaged in dialogue about racial equity but we transformed our peer coaching program to a peer equity–coaching program. At my school we hosted study groups, practiced vulnerability, and identified our own racial lenses and experiences in discussions. I, as a white woman, led my teacher leaders to continually identify and dismantle systemic barriers that students and families of color faced in our school. This sense of caring evolved from "caring about" or "caring for" students to believing that each child's unique experience be placed at the center of the work of everyone in our school. In talking about this change, I recounted the following:

> I can remember when people started the racial equity journey. It was still about how we were going to transform children. It was how the *children* were going to change. In fact, I'm going to take it a step further. It was about how I help children become successful so that they will be

able to navigate their lives. I think pivotally in the last three to four years, we have made this *aha* that it's not about that. It is all about me. About us. It's like "Where am I in my own racial experience, and how does that look?" And "This is the child's school and they're not changing. Nor should they change."

A good example of our change was a situation involving our school's resource officer, the white police woman assigned to our school. She was looking at student artwork hanging in the hall prior to a family event, and she became disturbed by a poster designed by a fourth-grade girl that contained an illustration and this question: Why do all the police officers shoot black people? The officer asked me to take the poster down.

I looked at it. I looked at it again. I read, and then I started thinking, "Well, maybe the student could change the word *all* to *some*." And then I thought, "Wait a minute. It's not my job to tell this fourth grader to do this just for being honest and for her honest thoughts. It's not right for me to go and say, 'Can *you* change?' Because there's nothing wrong. These are her thoughts, and wrestling with these thoughts is what we are about at this school."

In our training, we consider how our identity influences our decisions, so I considered how I would approach this. What influences me, and how have I been socialized to consider this? I talked briefly with our school's equity coach, an African American female, and then discussed with the officer my decision to leave the poster on the wall and honor student voice. I called the student's mother to discuss the resource officer's request and my decision. She thanked me for supporting her child's point of view. I also told her that the officer wanted to meet with her, her husband, and their daughter to help them understand that she was there to help and didn't hate all black people.

A few weeks after this conversation happened, I was on bus duty and was approached by an African American parent I had not met before. He asked me, "Are you the principal?" I had my jacket on, and I said, "Hi, how can I help you?" He gave me this really big hug. That didn't bother me, but I'm like in my head, I'm like "I don't think I know you, but obviously you know me, so that's OK." He said, "I just have to tell you thank you. I'm so and so's father [the fourth-grade girl]." "Oh! So nice to meet you." And he said, "I am so appreciative of your stance on this particular situation and how you took care of it. Do you know"—and this is him saying it—"that you could have dealt with it in many different ways? My wife and I appreciate how you took care of it." I said, "Well, it was a joint effort." "No, no, no, it was you."

I really think that if not for our school's focus on racial equity and how we encourage dialogue as a learning experience for everyone, this situation might have ended very differently. Instead, our caring for a student's perspective moved our focus from taking down the poster or changing the poster to adults engaging in dialogue about current events and youth understanding.

---

# 49. Dots

—Told by a teacher in a suburban elementary school

During the last week of the school year, my school district sent out an e-mail to all teachers. The memo was titled "Social-Emotional Learning Opportunity." I remember opening the e-mail reluctantly, thinking, "Oh great, one more thing to put on my summer 'to-do' list before coming back to school." It was a workshop that the district was offering over a few days during the summer for teachers who were interested in learning more ways to implement social-emotional learning (SEL) in their classrooms. Knowing that the district initiative for the next year focused on SEL, I thought this might be a beneficial use of a couple of days.

Before I knew it, it was July, and I was attending the three-day workshop. During those few days, I participated in meaningful discussions, strengthened my understanding of the importance of teaching the "whole child," and obtained a plethora of resources that I could easily use in my own classroom. I felt great heading into the new school year.

Throughout the course of that school year, my principal prioritized our development in SEL. We spent many of our school improvement days and faculty meetings focusing on SEL for our students and ourselves. In May, we had a school improvement day, and none of us were surprised to see SEL on the agenda. Our principal began by praising the work that we had also done during the year. We had not only made changes in our own classrooms but we had begun changing the climate of the school. It began to feel like our work was done, and the next initiative was to be revealed. Little did I know this was just the beginning.

Our principal began asking us questions and encouraging us to reflect silently at our seats. He asked us questions such as these: "What students have you connected with the most this year?" "What did you learn about your students this year that had nothing to do with learning objectives?" "What students changed the most during the year?" "How did you find ways to connect with students who had trouble sharing during SEL lessons?"

While we reflected, our principal began passing out a different color marker to each teacher. He then said that we were going to go into the gym where we would find a school roster with every student's name on it. Our job was to read every single name and put a dot next to the students with whom we felt we had made a significant connection to over the year. He was specific by what he meant by "significant connection." A significant connection was something different than knowing if a student excels in reading or struggles in math. Instead, a connection was considered significant if we could give details about an individual student that had nothing to do with proficiency in school but instead were about their personality, interests, and overall character. We were to identify the kids we knew as persons as well as students who had trusted us enough to tell us things, who we have taken the time to learn about and understand.

As I headed into the gym, I wasn't sure what to expect. The moment I walked in, it was a bit overwhelming. All four walls were covered with lists. Huge lists. We were assigned a place to start and began our journey around the gym. I read through each name. With each name, I took a moment to think about that child. By the end of the exercise, there was a rainbow of colors filling the long white sheets of paper. We headed back into the library and continued with the next item on the agenda. Little did I know that once we finished, the secretaries would go to work. Their job was to go through the list and identify students who did not have a dot by their names.

After lunch, we had one more item on the agenda. It simply said, "Reflection." As our principal welcomed us back, he asked us to reflect on the dot activity. Then he passed out sheets of white paper and asked us not to turn them over until everyone had one. He then revealed that this list contained the names of students who didn't have any dots. The list of students who didn't have any dots was not long, but it was significant. I remember a lot of silence. I couldn't help but think how I would feel if my own sons' names were on that list. How did we miss these students? I also remember thinking our work was not done. It was just beginning. If we were going to connect with every student we had to do more. We ended that meeting in May with a list of goals and ideas for the next school year.

Today, years later, I can still remember that moment like it was yesterday. It changed me for the better and has caused me to constantly take inventory of my dots.

# 50. Season of Giving

## —Told by the director of an education nonprofit organization

Each year around December 17, at a K–8 school in a large, urban district, a school with over 80 percent of the students receiving free and reduced price lunch, a group of teachers and staff members can be found furiously wrapping hundreds of books, toys, games, and clothes in the cafeteria. Laughter and music permeate the room, as rolls of tape are shared, scissors are lost, wrapping paper is unbound and torn, ribbons are curled, and names are assigned. While this is happening, another team—teachers, counselors, custodians, secretaries—are on their way to the house of one student with a Christmas tree, lights, ornaments, a turkey, potatoes, green beans, greens, stuffing, cakes, pies, and candy.

Each child in this elementary school receives one wrapped present with his or her name every year on the last day before Christmas break. One child will go home to find a fully decorated house and a holiday feast.

Because of the low economic conditions that the students in this school live in, many of their parents do not have the means to provide a traditional, Santa-approved Christmas. Many of the parents do not work or are a part of the working poor of Americans. Jobs are intermittent, one-parent households are the norm, and one house may have several children. Each year, the principal makes it clear to the staff that "all children deserve Christmas." So each year she secures funding from several local businesses to make sure that every child gets one wrapped gift before they go home for the holidays. Whatever is not donated or funded, the principal pays for herself.

On the last day before the break, when students come to school, they are immediately greeted by Santa and Mrs. Claus (if you look carefully, she may look suspiciously like the principal), who remind them to be good. During lunch, Santa and Mrs. Claus entertain in the lunchroom, and students come to the stage to get their presents. When the day is over and after the students go home, the staff is treated to a dinner by the principal, who gives each of them a small wrapped gift as well.

**Inside My School. Charlotte Kehler, Grade 3**

# 51. Evaluating Faculty With Challenge and Support

—Told by the principal of a suburban elementary school

"There are several areas on the rubric in which you scored *below standard*. If we don't see improvements in these areas over the remainder of the year, your contract will not be renewed." Principal Feldman was straightforward and clear, yet her words were delivered with kindness and care. She followed by letting first-grade teacher, Ms. Lewis, know that she believed in her and her ability to implement the changes they were discussing. Ms. Lewis, in her third year of teaching but first year in this particular school and district, quietly paged through the rubric attending to the areas of growth identified by her principal. After a few minutes, she asked some clarifying questions about expectations for conducting readers and writers workshops, seeking specific examples. The principal pulled out the first-grade benchmarks and in detail talked through some examples of practices that met these benchmarks.

Before the end of the day in which this coaching conversation took place, Ms. Lewis had e-mailed the principal asking for another meeting. She had more questions and wanted to partner with the principal on a work plan that would support her learning and growth. Mrs. Feldman responded promptly, always willing to provide guidance and specific feedback to her teachers. They met later the same week. Sitting side by side, they laid out together some actionable steps—a time to observe in another classroom and reflect on new learning with the assistant principal and some work sessions with the building instructional coach. They also discussed strategies for connecting Ms. Lewis's university learning and coursework with the practices expected by the school district.

By her next observation one month later, Ms. Lewis scored *developing* or *proficient* in all areas of the evaluation rubric. During the post-observation conference, Principal Feldman provided specific praise while acknowledging there was still work to be done. The overall tone of the conversation was celebratory with Ms. Lewis high-fiving the principal as she left the office.

Mrs. Feldman's conversations with staff, even the most challenging conversations, seemed effortless. In reality, she was always very thoughtful and intentional with her words. She considered each interaction an opportunity for relationship building. Further, she believed that the success of her staff was a reflection of her leadership. Her words held meaning and resulted in desired action because of the strong caring and trusting relationships she had built with staff members. Staff members demonstrated a sense of vulnerability and willingness to implement change because they felt that they were authentically supported.

# 52. Coaching With Care

—Told by a partner of an education leadership development organization

My work involves training school leaders to coach teachers through the process of building a positive and productive classroom as well as a school culture of high expectations, support, and care. A session early in my career as a coach stands out as an example of the urgency of developing these environments early in young students' academic careers.

As part of her coaching training, a beginning principal and I were observing a first-grade teacher during her morning routine. The teacher had given her students an assignment, and we were paying close attention to her actions and interactions as she made her way through the classroom, checking in on students as they worked. Although caring and attentive, she dedicated a disproportionately low amount of attention to one of the students, a non-neurotypical child of color. As I observed her, she seemed to avoid him, taking little time to connect or acknowledge his work, or even his presence as a member of this class. It became quickly clear that the teacher, who surely would have been genuinely disturbed and shocked to have it brought to her attention, did not see this student's potential and was allowing her low expectations of him to become a rationale to avoid any kind of meaningful engagement.

Much of the coaching we do involves putting an earpiece on the teacher and coaching through a walkie-talkie. This helps teachers be aware of and address challenges as they occur. Later in the morning, after taking note of this particular teacher-student relationship, we observed the math lesson for the day. The teacher had gathered her students onto the carpet and was posing problems. "What is three more than nine? Two less than seven?" And so on. She would call on different students to answer. The student we had observed earlier as receiving lower-than-average teacher attention sat on the carpet among his peers. His lack of eye contact, poor posture, and constant hand movements signaled engagement different from the other students. Looking closely, however, his hand movements suggested counting and attention to the math problems being posed. The teacher, in selecting students to answer her questions, repeatedly avoided calling

on him despite being in her line of sight and his atypical engagement with the material.

"What is three more than five?" the teacher asked. I quickly told the principal, who was on the walkie-talkie connected to the teacher's earpiece, to instruct the teacher to call on the child. The principal looked at me with doubt, so I repeated myself. She instructed the teacher, who, stunned, shook her head no as a baseball pitcher might shake off a catcher's call for a particular pitch. We cued the teacher again. The teacher took a deep breath, paused, asked the question again, and called on the student to answer. Every single child in the class turned their bodies toward the student, their surprise and interest evident. The student began mumbling and moving his fingers. After a few seconds, he answered, "Eight." The entire class erupted in cheers. The student beamed. The principal and teacher burst into tears.

The drama of this story indicates the importance of actively caring for students, even in the smallest ways. I have absolutely no doubt that this teacher *cared about* this student. And I have no doubt that this beginning principal cared deeply about this student and this teacher. But caring about a student or a teacher merely requires feeling for them. It's a passive emotion. Being *caring for* a student or a teacher requires an action and follow-through. It can also take challenging and pushing. In *caring for* others, you're demonstrating care by taking concrete steps to convince them of their potential for brilliance, the power of their voice, and their worth. Students will spend their entire school day around adults who *care about* them. Adults actively *caring for* them will turn compassionate feelings into action. They will lead students to realize their full potential.

---

# 53. Accepting Your Feelings

—Told by the principal of an urban elementary charter school

Tylie, one of our nonteaching staff members, walked into my office with no appointment, a good-news smile, and no urgency, so I knew she was going to surprise me. Since then, I recognize that this is how people act when they quit.

With Tylie sitting before me talking, I panicked. One of the main things this school needed was stability, and resignations cause instability. She was pulling at the supports of my plan. The school had been through tremendous change during the past few years. The staff had been open to changes in curriculum and in culture and accepted drastic changes in schedules, but they were exhausted. They had spent down their openness to change, and it was gradually being replaced by reluctance and fatigue. I had to safeguard their vulnerability by moving all of us forward without leaving anyone behind.

Tylie made things short and simple. She had decided to leave. She already had another school to go to. It was an opportunity she couldn't pass up. She was sincerely grateful for the opportunity to work here.

So, as she left my office, I began to think hard about what she told me. I turned her words over and over. The more I thought about what she had said, the more I noticed what she hadn't said. She hadn't given me a reason for leaving.

I decided not to let her go so easily. After a few hours, I saw her again and gently reopened the conversation. I wanted to convince her to give me an explanation. I had to give her all the control. I couldn't condescend. It had to be her decision to tell me.

Making some private time (it was a quickly ticking countdown to her last day on the job), I told her, "You must have put a lot of thought into this, and you must have had a reason." Taking responsibility, I said, "If there was anything I did, I hope you'll find a way to tell me so I can grow from it." I ventured delicately: "Something very specific must have happened. And if I am going to be successful at leading this school—and I know you care about the school's success—you have important knowledge that I need. What was it like to work here?"

She opened up. I think it was partly because of the compassion. I also think it was because I admitted all that I didn't know. She told me it was because of Rose, another teacher at the school. Rose! Rose was acerbic and direct, but I didn't think she would aggravate someone to the point of quitting.

Tylie gave a spoonful more at a time. Rose had been uncooperative, even though Tylie was just doing her job. Rose gave her responses to requests in a tone that said "over my dead body." Rose shot her looks that prevented any kind of genuine conversation, much less collaboration. I hadn't been witness to any of it, and this was the first I'd heard of it. I implored her to let me look into it and see if there was something I could do. I promised I would get back to her in a day.

When I called Rose into my office, she could tell something was up. I was sweating a little too because once you light a fire in a room, it's going to get hot for all of you. People will do anything to save themselves from getting burned.

The hardest part of this conversation was that I couldn't tell her who had complained. I had to fudge my honesty. Rose deserved to know what was going on, but what if Tylie stayed and they had to work together again? What if Rose only took her relationship with Tylie seriously but didn't change her tone for anyone else? There were many ways to lose.

I was frank. I told her that someone was quitting because of her, and I acknowledged that Rose probably didn't want that. Of course, Rose asked me over and over who had complained. She said she wanted to make things better, but it would have been plainly wrong to expose Tylie. Imagine being Rose and having to figure out how to make things better without having the opportunity to apologize or even acknowledge the person who was hurt.

She left her seat and stood for a while. The pauses got longer. She was reflecting. I caught my reflex to want to fill the silence, and I held my tongue. The longer I let the silence go on, the longer she would reflect. She repeated that this was extremely difficult to talk about without knowing who we were discussing. I held my tongue again.

Eventually, she offered that she probably could be nicer and more cooperative around the school. I told her that was all I could ask of her. I promised I'd let her know if things got complicated again or if I could share the person's identity. I said I'd let the person know how heartfelt her apology was. Her face brightened. It opened up, and she smiled as if she'd been looking forward to this moment. However, I don't think she had, and I don't think she was feeling particularly happy. Perhaps she was showing me she could do as she had promised.

Compassion is a powerful tool, but that sounds mechanical and strategic. Compassion is something we deserve fully. Withholding it is as unhelpful as withholding care for the needy. If we offer only meager amounts of compassion to others, we're basically taking the last portion from the plate over and over. That's self-serving, because you expect compassion for yourself without expecting it of yourself. It's also counterproductive. To earn people's trust, they need ample compassion to work with you. When you feed people what they're asking for, conversations can become harder, more honest, and agreements more durable. Compassion also means that we accept each other's feelings and experiences. Accepting your feelings is different from accepting your position or point of view.

After I explained to Tylie what happened—and raised her compensation a little more—she agreed to stay on. I got the stability I needed. Rose continued to be Rose but was noticeably more agreeable. She acknowledged my reminders when I offered them, and we began to develop a stronger, more trusting working relationship.

I was trained to look at schools for their data, but some of these data have an $n$ of 1, and the most important picture you can ever get is the experience of a single person.

# 54. Seth

## —Told by a teacher at an urban independent elementary school

Meet Seth. Seth is the younger brother of Jack by one year, both adopted by two moms from Central America. I had the pleasure of teaching both boys back-to-back. It wasn't easy being Jack's little brother. Jack was a rock star, excelling academically, athletically, and socially. For Seth, life was different. Seth had a medical issue that caused tumors to grow in his little body, leaving his moms terrified and his brain having to work harder than anyone in my class—and perhaps in the school. Each week, Seth saw a speech and language pathologist, an occupational therapist, a speech therapist, and a math tutor. He struggled to speak clearly, write legibly, and finish any assignment with success. Amazingly, these hardships were not obvious when you met Seth. Seth was one of the happiest boys I ever taught. He said "Good morning!" *with* eye contact every day as he entered the classroom—not the most common thing for a fourth grader to do. He cared for his peers, such as when he would rub their backs when they were sad and when he would come and tell me he was worried about his friends. He made people laugh. He participated in class discussions. Seth was someone every lower-school teacher wanted in his or her classroom. Seth was in the fourth grade, and next year, he would enter the middle school, and the big question that was on the table was whether Seth would continue to make it here.

Seth's moms knew that he struggled. It was undeniable. They were paying thousands of dollars on top of independent-school tuition just to get enough tutors and therapists to keep Seth's head above water. But Seth was part of our school community, and it terrified his moms that he might not be allowed to continue at this school. They wanted him here. *We* wanted him here.

But the most important question was what was best for Seth. When Julie, the head of the lower school, came to me in late October to schedule a *touch base* meeting with Seth's moms about his future, I knew it was going to be difficult. I knew the meeting was going to be frightening for Seth's moms.

The meeting was scheduled for after school. I was running around to get my fourth graders into their cars and to get back up to the mail room to grab the last of the coffee. As I swung open the door and dashed out of the mail room, I almost slammed into Seth's mom Robyn. "Hi!" I exclaimed. She barely looked at me as she quickly strode down the hall. "Can I get you some coffee?" I asked, trying to keep up with her. "No." She brushed me off and entered Julie's office with me trailing behind. This meeting was going to be worse than I thought.

I entered the office as Julie was offering a beverage to Mary, Seth's other mom. "Sure!" she said in a friendly reply. Robyn sat across from Mary, saying nothing and still fuming. Mary looked across the table at Robyn and gave her a look to tell her to pull it together. To say it was awkward is an understatement. I just looked at Julie. After some awkward chitchat, Julie took the lead.

"Let's just dive in," Julie began. "How are you feeling about how everything is going for Seth?" That's all it took for Robyn to explode. She sounded off about how everything is so easy for Jack and how that isn't fair for Seth. She said she doesn't know how to help Seth. She cursed. She was red faced. She was angry. She asked if I was the best teacher for Seth. That hit a nerve for me, and I became visibly upset by her question.

Mary stopped her and said fiercely, "Robyn, if you are going to act like this, leave!" It was the most raw parent emotion I have ever seen. Julie intervened. "Let's take a step back. Let's relax for a minute. We are here *for* Seth. So what do you want *for* Seth?" That's when the tears started flowing. Robyn sat quietly wiping her eyes as Mary stepped in. "We want Seth to be happy. We want Seth to learn and be whatever he wants

to be. We are scared for Seth. We are scared he won't make it here." The room was quiet.

Julie said, "We are not at this table to kick Seth out of this school. Let me be very clear. The question is how can we best support Seth?" I could feel the anger and fear leave the room. Julie's tone calmed the moms. She wasn't the authority figure in the room but rather a comforter and mediator to help the moms process Seth's situation. Julie reminded us to think about how Seth was feeling about his experiences in school. Are his struggles overcoming his confidence? Does he love school? Julie insisted that we keep Seth's feelings at the forefront of our conversation. This seemed to provide comfort for the moms.

Julie guided the conversation along. Her voice was calm and reassuring. She was fully present, focusing all her attention on the moms. There was no computer on the table, nor were there folders of information about Seth. Julie took no notes. It was all about making the personal connection and laying the foundation for future conversations and decision-making. As she was talking, Julie gave examples of Seth's experiences in school, about how she had gotten to know him by talking with him in the mornings when he was dropped off at school. She spoke about the things that made Seth happy. She was assuring the moms that Seth is known at school and that the school is being supportive and caring of him. There were no negatives spoken, only positives. Julie kept Seth at the center of the conversation. Julie spoke about how the moms could learn more about Seth's strengths and struggles. She asked the moms for their insight into Seth and his condition. She asked the moms for their advice about what resources might be most helpful for Seth at school. Along the way, Julie put to rest Robyn's concern about Seth being in my classroom, saying, "I would not want him anywhere else." That meant a lot to me, as I hope it did to the moms.

We all hugged at the end of the meeting. We didn't reach a decision about whether Seth would continue at the school next year. But Julie had established a connection with the moms that would make further conversations and the ability to make this decision less difficult. She was clear that we care about Seth, that we care about his well-being, and that we care about his moms and how they are navigating their support for Seth. She was communicating the school's values of caring, openness, and support. This was enough for a first conversation.

A week later, the moms returned to school with packets of information about Seth's condition and about resources they thought the school should know about. They began to trust and open up to Julie and to me. They engaged more fully with Julie as partners in Seth's schooling. And two years later, at the time this story was written, Seth was still at the school, ready to enter the seventh grade.

# 55. Learning Together

—Told by the director of an urban education foundation

Turnbull Elementary has a large population of Spanish-speaking families. The principal laments her difficulties engaging with non-English-speaking parents and desires to reach out to them more effectively. In advance of an upcoming open house, she posts flyers and sends home notices that have been translated to Spanish. At the event, she has a translator for parents.

During the open house, a teacher asks to have a conversation about how to better engage with Spanish-speaking families. With the aid of the translator, one parent suggests offering English as a second language (ESL) classes for parents after school. Another teacher raises her hand and says that she would like to learn Spanish. A representative of the local community literacy council offers to facilitate.

Soon, joint Spanish-ESL classes are offered at the school in the evenings, and the principal makes sure there is on-site childcare provided so that both parents and teachers can easily participate.

# 56. Helping a Teacher Build Relationships With Students

—Told by a teacher at a suburban K–12 independent school

As a special education teacher, I have worked with many challenging students. One year was especially difficult. I had a class of students with severe behavioral difficulties, and every day felt like a battle. Desperate to make things better, I went to my assistant principal, Ms. Rose, for help. She dropped everything to sit down with me and brainstorm solutions.

She gave me resources on creating a positive classroom community and helped me formulate a plan to focus on team-building with my students. Then she came into my class's morning meeting the next day and helped me implement the first stage of the plan. And once per week for the next three months, she took over the morning meeting so that I could spend time building relationships one-on-one with my students. Ms. Rose bent over backward to care for me and my students. While we still had tough days, the time that she invested in my class provided us with a foundation of trust that allowed us to overcome those hurdles.

# 57. Buddy Bench

—Told by the principal of a midsize-town elementary school
Adapted from Itkowitz (2016).

Christian, a ten-year-old student at our school, thought he and his family were moving to Germany for his dad's job. His mom showed him brochures of the schools he might attend. Christian knew he would be the new kid, the one without friends, the one without anyone to play with in the schoolyard. He was in first grade, but he knew what loneliness on the playground looked like and felt like. He had seen it at our school.

One German school he and his mom looked at had a solution for this problem. It was called the "buddy bench." If a child was sitting on the bench alone, it was a signal to the other kids to ask him or her to play. Christian's family never moved to Germany, but Christian is credited with introducing buddy benches to American schools.

Christian brought the idea of the buddy bench to me, and the two of us immediately set out to install one in our school's playground. Christian told me that he didn't like to see kids lonely at recess when everyone was playing with their friends. He thought the bench would help. It would give children a safe, nonjudgmental way to say they wanted companionship. Once a child is asked off the bench to join others in play, the hope is that they will have the confidence to go play with their new friends again the next day.

The installation of our buddy bench was covered by our local newspaper, and word of it went viral. It's been unbelievable. Christian and I have been featured on the national news. The story was picked up by *The Today Show* and *Huff-Post*. We were invited to give a joint TED Talk. E-mails have come in from all over the country. Christian has been invited to speak at schools as far away as Los Angeles and Honolulu to help them unveil their own buddy benches. A second grader from Los Angeles wrote me a letter and said, "I have had a hard time making friends on the playground, so I am going to use a buddy bench at our school." This second grader met with his principal, and his school installed one. Christian and his mother flew out there for its unveiling. Only a week or so after Christian's buddy bench story went viral, the mass shooting

**Let's Play. Lucas Little, Grade 3**

at Sandy Hook Elementary School in Newtown, Connecticut, occurred. A year later, Christian and I visited Newtown, where Christian was awarded the Charlotte Bacon Act of Kindness Award, named after one of the little girls who was killed.

There are new buddy benches popping up on school playgrounds all around the globe. I'm told that there are more than two thousand schools with benches across the United States and in about a dozen other countries. It's such a simple and powerful thing to do. As Christian says when he is invited to make buddy bench speeches at schools and conferences, "Amazing things happen when you share your hopes and dreams, and you may end up helping more people than you can ever imagine."

# 58. 360 Degrees of Caring
—Told by the principal of a small-town elementary school

In my time as a school principal, I often felt that there was an imbalance in the giving and the receiving of caring and kindness. Often my office was a place to vent frustrations, to share sorrow, and to be upset, and I did my best to find solutions and make things better.

This all changed when my husband died suddenly. I found myself on the receiving end of caring and kindness in a way that I had never experienced before. I knew that I poured myself into my job, but I was overwhelmed when the school community responded to my loss with an outpouring of caring, kindness, and love from every corner—students, teachers, staff, parents, community members, business partners, and colleagues from the district and other schools. I was surrounded by caring people, and their kindness carried me through a profound period of personal grief.

First, there was that afternoon. My husband was in the hospital. He died suddenly from a heart attack that seemed to come out of nowhere. I don't know how the word of his death traveled so quickly, but within a short time, his hospital room was filled with my colleagues from the school district. My family had not had time to arrive, yet I was surrounded by my mentors, mentees, and colleagues. That afternoon is seared into my memory, and I vividly remember thinking how fortunate I was to work with such a group of caring, servant leaders. I have often asked myself if I would have done that. Would I have gone into the room where someone had died (his body was still there) and offered to do anything to help?

A couple of days later, I arrived at my home to find out that one of our board of education members had delivered one of the delicious pound cakes that she was known for baking from scratch. I really didn't know her at all beyond introductions, but from there forward we cultivated a relationship based on her love for students, her showing me she cared, and pound cake! That same evening, one of our school business partners brought and served dinner for my family and friends.

During this time, I was on the receiving end of many of the usual gestures of grief when someone dies (flowers, visits, food), but one of the most precious ones was this. Several months after my husband's death when I had returned to school, I looked up from my desk and a second-grade student, who had *slipped* away from her class on their way to lunch, was standing in my door. She started by telling me that she hoped I could explain to her teacher that she had to talk to me and that she wouldn't get in trouble for leaving the lunch line. I invited her in, and she proceeded to tell me that she had heard about my husband dying and that she hoped I wasn't too sad. She told me that I could feel good because he was looking down on me, and he was in a place that was beautiful. She said that the streets were gold there and that no one was sick.

She said, "Don't be sad, I know this is true." She also stated that she knew I would be OK because they (the students) loved me.

As I walked this second grader to join her class in the lunchroom, I was simply amazed. Her theology wasn't surprising here in the Bible Belt, but her compassion and the urgency with which she *had* to talk to me caught me off guard. That day I made sure that her teacher knew that she and I had something important to discuss. And I will carry that conversation with me always. I like to think that the caring demonstrated by this young student was nurtured by the caring school community we had worked to build.

---

# 59. The Results Are In
## —Told by a teacher at a suburban elementary school

Everyone was gathered. The atmosphere was tense. She walked into the room and said, "The results are in." *She*, Carla Jones, was the principal of a diverse midsize elementary school. The statewide *high-stakes* test results were being distributed to the teachers at their building data meeting. The results were not good. The principal spent the next two of many hours guiding teachers in a discussion analyzing the graphs of each group and grade level, coming to some initial conclusions and problem solving for the next steps to be taken.

In her calm manner, the principal led the discussion, pointing out the positive growth the students had made as well as the challenges yet to be met. The scores were lower than in past years, and the school was considered to be on probation. Concern was etched on every face in the room. Teachers with a strong commitment to students already felt the stress of a demanding curriculum and pressure to close the achievement gap as well as to provide enrichment for students all while being under close scrutiny by the community. Test scores splashed across newspapers and public criticism added to the already-low teacher morale. The principal took this challenging situation and turned it into a positive call to action. She brought together all stakeholders—teachers, students, parents and community—with one goal: to do all that could be done to increase the academic gains of the students, thus test scores, by caring for the "whole child," meaning the social-emotional as well as the academic needs of students.

The principal worked with the teachers. She energized the whole staff; encouraged brainstorming sessions with teachers; and helped us identify, assess, and strengthen all the academic support programs currently provided to students. She helped us create additional ways to support small groups of students at specific grade levels. She sent teachers to professional development sessions on student academic motivation, math instruction, and general teaching strategies. She focused on strengthening their own professional community at the school.

The principal also worked directly with the students. Among the things she did was to try to relieve the stress and pressure that surround the tests and turn testing into a more positive, empowering experience for the students. She had *big* banners made, screaming "Show What You Know!" Then she hung them around the school. She worked with teachers to prepare a lighthearted video of teachers taking the test and their misconceptions and missteps of test-taking. It was serious but laced with lots of humor for the students. She filmed fifth-grade students imparting good test-taking strategies for the closing scene of the video. This video was shown at a huge kickoff assembly for third-through fifth-grade students on the first day of testing. The principal also gave a big pep talk. As students left the assembly, each was given a bag of healthy snacks and pencils with encouraging sayings. The bags were decorated by students in the first and second grades. Their lockers were also decorated with words of encouragement: "Rock the Test!" You Can Do It!" etc. And as they left the assembly, the whole school lined the halls and cheered as the students passed by.

The principal also worked with parents. Among the things she did was send a letter home to each parent of third- through fifth-grade students explaining the test and the results. She prepared a Q&A presentation for parents and community members to explain the test scores, current programs, and next steps the school would take to improve the scores. She encouraged parents to have their children get to bed early before test days, serve them a healthy breakfast, and give them an extra hug and encouragement as they sent them off to school. In the days leading up to the test, she asked parents to send little notes of positive comments and encouragement for their children. These might be written by parents or by siblings and grandparents. These notes were given to each child before the test each day. Students kept them on their desks as they took the test as a reminder that they were cared for.

The principal brought the whole school community together to care for students and to help them do their very best. She took a negative situation and turned it into a positive one. She rallied everyone around a common goal to increase test scores while caring for students at the same time. The test scores went up. Students felt proud of their accomplishments, and this experience brought teachers, students, and parents in the community closer together.

---

# 60. Always There for Me
### —Told by a teacher in an urban elementary school

A few years ago, while serving a public school district as an elementary special education teacher, my mother and only parent unexpectedly passed away. After submitting for bereavement leave through my district's online absence system, my principal immediately called me on the phone to talk. He extended his sympathy and reassured me that the school and entire staff cared about me and supported me. He, a white man, and many other staff members knew that I, a person of color, was very close with my only parent, and I remember him distinctly saying that the school wanted to do something to honor my mother. A week later, I was completely shocked and truly touched that over twenty-five staff members, including my principal, attended her memorial service.

In the months that followed, my life was preoccupied with estate work and what took me years to fully comprehend—significant grief and sadness. While I was confident of my skills in the classroom, I know my teaching suffered, and the time I would ordinarily take for planning and preparation became focused on my nonwork life.

While it has been a few years since this happened, I am still blown away by the care, compassion, and empathy my principal extended to me. He was someone I admired prior this tragic loss, but he would constantly check in with me to see how I was doing. He would continually reassure me that I was still doing a good job in the classroom. At the time, I hadn't realized how much my principal had fostered a supportive, empathetic culture at my school, where I found a sense of consistency, normalcy, and support that helped me through my grief.

I sometimes reflect on the complex roles of school leaders generally—and particularly principals. My principal was a sounding board. He was always accessible to talk to when I was struggling. At times, he even served as a de facto counselor. He helped me feel supported both professionally and personally. I will be eternally grateful for the care, dignity, and support he gives me.

# 61. Lunch With the Principal

### —Told by a teacher at a small-town elementary school

"Ms. T," the name given to her by her students, is the principal of an international school located on the coast of a small West African country. The school is known for its family-like atmosphere, a culture supported by Ms. T's leadership and caring for students and their families in and out of the classroom. She knows her students by name and interacts with each one as though they are the most important concern on her agenda that day. This kind of care extends beyond personal interactions and infuses Ms. T's whole approach to school leadership.

In preparing for the school year's anti-bullying month, Ms. T kicked off a contest among the upper elementary grade students to create posters that would encourage their peers not to bully one another. The winner would receive lunch with Ms. T at a local restaurant. Posters were submitted and hung on the hallway walls. Other school leaders voted to determine the award-winning poster. Whitney, a shy third-grade student, won and named her lunch with Ms. T as her best memory of a school principal. She told the story this way:

> So Ms. T made a contest to see who can make the best (anti) bullying poster.

And I won! I was passing through the hallways, and I realized that mine had the bow. So then what happened next is that Ms. T called me from my class, and I went to her office. She said that I get to have lunch with her at Pinocchio's. At the time I didn't know what that was. It was just a little bit up the road. I was really excited because the ice cream looked really good, and she asked me what I wanted and she bought it for me. She took me from school at lunchtime and brought me into her car and drove to Pinocchio's. So we ate there, and it was a bunch of cool stuff like this kind of drink—I don't know what it was called. I felt special because it's kind of like Ms. T is famous. There are so many kids in the school, and to me it seems like principals usually have to do all the work, so it felt cool spending time with Ms. T at a restaurant.

Ms. T does something special for her students every day. Her office door is always open to any student who wants to come in and talk or share a problem. She makes sure that every student in her school feels special and cared for.

---

# 62. School Welcomes

### —Told by the principal of a suburban elementary school

Building a caring community to facilitate the best in student learning was a hallmark of the principal who hired me as a beginning teacher. Through the years, she nudged me into leadership roles and was even direct enough to suggest that I be her replacement when she retired. This was a future I never envisioned for myself, but it ultimately came to be.

In the thirteen years that I was an elementary school principal, I developed habits and routines for welcoming new students and families to our school, and I can say without hesitation that all of the time invested in those habits and routines paid off well in my relationships with students, parents, and staff members. I was following in the footsteps of my predecessor, who made these welcomes an important part of her work.

Each August, a welcoming invitation was sent out to all of the new families joining the school community for a private tour of the school a week or so before it is open to the public. Many incoming kindergarten families attended but so did many of the families of older children who had recently moved to town due to job transfers, relocating to be closer to other family members, and myriad other reasons. During these tours, I was always happy to put a face to the name of a new student I'd seen on the paperwork we received from the district office's registrar. While it was not always easy to immediately remember the name of a kindergartner when faced with a group of twenty new children, it was very easy to identify the nine-, ten-, or eleven-year-old who was anxious to see his or her new school. Some of my fondest relationships with students began on this tour—making an early connection with them and looking out for their well-being as they make our school theirs in the coming weeks. These tours helped us connect early with parents too. Some stepped up quickly to become active school volunteers, happy to have their children treated so warmly and taken under a caring wing from the start.

While this introduction worked well for the families who are able to take advantage of the opportunity, it was important for all the students to feel welcome from the very beginning of each new school year. On the first day of school, after teachers have had their introductions and welcomes, the whole student body would meet in the gym for a welcome from me and introduction to the entire school staff. Since the first day of school was often hot and our gym is not air-conditioned, it was a brief meeting, meant to welcome everyone and allow students to see all the faces of all the adults who were there to care for them. It was always great to hear the applause for all of the students who were new to the school as they stood up and were greeted by the student body and staff. We emphasized that all of us—teachers, administrators, and staff—were at the school to help them, and if they were ever in a situation where they needed something, they could seek out help from the person they see first, or the person they feel most comfortable with, or really anyone.

**Welcoming Arms. Mina Huh, Grade 3**

# Stories From Secondary Schools

## 63. We Choose Relationships
—Told by the principal of a small-town middle school

My school has a passion for educating the whole student, supporting a child socially and emotionally as much as we do academically. In early fall, I gave our teachers three options for our professional development focus for the school year based on the three Rs: rigor, relevance, and relationships. Three-quarters of them chose to work toward the requirements for the relationships option. This spoke volumes to me because it was the only option that required teachers to give up their time after school hours.

Teachers who chose relationships as their professional development focus had to sponsor or form a club for our students that was tied to their interests. This year we started a video editing club, a coding club, a Minecraft club, a gardening club, a school pride club, an art club for band students, a creative writing club, a jazz band, and a hiking and fly-fishing club just to name a few. The cool thing was that I did not have to tell the teachers what club they would work with. They just followed their passions to connect with students more than we ever had before.

## 64. Small Steps
—Told by the assistant principal of a small-town high school

I maintain a snack basket in my office filled with crackers, nuts, dried fruit, and assorted healthy snacks. Students who visit my office know that they can pop in anytime I am there to get a snack as a pick-me-up during the day. And there are two teachers in our science department who keep a food pantry and let their students know that this is available to them. Students can fill their backpacks or take a bag of food home at any time.

One measure of care that I personally try to implement with students is to engage them in a positive conversation about a strength I've noticed or a faculty member has noticed. This is especially helpful after having a difficult conversation with a student who may not want to engage in a mutually respectful manner. I have found that when I follow up the next day with students, even if it's just a quick greeting in the hallway, letting him or her know that I care about them as individuals, it truly goes a long way to build that relationship.

I write notes of encouragement to students on a regular basis. We have cards that say "It's great to be a part of the Tribe!" (the nickname of our school). We frequently say that we are all "one tribe." I write notes to students on these cards to congratulate them on academic and extracurricular achievements but also the little things that often go unnoticed. For instance, I recently had a young lady bring me a twenty-dollar bill she had found in the hallway. After a week of the money going unclaimed in the lost and found, I wrote the student a note of thanks and enclosed the money.

I also have a student who for the previous two school years had spent two semesters at our alternative school. I had gone around and around with this student trying to get him to go to class and give his best effort. He was continually skipping class, leaving campus, being disrespectful to his teachers. When he started the school year with us, I met with him to let him know that I was excited to hear of his amazing progress with credits and positive contributions at our alternative school. I have frequently followed up with him while passing in the hallways, and I have sent him notes of encouragement as I hear positive things from his teachers. He has become such an upbeat and respectful student and one who I am excited to see each day. Taking small steps to build trust and rapport with students can really make the difference.

# 65. Getting You Ready to Walk

—Told by an associate director of a nonprofit education organization

Too often, I fear, our high schools treat students like kids—or worse, bad kids. When I think of my experiences as a student or, perhaps more so, during my time as a high school teacher, I think of how rarely student voice was proactively elicited and—at least as perceived by students—respected and listened to. We seem to control so much of students' time and work. We fail to trust young adults, to give them adequate freedom and free time, and we program every minute of their time in high school. I remember in my first year as a twenty-two-year-old teacher looking at my senior students and thinking how much they looked like college kids but how dramatically differently we were treating them and in turn how they were acting. It felt like college kids being treated and acting like middle schoolers. Everything was programmed—there was a tug-of-war over behavior and rule-following. They had no free time. Everything was programmed. There was a lot of control and oversight. And in a few short months, most of them were going to be in college. What a dramatic shift—maximal free time, minimal accountability and hand-holding, more rigor and ambiguity, lots of room for failure.

Over the years, I have been thinking about this issue and discussing it with my high school principal friends—how high schools could be a better bridge to the autonomy and responsibility required to succeed in college. I stumbled upon a compelling example of a school that was tackling this issue head-on. I was inspired by the vision of the school leaders and how they treated students with respect and dignity as mature young adults. They were preparing students for life beyond high school by scaffolding experiences of independence and responsibility. It sounded simple, but it felt kind of revolutionary. That school was killing it on student voice and an amazing approach of *supported autonomy*.

I went for a visit. This urban high school had a robust vision and set of collective commitments that were embodied in structures and systems. One such system was called RISE, a student self-directed version of Response to Intervention (RTI) with really tight feedback loops and ample safety nets, run during an open-campus, sixty-minute extended lunch block. It was an innovative approach to a common practice. Essentially, it was an intervention or recovery and enrichment period. But the design was extremely thoughtful and fine-tuned and incorporated a much broader vision of both support and autonomy.

The program sat on the architecture of a sophisticated system of assessments, rapid data feedback to students, and an advisory system to help direct students to needed interventions and support. Every Friday, students would take a common formative assessment. On Monday, they would get feedback on their work in every class before an advisory period that day, where they would set goals for the week, based upon their data, under the light oversight of the advisory teacher. Students had to implement their plan for the week with ample support and safety nets if needed. They had to take responsibility for their learning and to accomplish their goals.

The amazing thing was how students spoke about the school. One young man I spoke to described in detail how the school had researched the program, how they had visited a school in Florida for inspiration for the program, and how they had adapted it to their school. Students were crystal clear on the goals and purpose (time management, following through on goals, self-control, etc.), had internalized them, and regarded this as a singularly important and effective program of the school. They also saw it as a powerful means by which the school was supporting them by helping them to develop the skills they'll need after high school. As two students described it, "It's getting you ready for when you walk across the stage. And it's pretty much, they're getting us prepared for the real world. I see college." "Most definitely college. They don't baby us. At all." Another student remarked, "You've gotta be on your game and take responsibility for yourself." At the same time, "They are going to intervene quickly to make sure you stay on track. They will most definitely call home!"

Learning about this program through the students' experiences revealed the powerful way that leaders communicated with students. The students knew the research that was cited for why programs like RISE were adopted at their school. They had been given articles by school leaders, and they had read them. Students were going with teachers to training sessions and conferences about the program. It was as if the school leaders were treating students like key stakeholders, like board members rather than kids—or worse, *bad* kids. When I asked, "Do teachers and administrators invite student opinions about what happens in this school?" one student responded, "Yes. Yes. Yes. *Big time!*" This student proceeded to tell me about the Student Advisory Council that meets monthly with the principal and addresses matters of substance in the life of the school.

The overall impression I got was that this school had deep respect and cared deeply for its students. The school provided them opportunities to mature into capable and self-aware adults. Students knew it *big-time* and deeply appreciated it. The school had found a highly innovative and effective way of scaffolding autonomy and self-regulation that will be required of students after high school though a system of monitoring and support that "refused to let students fail."

# 66. Student Advocates
## —Told by the principal of an urban high school

We opened our new high school with a class of ninth graders. Each year thereafter, we added a new grade level to our nearly 100 percent African American student enrollment. At the same time, we built our staff, seeking to expand and diversify it racially. By our fourth year, when we had freshmen through seniors, we had hired thirty-two teachers, of whom eighteen were women, seven were African American, nine were Caucasian, and two were Asian American. The fourteen men consisted of eight Caucasians and six African Americans. This was a big change from our first year when we had only one African American teacher.

In the fourth school year, we hired two new staff members as student advocates to provide additional supports to all students but especially to our most troubled students. By then it was clear that we needed to have full-time staff just to advocate for our students and solve problems more deeply than we had been previously able to. These advocates would also contribute to our student culture team so that we could continue the high levels of support for all our students.

The student advocates we hired were both African American men who had grown up in the neighborhood and could relate to our students extremely well. Hiring African American men was important. We were losing more boys each year than girls to dropping out. Our boys had lower grades than our girls. The average GPA for our boys was 1.9, while our girls averaged 2.4. Our boys also had higher incidences of discipline referrals. Three of four referrals written were for boys. We needed staff to support all of our students but especially our at-risk boys.

Both of our new student advocates were extremely professional and excellent role models for all of our students, and because of their knowledge of and experience with the neighborhood, they were able to understand what our students experience and consequently understand how to help them. They made home visits to find students who were frequently absent from school and made plans with the families so the students could come back to school. They talked at length with students who were in conflict, trying to get to the root of the problem and teaching students skills to talk about their problems. They used mediation strategies to help students resolve conflicts without violence. They made behavior contracts with students who repeatedly received discipline referrals from their teachers. They compiled data so we could find discipline trends among students and teachers. They helped teachers with classroom management.

These advocates and the proactive approaches they took helped our students tremendously. They built trusting relationships with students to be able to advise them in real, honest ways. Our students learned quickly that they could reach out to the advocates for help and that the advocates would hear and understand them. The addition of our advocates helped us to fully transition from a focus on maintaining order to a focus on restorative justice—getting to the root of the problem and helping students learn alternative ways to handle conflicts. This also helped us solidify our school's culture of care and support and our sense of community.

# 67. Grab a Sandwich

—Told by a visitor to an urban independent K–12 school

It was almost lunch hour and Bruce Durham, head of the school, a white northeasterner in his mid-fifties, had but a few minutes to run down the hall for a quick consultation with Ann, the head of the lower school. Bruce could have called Ann on the phone, but he preferred to do as much as he could in person. And he had to be quick. He could not be late getting back to his office.

Each fall, Bruce invites the senior boys in the school to a small, private *no business* lunch in his office. Bruce provides the food and drink and feeds them all. Each year, one way or another, he eats a meal with every senior boy. It is a tradition he established, consistent with the hospitality of this southern school's community. This day was the last of those lunches—the lunch that the boys who did not sign up for earlier lunches were "invited" to attend. Perhaps these boys could decline the invitation, but once Bruce signed them up and notified them of the date, none did. Dashing past the trays of sandwich wraps, chips, and bottled waters and into the hall

to go see Ann, Bruce joked to a few of the boys who had gathered early for lunch, "See, I knew you'd eventually come around and have lunch with me!"

No sooner had he passed these students than Bruce came up behind a group of four upper school boys, three African American and one of Indian descent. As he approached, one spun around—"Dr. D! What's up?!?" Smiling broadly, they all turned around to face Bruce and, now walking backward, they extended their hands to shake his. One put his arm around Bruce's shoulder as they playfully bumped each other. Bruce greeted each by name and a personal remark: "Jamil, how's that college application essay coming?" "Tony, that work you are doing in Ms. Cullerton's class sounds fantastic!" As the boys started to turn into another hallway, Bruce beckoned to one: "Nate, remember that question you asked me the other day? I've been thinking and . . ." The two huddled briefly out of earshot of the others. "Cool! Cool! Thanks, Dr. D.!

I'll let you know how it goes," said Nate as he broke away to catch up to the others.

Bruce had his quick consultation with Ann and made it back to his office just as the last of the senior boys was finding his seat. Bruce sat among them, and with deadpan seriousness that turned to a big smile, he exclaimed, "So glad you were able to make it! Grab a sandwich, and tell me what's going on! Joe, you first!"

# 68. Welcome to Refugee High
### —Told by the principal of an urban high school
### *Adapted from Fishman (2017).*

If Wrightwood High School had a motto, it would be "Give me your tired, your poor, your huddled masses yearning to breathe free." Its immigrant population is about 45 percent of the school's 640 students, and many are refugees new to this country. Two years ago, Wrightwood welcomed eighty-nine refugees— nearly three times as many as the year before and far more than at any other high school in the city. The recent surge, fueled in part by an influx of Syrians, has made Wrightwood's student body a global mix, with thirty-eight countries and more than thirty-five languages represented. The third most common language spoken at Wrightwood, after English and Spanish, is Swahili.

Wrightwood has a long history of welcoming immigrants. When the school opened in the early 1920s, droves of newly immigrated Irish and German students enrolled. In the 1980s and 1990s, Wrightwood was an academically successful school, earning an international reputation for its educational progressivism. But after its long-serving principal retired, the school began to decline.

By the time Charles Abrams became principal in 2013, the school had been on academic probation for eight years in a row. Its four-year graduate rate hovered around 54 percent. Classrooms were barely half full, and incidents of violence were common. It was not a place where you'd want to send your kids. There was a lot of talk at the time that the school would need to be either turned around or shut down.

When Abrams started at Wrightwood, he observed a group of students participating in a summer program for refugees. He had never before met kids from all over the world and had never worked in such a diverse school. He soon realized that if you got to know these kids, you could see that they have an appreciation for a free education that sometimes Americans take for granted. It was a profound experience for him. He filed it away and spent a good part of his first year learning how the school operated. He noticed a large number of older students who were regular absentees. By the end of his first year, he had them go to alternative schools or to GED programs. He reasoned that an eighteen-year-old with three credits would likely have little motivation to come to school other than to hang out and mess around.

Since the school district had already allocated funds based on projected enrollment, Abrams had some extra cash to work with. He applied it to the school's English language learner (ELL) program, which was designed for refugees and other immigrants who speak little or no English. By reallocating those funds he was, in essence, creating a new priority for the school.

One of Abrams's most significant decisions was to put a teacher, Susan Lopez, in charge of the program. He had seen how passionate Susan was about the kids and what a great classroom teacher she was. Abrams and Lopez worked to reorganize the program around a *cohort* model. ELL students would travel together throughout the day not just to English class but to all core classes where they would get language support. They made sure to get the word out to resettlement organizations around the city that Wrightwood was turning a corner. The refugee agencies didn't really feel comfortable sending their kids anywhere. Abrams wanted Wrightwood to be that place for them.

Wrightwood is now the go-to school for refugees in the city, and its academic standing has also increased. The school has risen from the lowest level in the district's ranking system to a middle plus ranking. Abrams believes that Wrightwood is on track to reach the highest ranking soon.

Keeping up with growth and changes in refugee populations presents a constant challenge to Abrams and his faculty. New foreign conflicts around the world bring new groups of students to Wrightwood. What might have worked for a heavily Bhutanese group of refugees (there were some ninety such students in the school when Abrams first became principal) may not work with Syrian kids. Abrams admits to struggling a little bit. He doesn't know exactly how to manage it all, only that he has to do something. He believes that there is no other place in the world that is doing what Wrightwood is doing.

While Lopez and one of the assistant principals have focused on developing a supportive community in the school for all its students, and

in particular its refugee students, the financial responsibilities of growing and managing the ELL program fall to Abrams. Every year, the district's Office of Language and Cultural Education gives additional funds to schools based on their number of ELL students. Wrightwood received about $60,000 of such funds for each of the past few years. The problem is that new refugee students continue to enroll at Wrightwood on a near-weekly basis throughout the year, and the school receives no additional money for them until the next year.

Cuts in the district's budget haven't helped either. A year ago, Abrams had to lay off two ELL-certified teachers because he simply could no longer afford them. This left him no choice but to partially collapse the cohort model. He also had to put non-ELL teachers—including substitute teachers—in charge of ELL classes.

Still, Abrams remains hopeful. The district recently selected Wrightwood to be the city's first newcomer center, a designation given to schools that offer robust programs for refugee and other immigrant students. Wrightwood's selection means the district can provide a lump sum of federal funding each year, which could amount to an additional $300,000 annually. Abrams plans to use the money to hire additional ELL teachers and rebuild the cohort model. He knows that this money will make a big difference.

# 69. Do We Really Know?

—Told by the principal of a suburban middle school

Staff members of our middle school pride themselves on the positive relationships that they develop with students. It's really at the core of what we believe in. At a school leadership team meeting, a teacher leader asked if we, as a staff, had developed positive relationships with all the students in our building. We would like to think that we had, but we honestly didn't know! As the principal, I created a way for us to figure out the answer to this question.

A spreadsheet of all of our students' names was distributed to everyone in the building,

including teachers, nonteaching professionals, our office staff, custodians, and teaching assistants. Everyone was to write their name next to a student's name if they felt they had developed a positive relationship with that student. Team leaders then brought the completed spreadsheets to their team meetings and reviewed them. If a student didn't have a staff person's name next to his or her name, then the team created a plan for a staff person to begin developing a positive relationship with that student. We did this activity every November for many years.

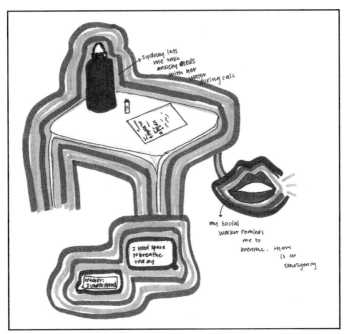

**To Breathe. Helena Loranz, Grade 12**

This year a teacher leader on our school leadership team asked a new question: "Do we really know that these positive relationships are felt from the student's perspective?" We honestly didn't know! I created a survey for students. It contained just three questions. The first question asked students whether they had an adult in their lives, outside of school, that they felt comfortable going to if they had a problem or just wanted to talk. This adult could be a family member, a coach, a religious youth group leader, a family friend, or any other adult. The second question asked students if they had an adult in the school who they felt comfortable going to if they had a problem or just wanted to talk. This adult could be a teacher, school nurse, principal, assistant principal, dean, custodian, an aide, a secretary, and so forth. The third question asked students to write the name of this adult in the school to whom they felt comfortable reaching out. Students were encouraged to list the names of all adults in the school with whom they felt comfortable.

After the students took this survey, I shared the results with our team leaders. The team leaders walked through the results with their teams. It was important to identify which students identified no adults in the school who they thought supported them. The teams began to create plans for forming relationships with those students. From the student survey, our school climate team will identify staff members who are not listed by any student and will plan professional development activities to help and encourage these staff members to form positive relationships with students.

# 70. Setting Rules and Policies

**—Told by the principal of an urban high school**

Administration and teachers agreed that in order to develop the atmosphere of high expectations and care in our new school, we would need to have clear policies and rules in place, and we would all have to work together to enforce school policy to create a safe and orderly environment. To help us define our expectations for students, I took the lead in developing a method to elicit parent and student voice in developing our school rules. We held a meeting for our parents and students in June and brought our questions to them. Not only did the administrative team attend this meeting to show support but so did a number of teachers. Sixty parents attended, representing nearly half of our incoming class of students. Parents and students had the opportunity to meet their teachers.

We started the meeting with snacks and small talk to help build community. Then we turned to developing expectations and rules. We introduced a particular topic for decision-making, discussed it, and then invited both parents and students to vote. One topic was whether we would require students to wear uniforms to school. We presented arguments for and against wearing uniforms, invited parents and students to discuss the matter, and then held a vote. Parents unanimously voted for uniforms while only half of the students did. Parents won. Uniforms it would be. Then we engaged parents and students in discussion to select the color of pants and shirts students would wear and if we should enforce tucking in shirts, wearing of belts, and so forth.

Parents also took a vote on how the school should establish other policies, including the use of electronics, tardies, and insubordination. Parents were able to explain from their perspective what they felt were fair consequences for violating such policies. Students were able to participate in discussions and voting, and we used all of this input to create our school policies. We used this opportunity to discuss with parents and students how each of us would have an integral part in educating our students.

I specifically remember the feeling I had at the conclusion of this meeting. I was very pleased that we received so much input and support from our parents. I could not recall ever seeing a school go about developing or realigning their rules in this way. I felt confident that we would be able to uphold our policies on our end and that our parents and students would do their part as well.

Midway through the fall semester, we found that a core group of students were consistently tardy, and there seemed to be little we could do about it. Warnings and consequences did not work. We had to come up with something different. Members of our school's leadership team and I began reading a number of books on understanding poverty and children's experiences growing up in poverty. We learned that children who live in poverty may not be as used to regular schedules or routines as children not in poverty. We learned, for example, that in many middle-class households, children know what time they must be home, what time dinner will be served, and when they must go to bed. In households in poverty, not only might dinner not be served but there may be no one home. We learned that sometimes children in poverty do not sleep in the same places each night. Routines are not established, and their lives often lack predictability. And, therefore, students may have a hard time understanding why their school is punishing them for being late or make a big deal about of it, especially if they are only a few minutes late. What are a few minutes to a student whose life is unpredictable? This all made sense to me. We had been looking at the issue from a completely different perspective.

A teacher on the leadership team drew on this information to create a Tardy Intervention Program for thirty students who were tardy most often. They were pulled into a classroom during their lunch period for one week. This program focused on helping students to use problem solving and understand that the school was trying to help them be more successful, not simply punish them for being tardy. The theory was that we would help students to solve problems together so that we could all be vested in the outcome. To make sure that this would not seem like a punishment, we took these students to the head of the lunch line so they could get their lunches first—a real lunch, not a cold peanut butter and jelly lunch. We then brought them up to the classroom to eat during the session.

The goal of this Tardy Intervention Program was to have the students themselves try to figure out what was causing them to be tardy to school, and what was within their control to change. We had them plan their evenings and mornings to the extent they could. We helped them go on public transportation trip planners to determine the fastest routes to school and to estimate what time they should leave their homes. They were to think about who else from the school they might see at the bus or train stops so they might have buddies. We helped each of the students with their schedules. We showed them that if they ironed their clothing at night rather than in the morning, they could save fifteen minutes, which would help them get to school on time. In some cases, we encouraged students to go to bed at a more reasonable hour so that they could wake up earlier in the morning. We even bought

alarm clocks for several students. In some cases, we contacted elementary schools where our students were dropping off their siblings in the morning to see how early they would take their siblings so that our students could be on time.

This program helped students feel a bit more in control of their lives, and it helped many to understand that the school was truly trying to help them, not punish them. This program worked for approximately half of the thirty students who participated in it. Those students began arriving to school on time, and they felt good about it. Although it did not work to solve our tardy problem completely, it gave us a new approach for working with our students.

---

# 71. No One Graduates Alone

—Told by a curriculum director of an urban charter high school

I had recently been named director of curriculum and assessment (Grades 9–12) for a network of charter schools. Having started as K–3 or K–5 schools and adding one grade per year, the charter management organization had experience managing elementary schools but not high schools. At the time I was hired to lead curriculum development for the new ninth graders who would start in the fall, I was the only staff member in the entire company who had ever taught in a high school. We were inexperienced, and we knew it.

Rory, the principal of the new high school, had been preparing for the role for several years. Hired as director of instruction in the middle school, he had assumed the title of principal over the seventh and eighth grades the previous year to prepare him to add the ninth grade the following year. In our planning, we wanted to make sure that ninth-grade students felt different—that ninth grade would not just be another year of middle school. We planned an orientation program during which students— about half continuing from the eighth grade and half new to the charter school—would begin

to experience high school for the first time. At the end of the two days, which included several fun, community-building activities, as well as introductions to the academic expectations of high school, Rory gathered the fifty incoming freshmen and all of the high school teachers in the biggest classroom in the school.

After giving out awards from some of the team-building activities earlier in the day and making some general announcements, Rory got to the point of the meeting:

Let me get real with you for a minute. The last couple days we've had a lot of fun, and that's great. But there's more to high school than playing laser tag with your friends.

In this part of the city, fewer than half of kids graduate from high school. I want you to imagine the stage at graduation four years from now. All of the chairs are set up. Your family is all in the audience. We've got some balloons and decorations, and you're wearing your cap and gown. And you're the only one on the stage. Would you be really happy at that moment? You still will have accomplished your goal, but I'll promise you that you won't be as excited as if you were graduating with all of your friends. Look around the room. Let's make this promise to each other: No one graduates alone. We're going to commit ourselves to doing whatever it takes so that four years from now everyone who is in this room will be on that stage.

And that's not just a commitment for you to make. Look around the room again. In this room are your teachers. They will do anything and everything they can to make sure that we achieve that goal. When you leave the room today, one of the teachers by the door is going to hand you a card like this [shows example]. On it are the personal cell phone numbers of each of your teachers. If you need help with your homework or studying for a test or if you just need to talk through something, you can call any of us, and we will be there for you. The teachers in this room

are some of the most amazing people I have ever worked with. One teacher in this room—and I'm not going to name names and embarrass anyone—stayed after school every day and sometimes came in on weekends last year to help a student who was behind in math get caught up. Another teacher in this room—when she found out that a student didn't have money for clothes—took that student shopping and spent her own money to make sure that the student had what she needed. That's the kind of people these teachers are, and you are incredibly lucky to be able to spend the next four years with them.

We know that there will be good days and bad days—we'll be there for both good and bad. If you're not getting to school in the morning or if you start falling behind, I'm going to stay on you, and your teachers will stay on you. And I hope your classmates will stay on you, and you will stay on them.

Before this week, I gave your teachers an assignment. I told them this: Make me a lighthouse. [The school and charter

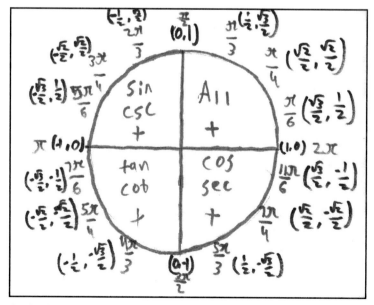

**Caring Unit Circle. Evan Huber, Grade 11**

network used the symbol of a lighthouse.] I didn't give them any directions and didn't tell them why. Mr. L's is in the back of the room there. [He pointed to a model made of balsa wood.] Miss K's is right here. [He held up a drawing of a lighthouse illuminating kids, turning the picture so that everyone could see. Those kids nearest the lighthouse have schoolbooks in hand, and those farthest away where the beam widens are wearing caps and gowns.] Since ancient times, the lighthouse has been a symbol of hope. When sailors would be out at sea, they could look out and see the beam from the lighthouse and know where the coast was, and the beam could help them avoid danger and get them home safely. Together, we are going to be a lighthouse for each other—to help keep each other on course, to rescue each other if we get too close to the rocks—and in four years, we will all be together on that stage at graduation, and no one will graduate alone.

In that talk, Rory not only expressed his care for the students but also helped to establish a culture and ethic of care for the school as a whole. A few of the teachers in the room had been at the school teaching middle school grades previously, but some were new. For them, this was enculturation and expectation setting by offering positive examples of "what we do here." For the students, it established a sense of belonging—being part of a group with a collective commitment—and communicated clearly that the adults in the building cared and would demonstrate care.

While some students transferred out of the school, 100 percent of the students who stayed all four years graduated. All were accepted to at least one college. Two have since returned to the school as teachers.

# 72. Responding to the Crises

—Told by the principal of an urban high school

Each year, we experienced shootings in the community surrounding our school that affected our students tremendously. Most commonly, our students were the victims of shootings that resulted in injuries and even death. One of our students from the class of 2011 was killed, one student was tragically injured and left as a quadriplegic, and many others were shot but not permanently injured. Each time a tragedy like this happened, it threw our school's culture into a tailspin, and we had to figure out how to best handle it. It also personally and deeply affected me and our entire staff. These were students who we had spent four years working with, cultivating, and shaping. I learned to make sure my school cell phone was next to me each night as I went to sleep. When it rang in the middle of the night, I knew exactly what the call would be. The only thing I did not know was who.

When I received the call in the middle of the night on a Friday that a senior, Tony Franklin, was killed, I was inconsolable. He had just brought his college acceptance letter to school on Thursday. It was the most excited I had ever seen him. I had the rest of the night and early Saturday morning to draft my plan to handle staff and student emotions and put the crisis intervention plan in place. I waited until 8:00 a.m. to begin calling my staff to tell them personally. I heard the pain and heartbreak for what could have been in each of their voices as I delivered the news. I also called a staff meeting Monday morning for 7:00 a.m. so that I would have the opportunity to inform our staff of the crisis plan for students. At the Monday morning meeting, we all cried together just before the students began arriving. Because Tony was a senior, as each senior student walked into our building, we ushered them into our auditorium. Our senior teachers were there, along with the district's crisis intervention team, and we all just sat around and cried, hugged, and talked about Tony. It was a free space where students had the opportunity to just feel and express emotions, and as students expressed their sadness and recuperated enough to feel prepared to leave, they exited the auditorium and moved on to their classes. At Tony's funeral, I spoke to the crowd that filled the church about what we, the whole school, loved about Tony. I was extremely proud that 90 percent of my staff was in attendance and at least half of our student body. Despite all of the problems we faced as a staff and a school community, we were there in solidarity to show our unity, and that meant a lot to everyone.

School staff and students rallied like this in all of our crises. When Jackie Watkins, another senior from the class of 2011, was shot in the neck and paralyzed, most of our staff went to the hospital to see her. In fact, when I told the nurses that I was Jackie's principal, they told me, "I want my children to go to your school. So many of your teachers and staff have been here to show their love. I've never seen anything like it." Months later, when Jackie was finally released from the hospital but confined to a bed and wheelchair and unable to return to school, my teachers went to her house to give her lessons so that she could still graduate. And she did.

Our students were often the victims of violence, but unfortunately sometimes they were also the perpetrators of violence. During the course of our first four years, many of our students were charged with crimes, and many times we experienced police officers coming into our school, entering our classrooms, and arresting students in front of their peers. This was shocking to me and to the staff at first, but we learned that this too was a reality that we had to deal with. For example, one of our smartest senior boys was arrested right out of his precalculus class and now faces twenty years in prison for attempted murder. Other students were apprehended at school for home invasion burglaries, armed robberies, muggings, drugs and weapons charges, and other crimes. Each time something like this happened, we had to work to rebuild our culture. Some students would find these events funny, or at least they responded in such a manner, perhaps to masquerade their true emotions. This could trigger angry reactions from other students, and we had to implement a response system to handle the conflicts that inevitably surround these issues.

Teachers also experienced a variety of emotions when things like this happened. I saw teachers lose hope in the work they were doing, feeling like they as individuals and we as a team were not having the impact on students' lives as we had hoped—and even that our work was futile. I also experienced teachers take a very negative outlook on students, viewing them all as criminals or potential criminals. But for every negative experience, we had ten positive ones, and these are the messages we constantly had to remind our staff and students of to give them the stamina to continue their work and their efforts.

# 73. Good Works Toward Each Other

—Told by the principal of a suburban high school

During my second year as principal, I was looking for opportunities to find new ways to connect with students and learn about their perspectives. Being principal meant getting a bit more deliberate when finding opportunities to meet and understand our students. Starting a Principal's Advisory Board (PAB) was one way for me to accomplish these things. In order to have diversity within this group, I asked our counselors to recommend students who were representative of our school community as a whole. To be sure, there were times when

**Sharing Is Caring. Katherine Hollister-Mennenga, Grade 7**

organizing and planning for their meetings was something additional to do, but the overall experience was completely fulfilling. As I got to know the students, it was quickly evident that many of them were involved in different ways and had diverse views of the school and the things where we needed to work.

One student I got to know was Lizzy. Lizzy was a flute player and in the band. Like so many band kids, she had a great network of students and was very active with the school. After her first year on the PAB (her sophomore year), I noticed that Lizzy needed to come to the school during summer to make up her final exams (one thing I did not do with this group was monitor their grades or look into absences). After doing some investigating, I discovered that Lizzy was seriously ill. She had been born with the life-shortening disease cystic fibrosis.

While this had not been obvious to me during my interactions with Lizzy, I did notice the impact over the next two years. During this time, her illness progressed in a serious way. But no matter how difficult things became, Lizzy

worked hard to manage her disease and to not allow it to interfere with her student activities. I came to discover that Lizzy's daily routine included four breathing treatments and chest physical therapy, and she was taking over twenty maintenance medications. She was hospitalized frequently and continued IV antibiotics at home after each hospitalization. Over this past year, her health declined significantly. She needed to be homebound throughout most of her senior year.

At one point, at the beginning of the second semester that school year, I was approached by another PAB student with the idea of starting a fundraiser. We agreed to have the PAB sponsor this effort and to promote it with the notion of also donating to the Cystic Fibrosis Foundation. Needless to say, the fundraiser was very successful, and at graduation practice, students were able to announce to the class that they had a significant check that they wanted to hand over to Lizzy.

I have found as principal that the most important aspect of caring about your students is the ability to facilitate their good works toward each other. Sadly, in large schools like ours, sickness, tragedy, and even death are things that we occasionally encounter. As a leader, it is essential that we take time to pause and recognize these times while we work hard to support those in need. Lizzy will require a double lung transplant soon. This is bound to be difficult. However, she can count on the students of our school to be a steady source of care and support.

---

# 74. Fostering a Caring Faculty Culture

**—Told by the director of a small-town independent girls high school**

A few years into my tenure as a new director of school, a group of teachers asked to meet with me. One was a relative veteran, and the other two were in their second year. They were from different academic departments. They didn't say what they wanted to talk about, and I was a little nervous. They had a proposal for me. They wanted to form a faculty conversations group that would convene a couple of times a month during lunch or other meeting times to discuss articles about teaching and to share what is working in their classrooms and what they want to try. They wanted to generate ideas for collaboration and for interdisciplinary teaching. They wanted to talk about successful technology integration. They didn't want the meetings to be required. They were OK with department chairs and administrators attending, but they didn't want these leaders to take over the conversation. In short, they wanted to form a grassroots professional learning community. They asked if they had my support.

I was thrilled. In my tenure as a head, I have discovered that the best way to encourage good teaching practices is to "encourage the heart." I try to reward innovation, to be what I call an *entrepreneurial* head. I support good ideas.

The first year, this faculty conversations group met, and other teachers came in and out, but soon a core group formed. They asked to visit other schools, and I gave them time off. They asked to visit each other's classes. This was welcomed with open arms. To encourage an open-door culture, they created the "Pineapple Board." In the faculty lounge, they posted a chart with the week's schedule on it. Teachers who are doing interesting things in their classrooms wrote a note on the board. The note served as an invitation for others to visit.

These classroom visits are one way my school is creating a supportive and open faculty culture, which is built on trust that teachers can try new strategies without fear of failing. This culture manifests itself in other ways as well. Whenever a teacher needs to be absent from a class, they put out a call for help with coverage. The sharing of ideas about teaching is breaking down walls, allowing faculty to care for one another and help one another out. In doing so, the students are the winners. They see their teachers invested in teaching them and in lifelong learning. They also see their teachers helping one another out and supporting one another. These relationships help model the way for students and encourage them as well.

In building a caring faculty culture, it is important to support faculty not only in the classroom but also in their personal and family lives. The director of Student Support Services at our school epitomizes care and concern for our students who have learning differences or emotional needs. I don't know a more dedicated or selfless teacher. She often goes above and beyond in her service to students and the faculty who teach them. This year, she has been eating lunch every day in the Learning Center with a student recovering from an eating disorder as a way for her to transition successfully back to eating with peers in the dining hall. Countless times, she helps another teacher modify assignments to meet a student's accommodation plans to ease their workload.

She is also a strict follower of rules and policy, a trait she learned in the Coast Guard. So when her husband, also in military service, returned from active duty in Afghanistan on a weekday, she asked if she could take the afternoon off to meet him at the airport. I insisted that she take the rest of the week off and enjoy spending time with him without it counting toward her paid time off. We found colleagues to cover the Learning Center during their free periods. For three- to four-month stretches when her husband is assigned out of the country, this teacher works a full day caring for students at school, and then she functions as a single mother of three with no family nearby enough to support her. By giving her the gift of time, I showed her that her school cares for her and the sacrifice she and her husband are making for our country.

---

# 75. Promoting Safety and Community Through Near Peer Mentoring

—Told by a teacher in a suburban high school

My last class of the day had just ended, the last kid who had hung around to chat had taken off, and I was beginning to gather my things and go to coach the dance squad. There was a knock on my door. "Melissa, hi. Got a minute? I'd love to share something with you." It was Justin Damon, a teacher at the school who had just become the new assistant principal for instruction. "Sure. Come on in."

After our usual pleasantries, he said, "You may remember when I was a teacher representative on the strategic planning team last year that I floated the idea of starting a new student mentoring program. And you may remember that it got into the strategic plan. Well, I'm on my way to the school board meeting to see if I can get it approved as a pilot program. And I'd like to know if you and Jim Thayer in the English department would like to flesh it out and run with it."

Justin's idea was to have a group of incoming juniors and seniors *adopt* and develop supportive *near* peer mentoring relationships with small diverse groups of freshman students. The hope was that this program would help freshmen get off to a good start at the school by forming close relationships with one another and with upperclassmen who could support them and give them personal and academic peer advice. For the juniors and seniors, the hope was that the program could become a springboard for their own personal and leadership development.

Upperclassmen who would be selected for this program would not necessarily be at the top of their class academically, but they would have a capability for developing strong relationships and for peer leadership. Overall, he saw the program as one among several efforts that the school was developing to create a more supportive learning environment for students, increase their connectedness and sense of belonging at the school, and provide additional academic and social supports—all helping to address persistent differences between white and African American student success at the school. Key pillars of the program were building psychological and emotional safety and community among program participants.

I spoke with Jim, and we decided to give it a go. Justin worked with us at the beginning to flesh out details of the program. He advocated for the program and for our leadership of it to the principal and the school board. And he helped us get the resources we needed to launch the program.

The program ran as a pilot for four years, and this year it was adopted as a program of the school. Although Justin has moved from the school, the administration continues to support the program and provide resources when we need them. The program has doubled in size since its first year. Today, more than 300 upperclassmen apply to fill about 125 student leadership spots in the program. The program has expanded

**The Lunchroom Table. Jane Vachon, Grade 12**

to involve nearly 350 freshmen, almost one-third of the entire incoming class. Student leaders are selected to be representative of the student body as a whole. The upperclassmen register for an elective course on leadership development for which they now receive course credit that counts toward their GPAs—a new development supported by the administration. Upperclassmen meet with freshmen during the school day. For several periods a week, as part of their leadership class, they go to freshmen study halls and selected freshmen courses to meet with their groups of three to five students. For the first month or more of the school year, the focus is on developing strong social relationships between upperclassmen and freshmen. These relationships become the foundation for both academic and social-emotional supports that freshmen can receive from their peer mentors. In their leadership class, upperclassmen learn not only about relationship development and peer leadership and support but also other aspects of leadership. In working with and supporting freshmen, they also learn a great deal about themselves and their own vulnerabilities, they learn the importance of being a good listener, and they gain in their own self-confidence.

The program has been in place long enough where Jim and I are now seeing students who participated in the program as freshmen now applying for and participating as seniors.

---

# 76. When It Is Actually Not Easy
## —Told by the principal of an urban high school

It turns out that kids want to be told "It's hard" and not "It's easy."

Caring for teachers who are struggling is one of the most important facets of my work. Listening to students so I know what they need and translating that to teachers in a sensitive way can be a complicated undertaking. But it is an important way that I care for both our students and our teachers.

Every month I have "Pizza with the Principal" lunches with about ten students attending each lunch over three lunch periods. Each month's lunches have a topic, but the conversation will go wherever the students want it to go. One month this spring, our topic was this: "How are we doing at creating a truly diverse and inclusive learning environment at our school?" Students were sharing what was working for them and what was not.

At one point, Anna spoke up, "What helps me is if it's hard, they acknowledge it's hard, and then they help me." Alex agreed. "My IB math teacher is good at making it clear that it's supposed to be hard. That makes it OK not to understand."

We take notes during these lunches and share them with the whole staff so that they can learn from what the kids are telling us. Everyone could learn that "Yes, it's hard, but you can do it!" is a great phrase that resonates with our kids.

A few weeks later, the issue came up in a different way. A parent had called to talk with me about her daughter's experience in a class. She wanted to make sure that her daughter would not have that teacher again next year. As I prefer to work with teachers to improve, rather than engage in teacher-switching, I asked the parent to come meet with me to figure out what was needed. To our meeting, this parent brought a page of notes from her daughter, and one of the notes said "When I don't understand and ask questions, he says, 'It's easy, you should get this.' That makes me feel stupid." I made an immediate connection back to what I had heard from other students at our lunch meetings.

This made it easier for me to have the tough conversation with the teacher, who I had been working with already on other issues. I was able to share not only that saying "It's easy" isn't having the intended effect, but that saying "It's hard" seems to be working positively for kids. The teacher agreed that he could shift his language in that way, and I affirmed that I know he wants the best for his students.

No teacher wants to hear that they are making kids feel stupid. Being able to frame the conversation with a useful strategy to share, as well as letting the teacher know that the information is coming right from the kids, helps me give feedback in a positive way—feedback that can receive and can actually lead to change.

# 77. Mama Bears

—Told by the assistant principal of a suburban high school

Regardless of how old my students may be, it is critical that I always remember that many of our parent partners still see the baby or toddler they knew long ago rather than the sassy teen we're having a phone call or meeting about in my office. I often have this conversation with new teachers who can be so overwhelmed by their new role that their responsibilities overshadow their better judgment.

At the high school level, we don't usually meet the kids until they're teenagers, and this is a very rough phase of life for some. We can remember that parents may still see their tiny baby faces, the infants who clung to them for every want and need. When I first became a department chair, I had pictures of friends' babies all over a wall in my office as a daily reminder of how parents might still think of their kids. I sometimes encounter a parent's fierce energy when I'm trying to understand a complaint leveled against a teacher, which 99 percent of the time results from a misunderstanding by the student conveyed to the parent. I typically refer to this ferocity as Mama Bear, and I remind parents that I wouldn't expect anything less than a passionate defense of their cubs. I also say that we need to assess the truth of the situation from all perspectives and see where we really need to focus that powerful energy.

This has been a productive perspective when working with a parent angry about her daughter's 504 Plan for accommodations being inadequate (at least in her eyes), with a student who desperately wanted to quit and be homeschooled because she had no friends, and with a mother who believed her daughter's heart issues were being ignored when we had not even seen any evidence of these health issues existing at school. Once I acknowledge that their defense and energy is coming from the love they have for their kids, they seem to relax a bit in knowing that I also care about them and their families.

# 78. Celebrating Matt

## —Told by the assistant principal of an urban high school

Matt passed away in October of his sophomore year. Word spread throughout the school within minutes of his younger brother Jake sharing the news in a text message to a few classmates. Matt had been diagnosed with leukemia one month prior. Although the entire school community knew Matt was ill, his death—the result of complications from treatment—was a shock to everyone.

In the twenty-four hours after Matt's death, our school's leadership grappled with what to do. Students were distraught. Teachers struggled with their own grief. One teacher looked at me through tears and asked, "What am I supposed to do about his empty desk?" Everyone shared a common question: "How can we help this family? And our school family?"

I thought of my own biological family. When someone dies, we move into action. We make arrangements. We collect photos. We make sure we have a dark suit dry-cleaned and ready. We clear our work calendars. We figure out where everyone will go for lunch after the funeral. It was Friday, and Matt's funeral was scheduled for Monday, which happened to be Columbus Day. School would be closed, leaving every student and teacher available to attend the funeral. As I thought ahead to Matt's funeral, I envisioned his family and a large percentage of our school's 950 students, plus teachers, administrators, and coaches attending. Where does a group that large possibly go after a funeral? There's only one space within twenty-five miles that can hold that many people—our school.

I picked up that phone and dialed Matt's parents. When his mother answered, I explained that in my own family, after a funeral and a burial, we usually all go to lunch. Tearfully, his mom said, "So do we." I told Matt's mom that I was sure the majority of our school community would be attending his funeral. I went on to say that although it might be a bit unusual, I wanted to offer the school as a spot for everyone to gather after the funeral. There was a brief pause before she said, "That would be amazing." From there, the pieces fell into place quickly. Tables were arranged in the cafeteria. Catering was donated by a local restaurant. The PTO organized parent volunteers to serve the buffet. Students worked on a slideshow of photos that would be displayed.

Matt's funeral was the saddest I have ever attended, but when it concluded, everyone—his brother, his parents, extended family, parent's coworkers, and all of his teachers and classmates—came together in the school cafeteria. We shared a meal, and throughout the room I heard stories of Matt. I stood in the corner with my superintendent, who said, "This might sound strange, and it's probably not the right time to say it, but this is the most incredible thing I've seen in a long time." As I reflect on it now, I think he was trying to say, "This is a unique example of creating a truly caring community for families in school."

Matt would now be twenty-three years old. His parents and I have stayed in contact over the years. We speak now and then and, in the way of our school community, we keep the celebration alive.

# 79. Everyone Has a Voice

## —Told by the principal of an urban middle school

Several students who were English language learners (ELLs) had complained for a while that Mrs. Murray was a bad teacher. When asked for examples, they would say she didn't care about them, she didn't explain things in a way they could understand, and she would get frustrated when they asked for help. Over time, these students were bringing concerns to the office more frequently, as a larger group, and not only about Mrs. Murray. They recognized differences between teachers who seemed to understand and acknowledge their needs as they learned the English language and those teachers who didn't.

The students wanted an opportunity to meet with the administrative team so the principal arranged for an after-school meeting, inviting an interpreter and the ELL teacher. When it started, more than forty students were present and wanted to share their concerns about how they were perceived, treated, and discriminated against in the building. Hearing and validating each and every concern, the adults present committed to meeting with the students on a monthly basis and working with them to address the concerns they shared. Several of the students wanted an opportunity to share their thoughts directly with teachers and did this through a series of videos titled "You Don't Know My Story." They also shared their thoughts face-to-face in dyads during specially planned staff meetings. It was common to see tears from both students and teachers and to hear teachers say things like "I had no idea you felt that way" or "I didn't know that's what I was doing."

The process led to involving students on committees in the school and getting their opinions before decisions were made to make changes in instruction. Very soon the strengths and experiences this group of students brought to the school became more widely recognized. Mrs. Murray became one of the greatest supporters of this group of students and took a leadership role in identifying other ways to get students involved in sharing their voices.

# 80. Our Work Is Really All About Caring

## —Told by a former high school teacher and administrator

During my thirty years as a master teacher, department head, coach for student teachers and beginning teachers, and school administrator, I have worked with many, many students and colleagues, primarily at international schools in Mexico. My experiences have led me to believe that my work—our work—is really all about caring. I understand that most enter the world of education caring about students, but not everyone enters knowing how to be caring of them. But I also understand that everyone can develop and practice emotional intelligence in their work. I know that being a caring educator takes practice and initiative, and I know that it means having the ability to focus on more than the daily work and to learn to step back and see the bigger picture.

As an administrator, caring meant many things—among them helping beginning high school teachers learn to work with students in caring ways. It is sometimes the case that new high school teachers will protect themselves behind the facade of the *tough* teacher and avoid personal contact or go to the opposite extreme of trying to be the *buddy*. I have tried to guide new teachers into how to find their space somewhere in between.

I have used numerous examples from my own experience to help beginning teachers think about their own practice and consider ways that they might make their practice more caring of students. Here are a few of the examples I have shared over the years:

> She walks into the classroom with the fashion magazine in her hands and defiantly sits in the front of the room paging through it while we are in class. It's learning to stop and observe—where is she coming from today? What is her message, intentional or unintentional? I talk to her after class—or in a transition when others are working because she is not in the mood to work in teams today—but it's not to reprimand, just to talk. What are her ideas? How would she do the assignment in her own style? Because for her, it is about style and her own sixteen-year-old sense of self. I invite her to participate but tell her that ultimately it is her decision, and with time she comes in a little bit more engaged, a little bit more ready to interact with others.

> Maestra, remember when I was in high school, and I was such a mess? I hated school, and your class was so hard sometimes! But I remember you told us that learning to write would be hard but that we would thank you one day. Well guess what? My first year in college, we had an essay assignment, and I was the only one who knew how to do it right! I felt so proud. Now I get it. Thank you.

> I see her from the corner of my eye during the exam, and there it is. I see her sneak a peek at her left knee, at the writing just under her skirt. Oh, I hate this part of educating, when kids do stupid things out of fear, out of lack of confidence, out of apparent indifference, and in this case what we call cheating. Do I say it? Do I call it out? How do I manage the essential lessons of actions and their consequences while staying conscious of the delicate state of self-esteem? So I call it, quietly. No rhetorical questions, no drama, but, yes, a conversation and, of course, the consequences, because otherwise there's no point. It's not because

**To Touch a Life Forever. Michael Ani, Grade ?**

I am angry or even disappointed. You took the risk, and now there are consequences. Let's talk about the *why*. Can I help you next time to feel more confident? Are there other ways to approach this horribly uncomfortable test-taking routine that can help you to succeed? Is there more effort that you need to put on your part? Remember, it is your choice. They are the consequences that you chose.

It's not always those who make the most noise that require the most attention. What about the invisible ones? Those who slip in and out of class, participate when called upon, hand in work without any comment, work silently but unengaged with others? They don't consider themselves the best students but not the worst either. They easily get sifted through the cracks precisely because they are invisible. So our challenge is to uncover their invisibility, to search for where the luster is, where the creativity is, where the deeper interest is, to invite, to challenge, to give enough flexibility so that each one is not invisible but individual. That is our challenge.

Am I really accepting each student where he or she is? Am I forcing myself to look beyond the parameters of the classroom to find individuality and beauty in each one? Do I dedicate myself more to the repetitions of history, of politics, of prescribed ways to doing things? Or do I dedicate myself to caring for each person who walks through this space?

# 81. A More Inclusive Culture

—Told by the principal of an urban Catholic high school

"How many students from China are coming this January?" I gasped. "The teachers are still reeling from the fall group!" This was my first semester at a small Catholic high school in a small city. I had already learned that the school's finances were smoke and mirrors and that the former principal had brought in Chinese students to infuse the finances with their tuition. In the fall, the number of Chinese students came to 5 percent of the student body. I was aware of these Chinese students but was completely blindsided by the fact that an additional number of these students were due to arrive for the spring semester, ballooning our number of international students to 13 percent of the student body.

"An Asian invasion" was the reaction of many parents. This was an urban area but one unaccustomed to cultures other than those already in the city. I met with the school counselor, who also acted as my assistant principal, to discuss what we could do to welcome the new students, help the teachers teach English language learners (ELLs), guide our current students in cultural sensitivity, and support our parents while not accepting their prejudices.

Fortunately, the agency that brought these Chinese students to us also provided an ELL teacher for them. The counselor and I met with her to discover what was going on with these students and solicit her advice. She was very grateful to be invited to speak and quickly let us know that a number of these students were very unhappy but that they would never let us know—they just would not return the next year. Financially, I was in a bind because our operating budget could use the tuition revenue these students would bring. I was also conflicted. We are a Catholic school whose mission is to welcome and develop all students through Christian principles; however, there were students in our own city who we might not be serving. I was embarrassed that we could not reach these children.

"What can we do?" I asked Mary, the ELL teacher. She had an answer. "We need to begin to look at our school and mission through the eyes of these new students—students who have been trained to obey without questioning and fear their teachers. These are students who have no concept of a Christian view of a higher being." The counselor, Jim, and I looked at each other soberly as Mary continued. "It is not uncommon for these students to be struck or beaten by their Chinese teachers, so they will not ask a question of the teachers and will always say everything is OK. Not only do they not share our religious beliefs, but they are trained that to be a good citizen of China, they must actively argue against and disagree with people who do believe in a God." "So why are they in a Catholic school?" Mary grinned and said, "That's easy. Some were told by your admissions director that religion class was optional, and the religious aspect of the school was downplayed to others."

After recovering from our shock, Jim, Mary, and I put together a plan to first address the comfort level of the students and help our teachers see themselves and the school through the eyes of our Chinese students. The first part was to change the faculty's idea that these students were "Mary's Chinese students"—as if they were not part of the whole student body. We started with a simple activity for the teachers once these students arrived. The name of every student in the school—not just the new students—was written on an apple: red for freshmen, yellow for sophomores, green for juniors, and blue for seniors. Every teacher was given a set of stars, and they were asked to place a star on the apple of every new student they had come to know personally, not just as a name but as someone they could converse with as a person. When the activity had ended, the teachers were asked to make observations. They all noted that there were no more than three stars on any of the Chinese students' apples. When pressed as to why that might be, after the initial excuses

of not teaching a certain Chinese student, I asked them to think about what could be done so that every Chinese student could have as many stars on their apples as non-Chinese students—even the freshmen who were native to the area. In the meantime, Mary presented myths and truths of the Chinese culture and the world from which our Chinese students had come.

After the presentation, I returned to the beginning activity, and the teachers were now eager to provide suggestions about how they personally could make their classrooms more welcoming as well as how we as a school could work with *our* Chinese students. We began as a team the next day with Mary acting as our barometer for the students and giving us monthly tips regarding how to better instruct our new students. I began to work with our parents. I spoke with them informally and bragged about the progress of the Chinese students and how they were adjusting to our school and American culture. I appealed to the Chinese students' foster parents to talk to other parents about their charges and about what they were doing during and after school. I made sure to include information about the Chinese culture in each newsletter and on our website. I made sure that Chinese students were pictured in the photographs we posted. My counselor worked directly with the teachers, particularly the religion teachers who were struggling to teach our new nonbelieving students. These teachers created a "Religion 101" course for all freshmen and other incoming students who were not Catholic, not just the Chinese. The counselor worked with students to discuss how to create an inclusive culture for everyone. This opened some great discussions with American students who also did not feel welcome because they were not part of the *in* crowd or from a certain parish. By the end of the year, only one Chinese student decided to return to China. We looked forward to having the rest among us the next year.

# 82. Enforcing the Norms

## —Told by the principal of an urban middle school

Mrs. Rodgers had been complaining about her student Laquisha for weeks. She described her as disrespectful, said she misbehaved constantly, and lamented that she was reading on a first-grade reading level in the sixth grade. Mrs. Rodgers would say that Laquisha needed intervention but that there was no time to provide the supports she needed in the English language arts classroom. It would take away too much time from the other students who knew how to behave and cared about their education.

Mrs. Rodgers came to the principal's office irate one afternoon. "She's done it. She's crossed the line. I want her out of my classroom immediately." Asked what prompted this anger, Mrs. Rodgers charged that Laquisha had stolen three small bags of chips from the prize bin. The principal asked Mrs. Rodgers to sit down and take a moment to relax. When asked again to explain what had happened, Mrs. Rodgers stated, "Well, first of all, she comes to school looking like she just crawled out of a garbage can."

The principal, voice beginning to shake angrily, said, "Please stop right there. I understand your concerns about her behavior and academics and the fact that she took something that didn't belong to her, but your commentary on how she looks is degrading and is unacceptable. We don't talk about students that way in this building. Please leave my office. If I ever hear you describe Laquisha or any other student in that manner again, you will no longer work in this building. Meet me tomorrow morning at 7:15 with your union representative. We'll talk more then."

Reflecting back on the confrontation, the principal realized that his reaction and his threat were over the top. And it probably would not lead to real change in Mrs. Rodgers's thinking or behavior. Mrs. Rodgers did apologize to the principal and promised to change her behavior, but the principal was doubtful. More had to be done

to work with this teacher and help her see the problems with thinking about and acting toward students in these ways.

The principal also took it upon himself to get to know Laquisha. He learned that food was always scarce in her house, helping to explain why she took the chips from Mrs. Rodgers's room. Laquisha was also taking extra food from the school cafeteria and from other sources to bring home and share with her siblings. The principal worked with the counselor to offer supports and also make certain there was a backpack of food for her to take home twice a week.

The principal also committed to providing an intervention time for Laquisha every day. What started as a fluency activity moved into comprehension and eventually math work. These twenty minutes weren't only about the academic intervention but also provided time to check in with Laquisha, set goals with her, and walk around the building and hear stories about her mom and grandmother and church. The principal learned that Laquisha loved apples but never got them other than when they were served in the cafeteria. After break, the principal started keeping a bowl of fresh fruit in his office rather than candy. It was available for anyone but was there especially for Laquisha.

Laquisha finally had an adult in the building she could trust and confide in. She had time with someone each and every day to give her attention focused on her as a person, someone to set goals with her and focus on her academic needs, and someone who connected with her and her family and worked to identify other resources to offer support. Laquisha had some modest gains academically and behaviorally that she and the principal celebrated together later that spring. Importantly, she had a smile on her face and seemed to enjoy coming to school more than she had previously.

The principal's encounter with Mrs. Rodgers had an influence on the faculty as a whole. The confrontation had been private, occurring behind a closed door, and the principal did not discuss it with anyone. Still word about it got out. The principal's actions, however problematic themselves, were seen as forceful reinforcement of norms of caring in the school.

He had held a teacher accountable for actions that violated those norms. Teachers and staff also saw that the principal found time in his schedule to support an individual student. He demonstrated that there were no excuses for anyone not to be able to find the time to provide extra help or one-on-one time for a student.

---

# 83. True Safety

**—Told by the principal of an urban high school**
*Adapted from Stewart (2018).*

I do not believe that metal detectors bring safety. I have worked in schools in Los Angeles and Chicago, both with metal detectors, and I can unequivocally say that there were weapons and guns in my classroom or at those schools often. Metal detectors are not, and will never be, the answer to the question of safety in schools.

Strong relationships with students will always trump metal detectors. More, I think the presence of metal detectors provides a false sense of safety. At our school, we have worked to encourage students to take ownership of their school. This is not my school; it is *our* school, and it is *their* school. I talk to parents all the time who tell me that students will not tell us the truth about what is really going on. I could not disagree more. We have an "everyone snitches" culture in our building. We hear from our students all the time, and we protect them in the telling.

We have had some guns and the threat of guns on our campus throughout the years. My first gun on campus was on my first full day of school. A student reported seeing a gun in someone's backpack. We secured the backpack and found the gun. Children want to go to school in a safe space. All children are well aware that schools should be safe. Even before we were able to build a strong school culture, students were willing to tell us when they felt unsafe.

True safety comes through investment in trusting relationships and investment in each other and in our school community. At our school we have put all of our resources in interpersonal trusting relationships, and it has served us well.

---

# 84. Gail and Her Girls

**—Told by a former teacher at an urban independent girls secondary school**

The first day of school was upon us, and I will admit that I had big butterflies in my stomach. I couldn't imagine what the day would be like that included the faculty "band" as a part of the launch of a new school year in such a tony environment. Apparently, the opening of school with a song was a tradition and a closely guarded secret. As we readied ourselves to sing on the play area that was filled with parents and overlooked the bay, I had to pinch myself that I got to be a part of something that felt so overwhelmingly joyous. I couldn't believe I got to work in a school where *joy* had a presence and priority.

That's the way life is in the company of Gail Greeley, head of this girls school. Her joy bucket

**Loving Hands. Amy Limplatya, Grade 12**

overflows and, I would come to learn, is contagious. Her school is a place where every day every decision is made with the clear purpose of furthering its mission—educating girls to meet the challenges of their time. Gail was, and is, fierce about "her girls." She models leading with her heart and has inspired me to do the same.

The girls come first, period, and for Gail this commitment takes many forms. She has a relationship with each one of her four hundred charges, and they know it. She challenges her girls to be their better selves and to explore and learn what their identities contribute to this school community. She is fierce about stewardship and developing resources that will further the experience of her students. I was on a trip with Gail once, and as we got off the plane, she introduced herself to the senior pilot, who happened to be a woman, and invited her to come and talk to her students. She said, "I want my girls to see someone who looks like them and is doing something extraordinary like being a pilot." That scene played out over and over, and I imagine Gail is still at it.

When Gail suggested that we load the entire student body onto buses and drive to the state capital to celebrate women's right to vote, there was a heavy silence around the table. Those of us who would take the concept to our teachers and help them make it happen were surely thinking, "How in the world are we going to do this?" Four hundred girls aged five through fourteen all going to the same place to do the same thing? I still recall what it felt like to see the whole school gathered on the steps of the state capitol, singing and honoring their history. My heart was bursting with pride and joy at what the girls and their teachers had done.

There is a palpable sense of purpose at the school. Gail's heart leads her into her purpose every day, and she leads the place lovingly and firmly. She teaches faculty, staff, parents, and those wonderful girls to bring their *whole selves* each day. She has a commitment to students getting outside of their typical bubble and understanding how to be active and involved community members. Participation in service learning and community events—which builds relationships with others—is central to the school experience.

Courageous and compassionate leadership is alive and well in the person of Gail. She laughs loudly, sings joyfully, loves furiously, and works tirelessly. I used to say that certain things were "sinning in the house of Gail." Her expectations for us, her team, were clear—be present, be your best self, be joyful. She made us want to meet and exceed her high expectations. The other amazing gift that Gail gave me was to learn that finding the path that brings me joy is going to be the path that allows me to bring joy to others. For that gift, I am grateful.

# 85. Our Food Pantry

### —Told by the principal of a township high school

Grand Bay High School is a comprehensive Grades 9–12 campus enrolling approximately 1,900 students. The demographics of our student body have changed a great deal over the past ten years. While our racial and ethnic diversity has grown somewhat, most of our diversity has come in terms of socioeconomic status and all the issues that surround it. Moreover, like many high schools across America, we have been responding to a mental health crisis in our community. Within a fifteen-month period, we lost six students to suicide. As a suicide survivor myself, I am well aware of the effects that death by suicide can have on survivors. But I had no idea about its impact on all the members of a school community. As we experienced mounting losses, I felt called to respond, looking for ways to better support our students academically, socially, and emotionally as well as strengthen our school community.

Our parents felt called as well. Motivated to action by what some in the community referred to as our "suicide situation," many parents came together and discussed with me ways they could help. I thought that we all felt that we had some responsibility for the six victims. Whatever the causes, they were our students. They were here in the same school building with us. They were members of our school community. Their deaths became a driver for action. Through multiple meetings with parents, several committees were formed to develop projects to provide tangible assistance to students and families going through difficult times, whether the issue related to mental health, unemployment, poverty, family strain and separation, death or illness, or other factors. The committee that gained the most traction was the one that developed our food pantry.

With economic disparity growing in our school and larger community and with the desire to do something that might have a real effect, this group of mostly moms focused its attention on an important issue—hunger and food instability. They wanted to develop a visible form of support for students and families, including those who might be struggling with mental health issues. This group wanted any student in need of food to be able to receive support without having to *qualify* for it. The only requirement to receive a food bag multiple times a week was to ask. The ask didn't need to come directly from the student either. A friend or adult within our building could reach out to the food pantry, and the student would be taken care of. I worked with this group of parents to identify space within the school for food storage and distribution and to work out a system whereby school staff, parent volunteers, and students keep the pantry stocked and organized and students could pick up bags of food. I also relentlessly and with great pride promoted this project within the school, among our parents, and in our community.

The food pantry is now in the second full school year of operation and is serving nearly forty students and their families. Each food bag we distribute provides a meal along with additional items. And each week there is a meal theme that helps us manage our food supplies and draw student interest. For example, if the theme of the week is Italian, a favorite among students, each recipient will receive all of the fixings for a pasta meal. Accompanying that meal are also breakfast items, canned vegetables, healthy snacks, and other items that fill up the bag.

Support for this program is amazing. We need to find a new location for the pantry within the building. The current space, discretely located inside our student book and supplies store, has been outgrown. Our school community has wrapped its arms around making certain the pantry is restocked continually. A student group formed and took ownership of "food drives" at many of our school events to bring awareness to the need and encourage participation by many stakeholders within our community. Monetary donations are accepted and used to purchase special "health requirement meals" that include specific items for particular families who might have allergies or other needs.

This seems like a small way that many people can respond to a need within our building and afford students with food insecurities and their families a guaranteed support system. We most definitely feel the need to continue to wrap such services around our students, going well beyond the academic supports that they need to earn a high school diploma. While our focus has been on providing students and families in need with food, our food pantry has helped strengthen the sense of community within our school. Students, staff, and parents are involved and take ownership of it. The food pantry has given us a way that we can all be more caring toward each other.

# Stories of
## Fostering
## Caring in
## Families and
## Communities

# Introduction

The third collection of stories illustrates the work of principals and other school leaders to foster caring in families and communities beyond the school. These stories tell of efforts to expand and strengthen the broader systems of caring that children, youth, and families may experience. They tell of school leaders' efforts to be caring of families; to provide assistance to address families' needs; and, in the process, to help them be more caring and supportive of their children. These stories also tell of efforts by principals and other school leaders to foster caring in the community beyond the school. These are stories of leading in the public on behalf of children and families, educating the community, and public informing and advocacy. These stories reveal school leaders working with community organizations to strengthen their efforts to support families and children.

Like stories in the other collections, each story here makes visible in one way or another the aims, positive virtues and mindsets, and competencies of caring. As you read these stories, we encourage you to recognize that taking caring out into the world can look different than engaging in caring leadership within one's school. Not only may there be more and different people involved, but the expressions of caring may be different. Actions may not look like direct caring but may serve to promote the broader interests and well-being of children and families and expand the broader network of caring that students experience. Consider a school leader writing an op-ed piece for a local newspaper to educate the community about a particular issue. Or consider a school leader participating in

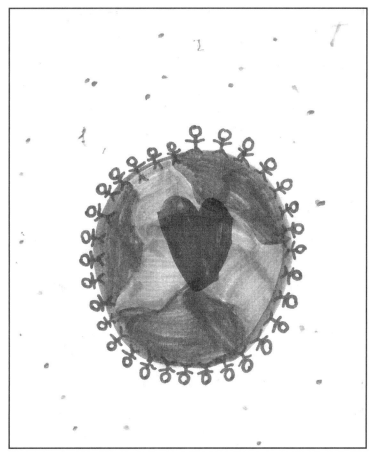

**Encircling My World. Maddie Grover, Grade 3**

a local rally to advocate for a community program or policy to address a particular need of children and families. Look for these differences, remembering the overall purpose and function of this arena of caring school leadership as described in the Introduction to this book. Like stories in the other collections, not all of these stories may be considered positive examples of caring. Some of them you may consider negative examples even as they may arise out of the best of intentions.

Like the stories in the previous two collections, these stories are not presented in any particular order. Unlike the previous collections, we do not divide this smaller collection according to level of school. We recognize, as we did with the other collections, that these stories do not represent the full extent of ways that principals and other school leaders might be caring and foster caring outside their schools. Across this collection of stories, pay attention to the importance of knowing and understanding families and communities. Consider the role of school and community context and how principals' and other school leaders' knowledge, skills, assumptions, biases, and sense of professional role may affect this work.

A number of the stories in this collection tell of experiences of parents and families being cared for by school leaders, and many tell of direct assistance that principals and other school leaders can provide them. The stories in this collection also illustrate principals' and other school leaders' efforts to connect parents and families to one another and to community support services. Several stories provide examples of leader modeling and other vicarious learning experiences accorded parents.

In addition, this collection contains stories of principals and other school leaders fostering caring in communities. These stories tell of community projects and efforts to develop the capacity of community organizations to better serve children and families. Finally, several stories in this collection tell of principals and other school leaders engaged in public education and public informing to help others identify, understand, and address key issues of concern to students, parents, families, and communities. Some stories tell of principals and school leaders engaged in advocacy to strengthen communities on behalf of children and families.

Figure 3.1 shows the stories, by number, in which examples of these caring school leadership practices can be found. You may use this figure to navigate through the collection.

**Figure 3.1**

**Caring School Leadership Practices Represented in Collection III Stories**

| Practices | Story Numbers |
|---|---|
| Modeling | 89, 93, 94, 95, 98 |
| Being caring of parents and families—experiential learning | 86, 87, 88, 93, 94, 98 |
| Providing direct assistance | 87, 88, 89, 91, 93, 94, 96, 99 |
| Connecting parents and families to one another and community services | 91, 92, 93, 94, 99 |
| Supporting community-based projects | 91, 92, 97 |
| Helping community organizations serve children, families, and communities | 97, 100 |
| Informing and educating the public | 90, 97 |
| Advocating for children and families | 90, 97 |

# Questions for Reflection and Discussion

## General Questions

1. How does each story reflect the three foundational elements of caring school leadership described in the Introduction to this book? (a) The aims of caring? (b) Positive virtues and mindsets of caring? and (c) Competencies of caring? In what ways might these three elements be strong or weak in the story? How might these strengths or weaknesses shape the actions and interactions of the school leader and any outcomes apparent in the story? How might caring in the story be seen as a part of the everyday work of school leaders rather than something *extra* that they do? How can the caring demonstrated by school leaders in these stories help others to be more caring?

2. How might the school leader's assumptions, understandings, and biases affect the way each story unfolds and the outcomes that are apparent? How might different contexts affect the story? The qualities and characteristics of interpersonal relationships? The organizational context of the school? The environment beyond the school?

3. What do you see as the main lesson or lessons of each story? If you were to write a moral for each story, what would the moral be?

4. What is your personal reaction to each story? Why do you react this way? What might be influencing your thinking?

5. Imagine that the school leader in the story met you and asked, "What do you think about what I said and what I did?" Looking through the eyes of different people in the story, how would you respond? What advice would you give this school leader?

## Collection-Specific Questions

1. How do the stories in this collection suggest ways that principals and other school leaders can help parents and families be more caring and supportive of their children? How might they help reduce the stresses and impediments that make caring difficult for parents? What might they do to help develop parents' knowledge and skills related to caring? How might they model caring and support? How might the ways in which principals and other school leaders are caring and supportive of parents help parents become more caring and supportive of their children?

2. How do these stories help you think about what principals and other school leaders need to know to be caring and supportive of parents and families? How do they help you think about ways principals and other school leaders identify and understand need and opportunity? About ways to help students feel that they can see their schools and school leaders as sources of caring and support for their parents and families? How do these stories help you identify and decide what kind of assistance might be needed and helpful?

3. What ways do these stories illustrate how principals and other school leaders can be leaders in their communities? How can school leaders address the needs and promote the well-being of children and families in their communities? Can you think of other ways that principals and other school leaders can be community leaders and act on behalf of children and families outside their schools?

4. What might principals do to arrange their work within their schools to help them engage in the forms of community leadership illustrated in these stories? What might they do to help others understand and support their community work on behalf of students and families? Their students, faculties, and staff? Their central offices? Families and communities themselves?

5. What dilemmas of professional roles do these stories suggest? What challenges do these stories suggest to the primary professional foci of school leadership on student learning and well-being within schools? Where do these stories suggest that professional boundaries be drawn between school leadership and community leadership?

## Application Questions

1. How might your own assumptions, preconceptions, and points of view influence how you read and make meaning of these stories? Consider your understanding of yourself as a caring person and a caring school leader, including your strengths and weaknesses in being caring of others. Consider your understanding of what the professional role of a school leader requires of you; what your situation calls on you to do; and what your students, your staff, and your community expect of you. How does your thinking and sense of self affect how you practice caring in this arena of leadership?

2. Put yourself in the position of the school leader who is the focus of each story. Would you think and act in the same way in the situation described in the story? Why or why not? In what ways might you think and act differently? Why?

3. For each story, recall a similar, actual situation in your school or your community. How would you retell the story for your own families and community, with yourself as the focal school leader? In what ways would your story be similar? In what ways would your story be different? Why?

**My Neighborhood. Kevin Mehr, Grade 4**

4. Consider the positive ways that school leaders in these stories are caring of parents and families and foster caring within families and the broader community. How might you adopt and adapt these positive practices in your own setting? How might you provide direct support and assistance to families? What might you do to help parents be more caring and supportive of their children? To help your community become the village that it takes to raise the child? What factors—personal, professional, and contextual—might support or impede your effort? How might you address the impediments to make your effort more successful? What role might your district central office play? How might you engage your central office to support your efforts?

5. Consider the difficult aspects of caring in this arena of leadership practice that are revealed in these stories. Do you see similar difficulties within your setting? Are there other difficulties? How might you address these difficulties? How do you think about fostering caring in families and communities when your work within your school is so important and demanding? What might you do to make it easier to be a leader not only in your school but also in your community?

6. What other leadership practices and strategies, beyond those illustrated in these stories, might be effective to strengthen caring in families and the community beyond your school? Explain why you think these practices and strategies might be effective in your situation. Explain the groundwork that might need to be done to increase the likelihood of their success. How might these practices and strategies relate to other practices and strategies you may use to develop caring within your school?

# 86. Engaging Parents in Equity Dialogues

—Told by the principal of a suburban elementary school

In my school, as part of our efforts to strengthen our racially conscious community, I created a voluntary, ongoing dialogue group for parents and staff, which we called the Equity Learning Community. This group met monthly to learn about race as a social construct; the impact of racism throughout our society and in schools; and how to identify, question, and interrupt biased actions. We wanted to address the question "How can we raise racially conscious children?" Most of the members were parents of color with our equity coach, a Latina woman, and me, a white male, leading the discussion.

After the group had met a few times, I called the father of one of our African American students to update him about something at school. After we finished the discussion, he said, "As long as I have you on the phone, can I say something?"

I said, "Sure." He said, "I want you to know you've changed my life." I said, "Oh. In a good way, or—" He said, "No, no, no, in a good way. I started going [to the Equity Learning Community], and I didn't know. I didn't even know that was a thing. I just thought that was the way my life was. I didn't know there was research out there about how black people are treated. So by going there, I know that I have a voice in this conversation," he said. "It's changed my life, and it's changed how I view myself. And I want to study these things and become a better dad and a better person."

While we're not moving as fast as I think we should be to end racism, it is times like these where I know we are making it better for the next generation.

---

# 87. The Fire

—Told by the principal of a small-town elementary school

I'm sitting in yet another district administrator's meeting when my cell phone buzzes in my pocket. I hate being out of my building during the school day, and this meeting has droned on without a clear end in sight. I silence my phone at first and try to ignore it, but just seconds later, it is vibrating again. This time, partially gleeful that I have a legitimate reason to step outside, I answer the phone, and it's Mr. Fielder, one of our bus drivers, on the other end.

"You hear about the house fire in Marks?" he asks, referring to a small rural town up the road from my school.

I'm puzzled now, and my contentment fades, "No. What happened? Who?" "It's the Bowmans. Their whole trailer is gone. Destroyed."

"Is everyone OK?" I ask.

"Yes, the mama and the baby girl got out just fine."

I exhaled, relieved. Sadly, house fires are an all-too-common occurrence in this rural area, especially in winter when poor electrical wiring and the use of space heaters in close quarters had caused several lethal fires only weeks ago.

"Thank you for calling me. I appreciate you."

Immediately, I called my assistant principal, who was back at school, to inform her of the fire. Three of the Bowman children attended my school, and I was immediately worried for them and how they would deal with the news. The oldest Bowman, Trevon (Tre), was nearly twelve and was the tallest kid in the third grade. He and his siblings had been to at least five different elementary schools, and all of the moves had taken a toll on his academic record. He had repeated each grade at least twice. After two years at our school, the kids seemed to be gaining their bearings, and Tre was placed in an accelerated class to complete both third and fourth grade in a single year. He was earning better grades, and things seemed to finally click. I was concerned that the fire would trigger yet another disruptive move, and our plans to get Tre closer to his *right grade* would be over.

I returned to the conference room for the meeting, but I couldn't get the Bowmans out of my head. Again, my phone rang, and it was the assistant principal. "I pulled the kids from class and told them about the fire. They are OK. They weren't concerned about the house. All they wanted to know is that

their mom was all right. When I told them that, they were relieved. They're going to be all right." I returned to school, and the entire faculty sprung into action. Our parent liaison gathered items from the uniform closet, and I called Ms. Bowman to let her know that the school was here for her and the children. She told me that she and the kids would be moving about twenty minutes away to Clintonville to live with a relative until they got back on their feet. She wanted them to continue to go to our school, and I breathed a deep sigh of relief because I lived in Clintonville, and the kids wouldn't have to transfer schools at all. I agreed to pick them up for school and bring them home each evening through the end of the school year.

# 88. Family Support
### —Told by the assistant principal of a small-town elementary school

It was the start of a new school year, and I was sitting in the main office the week before teachers would report. Throughout the day, parents who had moved into the area over the summer would stop by to get their paperwork to enroll their children. Near the end of the day, Shelby came in with four children in tow. It was obvious that she was overwhelmed and was being pushed to her limit. We engaged in some small talk, and I learned that all of the children were her nieces and nephews and that she had temporary custody of them. Two of the children would be attending our school for the upcoming year—Matt and Laura.

After Shelby completed her paperwork, she asked if she could speak with me in private. We set up in the conference room beside the office where she almost immediately began to cry. She was struggling financially, as many of us would be when four extra mouths were suddenly added to the family. But that wasn't what she was the most concerned about. She was most worried about how the children would be treated, as they were African American and our student

body was almost completely white. I did my best to assure her that her children would be cared for, loved, and protected just like all of our students. She did not seem completely convinced, but she could not afford to pay tuition for them to attend a nearby school that she would be more comfortable with. As she left that day, I committed to making sure I took extra time so that these children would feel welcomed and loved.

As the year progressed, Shelby's children did have a tough time adjusting. They had been torn away from their birth parents and were now going to a school in which they saw themselves as outsiders. Their teachers and I continually poured love and grace onto them, but they couldn't help but still feel different from everyone else. Matt would often become angry and lash out at the students around him. Laura was overly concerned with how the students around her viewed her, and she often misconstrued their intentions.

As Christmas approached that year, I was speaking with Shelby about a small behavior problem with Matt when she confided that she wasn't sure what Christmas would look like for the kids that year. I let her know that someone had expressed a desire to help out one of our families and that I would contact that person and see if he could help. Shelby didn't know that this someone was me.

I waited until the next day to phone her so that she wouldn't guess my identity. My wife and I purchased Christmas gifts for all six of her children (she had two children of her own). We also took up money from our Sunday School class at church and gave her a gift card to spend on groceries. Members of our church began to think about how they could support this family in the coming year.

It has now been two years, and Matt and Laura are doing well. I know that Shelby trusts us and knows that whenever Matt and Laura come to our school, they are coming to a place where they are loved and cared for. And our church played an important role in supporting this family.

# 89. This School Is Here for You

—Told by the head of an urban K–12 independent school

You never know who might call on a late July morning at school, but it's usually not easy news to hear. This summer it was a former colleague, now retired in the San Francisco Bay area, who had been contacted by a former teaching fellow's parents with the news that their daughter, who had worked here as a second-grade teacher, had passed away.

The young teacher had left lasting memories here, partly because of her artistic abilities and help with the creation of our school's centennial history book for children. She coordinated beautiful group projects grade by grade for this unique K–4 project, now a legacy document. From our campus, she moved across the city to a neighborhood school, where she was, by all accounts, beloved.

For some complicated reasons, that school was not able to host a memorial gathering for her. Nor was her church, where deep sadness and a rift in

Surprise Flowers at My Door. Roz Beile, Grade 12

the congregation followed her faith-inspired deferral of treatment of a very treatable form of cancer, a decision that proved fatal. It was, as we learned later, a painfully difficult situation for her and her family and friends. I said that we would host the memorial at our school.

We were only a few weeks away from welcoming faculty back for the new school year. Many of us had taken the chance to enjoy a vacation during the window between the end of summer programs and the beginning of classes. My decision to host the memorial meant that many colleagues would need to appear on a Saturday morning to open our doors to a grieving family and community. Everyone I asked to help said yes. What was expected to be a group of fifty attendees ended up being four times as many. All we could do was all we could do. We were able to say yes, and we brought some consolation to this family—to her parents and spouse and daughter and in-laws. Sometimes moments find us, and we should be grateful for that.

# 90. An Open Letter to Parents of Children Throughout New York State Regarding Grades 3–8 Testing

—Written by New York State principals and cosigned by more than 530 additional principals and nearly three thousand parents and teachers; see www.newyorkprincipals.org
*Adapted from New York Principals (2014).*

Dear Parents,

We are the principals of your children's schools. We serve communities in every corner of New York State—from Niagara County to Clinton, Chautauqua to Suffolk. We come from every size and type of school, with students from every background. We thank you for sharing your children with us and for entrusting us to ensure that they acquire the skills and knowledge they need to achieve their dreams and your hopes for them.

This year, many of your children experienced the first administration of the newly revised New York State Assessments. You may have heard that teachers, administrators, and parents are questioning the validity of these tests. As dedicated administrators, we have carefully observed the testing process and have been learning a great deal about these tests and their impact. We care deeply about your children and their learning and what to share with you what we know—and what we do not know—about these new state assessments.

**Here's what we know:**

1.  **NYS Testing Has Increased Dramatically:** We know that our students are spending more time taking state tests than ever before. Since 2010, the amount of time spent on average taking the 3–8 ELA and Math tests has increased by a whopping 128%! The increase has been particularly hard on our younger students, with third graders seeing an increase of 163%!

2.  **The Tests Were Too Long:** We know that many students were unable to complete the tests in the allotted time. Not only were the tests lengthy and challenging, but embedded field test questions extended the length of the tests and caused mental exhaustion, often before students reached the questions that counted toward their scores. For our Special Education students

who receive additional time, these tests have become more a measure of endurance than anything else.

3. **Ambiguous Questions Appeared Throughout the Exams:** We know that many teachers and principals could not agree on the correct answers to ambiguous questions in both ELA and Math. In some schools, identical passages and questions appeared on more than one test and at more than one grade level. One school reported that on one day of the ELA Assessment, the same passage with identical questions was included in the third, fourth AND fifth grade ELA Assessments.

4. **Children Have Reacted Viscerally to the Tests.** We know that many children cried during or after testing, and others vomited or lost control of their bowels or bladders. Others simply gave up. One teacher reported that a student kept banging his head on the desk, and wrote, "This is too hard," and "I can't do this," throughout his test booklet.

5. **The Low Passing Rate Was Predicted:** We know that in his "implementation of the Common Core Learning Standards" memo of March 2013, Deputy Commissioner Slentz stated that proficiency scores (i.e., passing rate) on the new assessments would range between 30%–70% statewide. When scores were released in August 2013, the statewide proficiency rate was announced as 31%.

6. **The College Readiness Benchmark Is Irresponsibly Inflated:** We know that the New York State Education Department used SAT scores of 560 in Reading, 540 in Writing and 530 in Mathematics, as the college readiness benchmarks to help set the "passing" cut scores on the 3–8 New York State exams. These NYSED scores, totaling 1630, are far higher than the College Board's own college readiness benchmark score of 1550. By doing this, NYSED has carelessly inflated the "college readiness" proficiency cut scores for students as young as nine years of age.

7. **State Measures Are Contradictory:** We know that many children are receiving scores that are not commensurate with the abilities they demonstrate on other measures, particularly the New York State Integrated Algebra Regents examination. Across New York, many accelerated eighth-graders scored below proficiency on the eighth-grade test only to go on and excel on the Regents examination one month later. One district reports that 58% of the students who scored below proficiency on the NYS Math 8 examination earned a master score on the Integrated Algebra Regents.

8. **Students Labeled as Failures Are Forced Out of Classes:** We know that many students who never needed Academic Intervention Services (AIS) in the past are now receiving mandated AIS as a result of the failing scores. As a result, these students are forced to forgo enrichment classes. For example, in one district, some middle school students had to give up instrumental music, computer or other special classes in order to fit AIS into their schedules.

9. **The Achievement Gap Is Widening:** We know that the tests have caused the achievement gap to widen as the scores of economically disadvantaged students plummeted, and that parents are reporting that low-scoring children feel like failures.

10. **The Tests Are Putting Financial Strains on Schools:** We know that many schools are spending precious dollars on test prep materials, and that

instructional time formerly dedicated to field trips, special projects, and thearts and enrichment, has been reallocated to test prep, testing, and AIS services.

11. **The Tests Are Threatening Other State Initiatives:** Without a doubt, the emphasis on testing is threatening other important State initiatives, most notably the implementation of the Common Core State Standards (CCSS). Parents who see the impact of the testing on their children are blaming the CCSS, rather than the unwise decision to implement high stakes testing before proper capacity had developed. As long as these tests remain, it will be nearly impossible to have honest conversations about the impact of the CCSS on our schools.

**Here's what we do not know:**

1. **How These Tests Will Help Our Students:** With the exception of select questions released by the state, we do not have access to the test questions. Without access to the questions, it is nearly impossible to use the tests to help improve student learning.

2. **How to Use These Tests to Improve Student Skills or Understanding:** Tests should serve as a tool for assessing student skills and understanding. Since we are not informed of the make-up of the tests, we do not know, with any level of specificity, the content or skills for which children require additional support. We do not even know how many points were allotted for each question.

3. **The Underlying Cause of Low Test Scores:** We do not know if children's low test scores are actually due to lack of skills in that area or simply a case of not finishing the test—a problem that plagued many students.

4. **What to Expect Next Year:** We do not know what to expect for next year. Our students are overwhelmed by rapidly changing standards, curriculum, and assessments. It is nearly impossible to serve and protect the students in our care when expectations are in constant flux and put in place rapidly in a manner that is not reflective of sound educational practice.

5. **How Much This Is Costing Already-Strained Taxpayers:** We don't know how much public money is being paid to vendors and corporations that the NYSED contracts to design assessments, nor do we know if the actual designers are educationally qualified.

Please know that we, your school principals, care about your children and will continue to do everything in our power to fill their school days with learning that is creative, engaging, challenging, rewarding, and joyous. We encourage you to dialogue with your child's teachers so that you have real knowledge of his skills and abilities across all areas. If your child scored poorly on the test, please make sure that he does not internalize feelings of failure. We believe that the failure was not on the part of our children, but rather with the officials of the New York State Education Department. These are the individuals who chose to recklessly implement numerous major initiatives without proper dialogue, public engagement, or capacity building. They are the individuals who have failed.

As principals of New York schools, it is always our goal to move forward in a constant state of improvement. Under current conditions, we fear that the hasty implementation of unpiloted assessments will continue to cause more harm than good. Please work with us to preserve a healthy learning environment for our children and to protect all of the unique varieties of intelligence that are not reducible to scores on standardized tests. Your child is so much more than a test score, and we know it.

Warmly,

Sharon Fougner, Principal, E. M.
Baker Elementary

Sean C. Feeney, PhD, Principal,
The Wheatley Candlewood Middle School

Carol Burris, EdD, Principal,
South Side High School

Andrew Greene, Principal,
Candlewood Middle School

Peter DeWitt, EdD, Principal,
Poestenkill Elementary

Elizabeth Phillips, Principal, P.S. 321

Tim Farley, Principal,
Ichabod Crane Middle School

Katie Zahedi, PhD, Principal,
Linden Avenue Middle School

---

# 91. Community Career Fairs and Pop-Up Food Banks

**—Told by the former principal of an urban high school**

When I took over as principal, I knew I wanted to build significant connections to the community as the school sat in a zip code that was on every list for the wrong reason: highest incidents of poverty, highest STD rate, highest crime—all the things that signal trouble. The state representative for this area was a man who also had a vision for his district that was beyond the traditional rhetoric and shared a solutions-oriented stance about it like I had. So we got together and brainstormed that a quarterly career fair for students and their parents would be just the kind of partnership the area needed. He used his connections to the local workforce development board to get prospective employees. I networked with other principals and got the word out to students and their families.

On several Saturday mornings, I got up early and met this representative's legislative assistant and a friend of his campaign to move tables into our gymnasium to prepare for the career fair. No one wanted to pay overtime for custodians, so we were the moving crew. Each fair hosted about fifteen to twenty different employers, and the press covered the first one we did, running announcements leading up to it and sending someone to do coverage the day of the event.

Many parents and students walked out with either follow-up interviews or offers of employment. Seeing students come through wearing interview clothes, being incredibly nervous, and practicing their interview responses with me in the lobby before going into the gym were just a few points of pride that made my heart swell with love. I would follow up with other principals to let them know how well their students did.

Being a principal means thinking outside of the box about what your community needs and how you can build bridges to other people and organizations doing those things. Often, offering the gym or other meeting space can be the final piece in making a powerful change or meeting a need. It starts with the vision that your scope of influence is not just the four walls of your school. Think of your school as not having walls. Think of your responsibility to include serving the community surrounding your school. What new possibilities are there with this new reframing of responsibility?

Another initiative to support families was spurred by our recognition that parent-teacher conferences at the high school level often leave something to be desired for staff and students alike. Parents sort of assume by high school the child has it figured out, so turnout is typically much lower than for elementary or middle schools. As I thought about how to reformat conferences to be a value-add to families, I started thinking about what they may need. Since the conference itself is held during dinner time, I thought that would be a natural starting place. I couldn't afford to feed all the families from my dismal school budget, but what if I connected us with an agency who fed people as part of their mission? I started asking around and found an agency that operates what they call *pop-up food banks*, where they take the food to a location to distribute from directly instead of asking people to come to their warehouse. Perfect! So I got in touch with the director of community outreach, and she loved the idea. We'd need volunteers to hand out the meal kits, and I knew this was something our National Honor Society would be on board with as a service project.

The premise that really made this initiative something that was truly different was every family that came through the door was able to get food; no one had to prove need or financial hardship to get the meal. By normalizing the handout process, it alleviated the stigma from accepting food and allowed everyone to benefit. We handed out over one hundred meals that night, and families were so happy to walk out with fresh food, including a loaf of bread, bag of apples, and ingredients for a salad, not exclusively canned goods.

Although it was a small thing, it concretely showed our families that we valued their time and understood they may have had competing priorities that evening, feeding their family dinner, and getting report card information. Hopefully, we made it a little easier that night and demonstrated that school is a place to get other needs met, not just an education.

---

# 92. Born and Bred

—Told by a teacher at a rural regional secondary school
*Adapted from Randall, Clews, and Furlong (2015).*

Tomorrow is going to be a big day. I've been offered the position of vice-principal of Glendale Regional School, where I am now a teacher. As a thirty-year-old *woman,* this opportunity is nothing to sneeze at. It may be the smallest school in the district, with fewer than three hundred students from Grades 6 through 12 and only fifteen teachers, but the next step, they tell me, could be principal and one day, who knows, regional superintendent! And tomorrow I need to tell the superintendent if I will take the job.

I'm one of the few staff members who actually grew up in Glendale. I know it like the back of my hand. And I know the people, too—at least most of them. Plus, I know more of the skeletons in their closets than you can imagine. I was homecoming queen and valedictorian, and I was voted "most likely to succeed," which, unofficially, meant I was

the one most likely to get out of here as soon as I could! But that wasn't me. I loved this school, and I loved—I *still* love—Glendale. And it's not just the people but the beauty around it—the hills, the fields, the river, and the bay.

Ever since the mines shut down back in the 1970s and the railway stopped running through here, plus a few other setbacks, Glendale's economy has been limping along. If it wasn't for Morton, thirty miles north, where many of our people travel every day to work, or the national park, twenty miles south, where lots of folks get hired every spring and summer, Glendale would be in a sorry state. You don't have to look far outside of town and inside it, too, to see some pretty grim examples of honest-to-goodness poverty with all the problems that go with it: domestic violence, alcoholism, illiteracy, drug abuse, even incest. With family breakups more and more the norm, the local population has become far more transient than it was when I was young. There are people now living in the area whose backgrounds no one seems to know.

We have kids who come to Glendale in the middle of the term, having moved more than twice already during the school year. Many of them are kids with single parents from somewhere else, usually the city, in need of affordable housing (often on back roads in substandard units) and with ex-partners constantly hounding them about custody issues, and so on. Of the more than thirty schools in our spread-out district, Glendale has the highest rate of student mobility and the second-lowest scores in the district in basic literacy and numeracy.

I've developed a reputation as a go-getter in the school at large. Maybe that's one reason why I've been asked to become vice-principal. I also have time to do a number of other things *outside* the school that extend my role as teacher in important ways and, I like to think, benefit the area as a whole by expanding people's horizons and help Glendale become a better community in which to live. Once you scratch the surface, you see a place brimming with possibilities—possibilities that people who've lived here all their lives often can't see at all. But *I* can see them.

The present vice-principal at Glendale will soon become the principal. He is leaning on me hard to take over from him, and I think that could work out well. I've worked with him already on a variety of committees and projects across the years, such as the Anti-Bullying Task Force, the schoolwide talent show, and the transportation committee, to name a few. I think the two of us could work very well together.

What concerns me, though, is how busy I've seen him become since taking over as vice-principal five years ago—how many headaches; how much paperwork; and how much administrative work, such as scheduling courses and classrooms, organizing school assemblies, lining up substitute teachers, conducting staff evaluations, attending meetings of the school board and the

Parent-Teachers Association, responding to the district office to set up this program or that, fielding complaints from parents, and handling discipline issues. All of these are necessary in the running of the school, and they will be the same ones I'll be responsible for as well.

Despite the added work and the added hours (starting a family will clearly not be easy); despite moving to the *wrong* side of *us and them* as far as staff relations are concerned; and despite not having much time to get involved in organizing school concerts, drama productions, and the like (which I have loved to do), it's the feeling that, all things considered, I'm in a better position to make a difference on a broader scale. I'll have to figure out how to delegate some of these things to other teachers, or to committees. Then I can get on to some of the possibilities I've considered before, some things that would help the school become a learning center for the whole region—not just a building where people send their kids for *readin', ritin',* and *'rithmetic* but a hub of growth and development for folks of every age.

I imagine that I could round up a select group of teachers and other key people in the community, plus some students, and enter into an arrangement with the Department of Extended Learning or the Department of Rural Studies at the nearby community college, and we could use Glendale school facilities for adult education workshops, information sessions, or full-fledged retreats on all sorts of topics. We could explore a partnership with the penitentiary, an hour away. Surely there's a way some of our more mature students—properly briefed and supervised—could get involved in visiting inmates and maybe tutoring them in particular subjects. Then there's the project I've been wanting us to get started for a while now. We could forge stronger ties with the local nursing home by getting some intergenerational activities underway. What a learning opportunity it would be for our students to visit and work with the residents there in terms of lots of things. It would help develop their conversational skills; their literacy skills; their knowledge of local history; and their appreciation for the full, rich lives of their community's oldest citizens. And the residents would learn from our students and benefit from the companionship and care our students would give them.

I could go on and on, but that's probably enough. Every time I get talking about what I do and what I—what *we*—could do, I get so excited. Yes, the challenges of teaching in a school this size, in the kinds of community like this, are huge but so are the possibilities. It's the possibilities I like to keep in mind. I think I'll take the job.

---

# 93. We Are Going to Be Together in This
### —Told by the parent of a suburban middle school student

During her years in middle school, our daughter put us through the ringer. Smart, funny, extremely social, and a huge risk-taker, she hung with a tough group of kids. Some of these kids were dealing with bad situations at home, some were showing behavioral problems, some were starting to cut school, and some were beginning to use and abuse drugs and alcohol. Several of these kids, including our daughter, had been in trouble at school. A few had encounters with the police.

In February of her eighth-grade year, we received a telephone call, out of the blue, from the assistant principal of the high school that our daughter would attend in the fall. He invited us to an evening meeting of a small group of parents of eighth-grade students. The purpose of the meeting, he said, was to begin preparing for transition to the high school. "OK," we thought. "A little early?"

When we arrived at the meeting, we discovered that the parents who had been called together were the parents of that group of eighth-grade kids. And we knew very quickly that this was not going to be a routine parent meeting about the middle school to high school transition. Joining the assistant principal at the meeting were several deans and a social worker. Also, there was the director of youth services for our township. We were confused and nervous.

Once in our seats, the assistant principal welcomed us warmly. He introduced each of the deans, the social worker, and the director of youth services. Then he got right to the point. "You are, no doubt, wondering why we invited you here tonight. I'm sorry that I was not more direct with you about the purpose of this meeting when we spoke on the phone. Your eighth graders are part of a group that we have been watching and speaking to the middle school about for a little while now, anticipating their arrival to the high school in the fall. I wanted you to know that we are concerned about them. We are preparing to welcome and support them when they arrive here." You could have heard a pin drop.

He continued, "I'd like to spend a little time with you tonight to tell you what our concerns are about your children as they come to high school. I, we [referring to the deans and social worker], would like to spend time telling you what we are working on to welcome and support them. We will have plenty of time to hear your questions and concerns about your kids and what we want to do for them. This is the first in a series of meetings we would like to have with you throughout the rest of the school year. We want to keep you informed about what we are doing, but also we want to learn about your kids from you and to get your insights about how we might serve them well."

After a long pause, the assistant principal said, "Importantly, though, this meeting is for you. We know how tough this period is for kids socially, emotionally, and academically. We know how

**Riding Together.** Daniella Chapman-Rienstra, Grade 11

tough it can be for parents. An important reason for calling you together as a group is to make clear that you are not alone. We are here, and other parents are with you. There are things that we can do together to help you be good and strong parents for your children. There are resources and professionals we can make available to help you best care for and support your kids. We can provide opportunities for you to get to know other parents and help and support each other. Our deans and social workers can be of service to help you support your kids. And the director of youth services can be a source of support outside the school. That is why she is here tonight, to give you an idea of how her office can support you as well as your kids." He concluded his introduction by saying, "We are going to be together in this."

My spouse and I glanced around the room. Most of the other parents, like us, were mixed parts stunned and comforted. The sense of loneliness we felt in parenting a difficult child had been penetrated. We began to realize that our daughter would be supported and that we would be supported too. The start of her freshman year was seven months away, and they were already on top of this. No one got up to leave. After a few seconds of silence, the assistant principal said, "Let's introduce ourselves again, starting this time with the parents. Please introduce yourself and your son or daughter by name. If you wish to share something now about how you feel, a concern you have, or something you'd like to see happen for your child, please feel free to share. If not, don't worry. Your names will be just fine for now."

So it began. As the introductions went on, parents started to open up with fears and concerns they had about their kids and about their own ability to guide and support them. A few spoke about the stresses they were under, to the nods of other parents. Yes, over the course of the evening, the assistant principal, deans, the social worker, and the director of youth services summarized their own concerns and described some of the things they were working on. But most of the time was taken up by parents in this *introduction*. While we did not see it at the time, that appeared to be the purpose of this meeting all along—to take a first step in developing relationships among parents and between parents and the school as well as to introduce parents to the human faces of parenting resources and supports available to them in the school and community.

# 94. My Mom Is in Trouble
## —Told by the former principal of an urban high school

Isaac was a reserved, quiet student, and I was drawn to him because I know adjusting to high school can be tough, especially for introverted students. He didn't know many other freshmen, but when I talked to him, he showed an interest in coding and robotics. I got him connected to the coding club teacher and also the robotics sponsor. In those spaces, he was able to build some peer networks and find his community.

For the duration of his freshman year, I chatted with him in the halls and at lunch about how stuff was going. I checked on him when I visited his classrooms to observe his teachers and worked hard to ensure he knew I *saw* him and cared about how he was doing. Sometimes we'd eat lunch in my office together just to give him a space outside of the cafeteria to have some quiet time and a chance to check in with me.

I noticed a shift when he returned to school at the start of his sophomore year. His shoulders were hunched more forward, and despite growing an inch or two, his weight had declined, leaving him even skinnier than the previous year. His eyes lit up when he saw me that first day back, and he ran up to give me a hug and chat with me. He said very plainly and very directly, "I need to talk to you, in private." So in the hectic nature that is the first day of school, the morning got away from me, but I saw him again at lunch. He was busy catching up with friends, and I didn't want to interrupt. He found me after the lunch bell rang and asked if we could chat in my office. We walked in, and I took my desk chair as was custom—although Isaac didn't sit down right away. He stood by the door and asked if he could shut it, something he had never directly asked me to do, standing with his hand on the knob, waiting for my approval. Something was gravely wrong.

Now my heart began to quicken, as my intuition was correct and clearly something had changed. And Isaac knew he needed to let me in on this secret he had been carrying. He closed the door and sat down, clearly thinking hard about how he was going to share this news. He said, "My mom is in trouble. Her boyfriend is hurting us." My heart sank. I asked about any other children in the house, and he described his five siblings, one older but also a sophomore, a fourth grader, a first grader, and a four- and two-year-old. He described how they weren't getting enough food and had to lock themselves in their room at night. He went on to explain how his life had become a complete hell. I asked, "How can I get in touch with your mom?" He responded, "She is with him right now. You can't call her." I asked if the Department of Family Services had been involved, and he said yes; it closed the case a few months ago. I gave him my cell number and let him know I would help him and his mom; she just needed to get in touch with me so we could put a plan together. That evening, after the buzz of after-school activities had died down, I sat in my office and pondered what I was actually going to do when his mom called. I had no idea what I was doing and concretely knew I was in over my head but didn't care: The system had clearly failed this family. Isaac meant the world to me and to know what was happening to him set my soul on fire. I talked briefly to the social worker to update her, but since she was only assigned to be part-time at our school, she couldn't be much help. I let her know the mom would be calling me in the morning and that I would probably need some guidance from her.

The next day, Isaac arrived on the school bus and immediately came to my office, around 6:20 a.m.. I hadn't heard from his mom yet. He insisted, "Call her now." So my fingers clumsily typed the number he gave me, and I tried to contain the shakiness of my voice. She answered from a bus, riding from her overnight shift at Walmart back home where the boyfriend was waiting for her to return. She said she needed help to get out and felt she had no one because she didn't have family locally. She said she would call me back later that day—around lunch—but that she couldn't really talk now. The look of disappointment on Isaac's face was hard to stomach; I knew he was hoping for bigger action during this phone call. I let him know we would meet up at lunch and that he was welcome to find me so we could make another call. He pleaded with me, "Does this mean we will be able to get out of the house tonight?" I answered, "That's the plan, Isaac." However, no answer I could give would have been sufficient. By that time, the first bell had rung, I gave Isaac a hug, and he went off to advisory. I stood there wondering how his day would go and if I could really make good on my word.

At lunch, he was at my office within seconds of the bell dismissing students from class. He was very jittery, clearly a bundle of nerves. I dialed the number, and his mom answered, "Hello." She was speaking to an unknown male voice in the background. "It's the school. You need to be quiet. You don't want any trouble." She whispered into the phone, "Give me a few minutes. I'll call you back when I leave to go to the corner store." Then she abruptly hung up. Within ten minutes, she was calling back and confirmed that, yes, he was abusing them, specifically her; withholding food; and depriving them. She said she needed help getting out and was really scared because she had no transportation and six kids. She didn't think a shelter would take them. I asked, "The two children who are with you, could you get them to my school? She said she could do that, and although she didn't have her own transportation, she could call the police from a friend's house to pick them up. "What about my other children?" she asked. I quickly answered, "I'll work with the district security team and the other principals to get them to my school safely." She agreed to this plan. We would all rendezvous at my school after they got off school. The youngest wasn't done until 4:00 p.m., but the two high school students finished at 2:07 p.m., and going home first was not an option. We hung up with a tentative plan in place. Isaac was grinning from ear to ear—the first smile I had seen on him. He stated, "We don't have to go there tonight?" and I was finally able to respond, "No, you are going to be somewhere else." He then headed off to his afternoon classes, walking with a new lightness I hadn't seen in him since the previous school year. I contacted the other two principals of his siblings and let them know what was going to go on. I called district security with the update, and they got in touch with two different sergeants who would be transporting the children from the other schools to mine for the rendezvous.

At dismissal, Isaac happily walked in my office and exclaimed how he was excited to show his school off to his siblings, completely changed in his demeanor from the previous day. By 2:30 p.m., his older sister arrived, and he gave her a quick tour around our school, showing off the coding club where he was supposed to be that day. By 3:30 p.m., the police had arrived with his mom and the two youngest siblings. District security arrived with the last two children, and by 4:15 p.m., all six children and mom were together in my office. I was able to provide food from our after-school program, and all of the children ate everything I put in front of them—yogurt, chips, pretzels, juice boxes, crackers, anything.

Mom had to make a call to a women's shelter to see where there was room that night. That morning, I had contacted our district coordinator for students in transition, and she was able to find space in a shelter that would accommodate the whole family so that piece was prearranged and confirmed. She just had to complete the lengthy intake process. So, by 5:30 p.m., we had ordered some pizzas while we waited for the process to get finished. My office was filled with the laughter of children who were busy drawing, playing, and just enjoying the company of each other despite their situation.

By 6:30 p.m., two cabs were dispatched by the shelter to transport the family to their resting place for the night. As I walked out with them to say goodbye, I was scared but hopeful that they had been able to take the first step, getting out, and were now connected to resources that would know more about the following steps than me.

I walked back in my office amid empty juice boxes and toys and drawings and colored pencils scattered everywhere, sat at my desk, and cried—the deep, heavy sobs where you lose yourself fully in the emotion and don't hold back anything. I had been in emergency response mode, and my body was finally able to release the emotions I'd locked up inside all day. I cared so deeply for Isaac and his family yet, in reality, had so little I could offer to help them. The world didn't care about how he liked robotics or was interested in being a coder for video games someday. He was *just another kid* who I loved fiercely and beyond the limits of what I knew was possible. I leaned into that love and encourage others to do the same, every day, for every student.

# 95. We Just Couldn't See It
—Told by a division head of an urban independent elementary school

It was summer break, and I was finally getting back to my local gym after a long hiatus. I was starting with a warm-up on the stationary bike, easing myself back into the exercise routine. As I was half paying attention to the cooking show on the TV hung above the bicycle (*Why* were they showing cooking shows at the gym???), I saw *her* walk in. My heart sank, and my throat tightened. I briefly thought about darting for the locker room, but she had already spotted me and was walking toward me. She sat on the bike right next to mine and said hello. I mustered a smile and uttered a nervous hello.

*She* was the parent I dreaded seeing again after she had angrily withdrawn her son from my school three years ago. In the two years her son had attended my school, I had had numerous meetings and phone calls with her and her husband about a variety of issues, all ultimately related to her son's grade placement. She was a prominent attorney in the city, who had married into a well-known political family. Every encounter we had turned into a trial by fire. There was a rebuttal to every statement either her son's teachers or I made, there was questioning of evidence we presented to back up our observations, and there was belittling of the teachers and their approach, teaching qualifications, and language. The conversations became downright hostile when the teachers and I made the recommendation that her son repeat his current grade. That was the ultimate reason she withdrew him.

Nervously, I made small talk with her, asking about her work. I had seen in the local paper she had just received a huge promotion, so I congratulated her on her new position. Eventually, I asked how her family was doing, specifically her son. She told me he was joining a new school that year, as they had not been happy with the public school he had attended the prior year. I had heard through the grapevine that was actually his second school since he had left us, so he would now be moving to his third new school in three years. I knew some administrators at the new school and told her that I had heard it was a wonderful school and hoped he would be happy there. She smiled and said thank you, and then she said the three words I thought I would never hear.

"You were right. You were right when you told us we should have had him repeat." I was so shocked I nearly fell off my bike! She continued, "We should have listened to you. He's had such a hard time in school, being the youngest in his grade. You tried to tell us, but we. . . . Well, really me. His dad agreed with you. I couldn't see it. He was our only child then, and we thought he was perfect! But everything you said was true. He's really struggled to keep up with his classmates. He's smaller than everyone else. And now he's noticing the difference, and he talks about it. It was my pride and my guilt that got in the way. As a working mom, I just couldn't hear anything negative about my child, because I thought it was my fault."

I felt all the anger and fear I had felt toward this woman for too many years immediately fade away, and it was replaced with compassion and sadness. I didn't want to be right about her son facing difficulty, but I had seen it too many times before that I knew what was coming. So in trying to learn from the situation, I asked her, "What could the teachers or I have done to help you with your decision? I know we had several conversations and even connected you with a mother who had made the same decision for her child. What could I have done differently?" "Nothing," she replied. "You were always so honest and straightforward with us. My husband and I liked that—I think especially being lawyers!" She laughed. "But I think for me, I couldn't make a logical decision

on this. It was emotional. It was my guilt, my sense of failure as his mother. I felt like I hadn't done something I should have done. It was my issue, not his. But it's not your job to be my therapist! Even talking to that other mom, she was very nice, but she was a stay-at-home mom. She didn't have that working-mother guilt. So maybe talking to another working mom would have helped? I'm not sure, because it was about me. Maybe just call me out on that!"

We both laughed, and I thanked her for sharing her story with me. This family's departure had haunted me for three years, and I worried about her son's experiences in school since leaving. He was a bright and energetic boy, with an advanced vocabulary, but also quick to cry and throw a tantrum when not getting his way. I had heard he was quieter now, more of an observer and somewhat withdrawn. It saddened me to think that change may have occurred because he was feeling overwhelmed and left behind from his older classmates.

I knew the mother had two more children since leaving us, so I asked her about them. She beamed as she talked about her three boys, joking that she lived "in a house full of testosterone." She told me she is now "a repeating advocate" and has already asked her younger sons' teachers if they were on track with their peers or if they should repeat. I asked her if I had any current parents who were faced with the same decision if I could give them her phone number. She replied, "Of course! Especially any working moms. They need to know it's not about them. You have to take the guilt and emotion out of the decision. Maybe it's just better to let the dad make the decision!" We both laughed and hugged after finishing up our workouts.

---

# 96. Our Next Mayor

—Told by the principal of an urban charter middle school

Normally, when we boarded buses, we were shepherding hundreds of middle schoolers home for the day, with backpacks, lunch bags, and books in tow. This afternoon was different.

We weren't boarding buses with our students. We were boarding buses with our students, parents, families, and staff.

Our city was on the verge of electing a new mayor, and we were heading to the last mayoral forum—a forum focused on education. Many of our parents had been asking questions about the election, but because so many of them did not speak English as their first language, they had a difficult time following the conversation about the candidates.

So we packed two buses, with our students, their parents, our principal, our teachers—and two interpreters—to bring the conversation about the future of our city to our school community.

A parent leaned across one of the seats and asked me, "What do you think about the first candidate we are going to hear? I heard he was on the school board, but the second candidate founded a charter school. Who do you think would be best?"

"I'm not sure," I replied. "Let's find out."

# 97. Promoting Early Childhood Education in Families and the Community

### —Told by the director of a suburban preschool

As director of a preschool in a suburban town, I knew the directors of five other schools. We met informally several times a year to talk about issues we face in our programs and to share resources and ideas. But for the most part, we all were operating in our own isolated silos.

One winter day in 2001, I was visited by the president of the local elementary school board. As board member and president, she was frequently hearing reports of the number of children entering kindergarten poorly prepared, while other children were thriving and achieving in kindergarten. In a quest to learn why there was this sharp disparity, she and a former school board president had begun to study the issue and soon learned how important the first five years of a child's life are in preparing them for success in life and school. I was contacted along with many others involved in the lives of young children—administrators, social workers, therapists, medical personnel, school officials, village government personnel, college professors of early childhood education, concerned citizens—and we were all invited to a meeting to discuss how we could address the needs of young children in our community so that all of our children would enter school enriched and ready to succeed. Out of that original gathering, the Consortium for Early Learning was formed with some meager financial support from the five taxing bodies in the community and a number of committed volunteers.

After working through the process of mission statements and bylaws as well as achieving 501(c)(3) status, the first endeavor of this new organization was to ask four local kindergarten teachers, myself as director of a program, the director of another preschool, two home childcare providers, and a teacher of early childhood in a local school to meet for dialogue. For a year, we met monthly to talk about what kindergarten teachers expected of those entering each fall, what they were finding to be missing for some children, and what the goals of those of us caring for and teaching young children had in our programs as well as exploring best practices in early childhood settings and having many more rich conversations. After a number of months, we proposed expanding the conversation through a Saturday morning symposium. The chair of the consortium set the goal for 50 attendees and was surprised that 140 attended. We were seated at round tables. At each table was one administrator, one home provider, one kindergarten teacher, one or two early childhood teachers, an assistant teacher, one speech therapist, one college teacher, one social worker, and so forth.

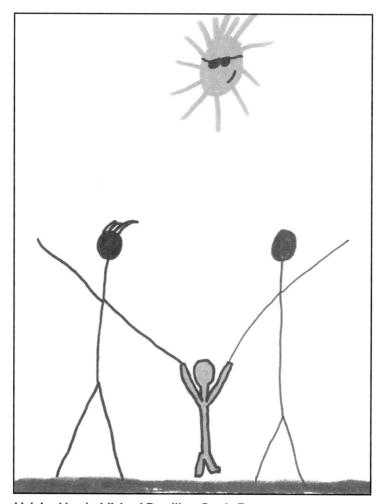

Helping Hands. Michael Readling, Grade 7

After a keynote address, each table was given thirty minutes to brainstorm the question "What are the characteristics of a successful learner?" The sticky note answers were placed on two large cutouts of a child, and the responses were then condensed to the most frequent responses.

The next question posed was "What experiences and activities in the first five years of a child's life support the development of these characteristics?" Again, all of the sticky notes were attached by characteristic, and five committees were formed to work over the next few months to consolidate or expand each area. A group of four of us then turned the results of this dialogue project into a flip book with five chapters for teachers

to use in their classrooms to support: Children as Social Beings; Children as Active Thinkers, Learners, and Explorers; Habits of Mind; Habits of the Heart; and Children as Physical Beings.

At the second annual symposium, the flip book had been self-published and was given to each person in attendance. The consortium then hired a master classroom teacher from my school to visit monthly twelve targeted preschool programs to conduct a training session during children's nap time by using the content of the book as the basis of the training. Each teacher in each preschool received a copy of the book, and they were encouraged to focus on one area each month and use ideas from the book to support their practice.

The twelve programs chosen for this training were ones that served lower-income children and that had historically been unengaged with quality improvements. The consortium has thrived since those early days, and its annual symposium is now attended by 350 to 400 early educators, and many of the staff from those original twelve programs are actively involved and continuing to grow professionally. A couple of the programs have closed, and others have opened. The consortium continues to engage all in the community who are educating the youngest among us in a variety of supports and opportunities for growth, including parents and home care providers.

My involvement in the consortium has been fulfilling and exhilarating as improving opportunities for all young children to develop and have a better opportunity to reach their potential goes beyond the doors of my preschool. Being a part of a community-wide effort to invest resources in the first five years and to expand the understanding of why that is so important to the decision makers in the community has been an energizing focus that has benefited all of our programs. As the community, parents, and providers grow in skill and knowledge, it is the children who benefit, and it is—above all else—all about the children.

# 98. Visiting With the Kids

### —Told by a former principal of a suburban elementary school

Jim was the principal of an elementary school in a rural part of the state. The families in the community his school served were mostly low-income, and most were under a great deal of stress. Some parents worked multiple jobs to make ends meet. Some parents had children early in life and had not finished high school. Rates of single-parent families were high. Over the years he served as principal, and as a teacher before that, Jim had come to understand that many young parents in his school's attendance area lacked the understanding and the skills to be good and caring parents to their children.

On most weekends throughout the year, Jim got in his car and visited the families of students in his school. He made a particular point of visiting those young parents who he thought needed parenting support. He wanted just to visit, to be present, and to help them talk about any issues they were having in supporting their children. Often, Jim would take his own children on these visits. His purpose was twofold. His children might entertain the family's children while he and the parents talked. But, importantly, he wanted these young parents to be able to see him in interaction with his own children, to see how they would interact with each other, how he might express love and support, even how he might guide and correct them.

# 99. Parent University

### —Told by a board member of a suburban community organization
### *Adapted from Sikora (2019).*

With reports of mental health issues increasing among youth nationally, River Park High School founded a Parent University

with community partners as part of the school's Mental Wellness Collaborative. The collaborative is a partnership of the school with the local chapter of a national association on mental illness, a local community foundation's youth program, the municipal government's mental health board, and the municipality's youth development program. Parent University recently held its first series of workshops at the school, inviting all parents of area youth to attend.

The principal and her administrative team at River Park developed the collaborative in response to the results of a state youth survey that found that nearly 20 percent of sophomores and seniors at the school had seriously considered attempting suicide. Nearly one-third of sophomores and seniors reported feeling so sad or hopeless every day for two weeks or more in a row that they stopped doing their usual activities. The mission of the collaborative is to ensure that students, teachers, and parents of the school have access to community-based resources to promote positive mental health. The collaborative formed Parent University to better connect parents with these resources and with one another and to help parents better care for and support their teenage children.

Parent University is designed to address many of the issues facing youth today. The university's first session offered workshops for parents focused on helping teens find a healthy balance in their lives and helping them master the executive function. Other sessions focused on the teen brain; screens, phones, and technology; vaping; and helping teenagers manage stress. These topics and the format of the workshops and sessions were inspired by results from a parent survey. Developed to better hear the *parent voice*, this survey asked parents what they were seeing in their students and what kind of information and tools parents might find helpful to better support them. The survey also asked for details about how parents wanted to receive this information and how often opportunities for learning might be provided.

Plans are being made for Parent University to convene at least twice a year. Its organizers are also working to make sure that between meetings parents are provided information about where they can find information, other sources of support, and professional services to help them better support their children.

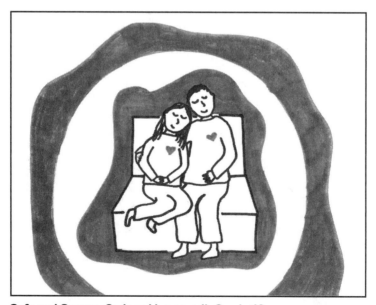

**Safe and Secure. Sydney Hunnewell, Grade 12**

# 100. What Can We Do?

**—Told by the program director of a suburban community organization**

We were having a problem at the residential group home where I serve as program director. Our kids were not only struggling in school academically but each year, after summer break, they seemed to be getting farther and farther behind. The gains they made the year before seemed to vanish. School is tough for most of our kids. They come to us after being removed from their families by the state because of harm or abuse. They live in the home—some for a few months while they are being diagnosed for services and some for a year or more until they can be placed in foster homes or reunited with their families. We really wanted to do something more to help our kids be more successful in school. They were already welcomed and supported by the community's elementary and high schools. We were looking for things that we could do in the house to further promote their academic success.

Our director, Anne Marie White, had the idea of pulling together a group of educators from the community to advise the home about what it could do. She reached out to Mary Abuz, a friend and an assistant principal at the high school, who was volunteering as an academic adviser at the home. Both Anne Marie and Mary shared a long history in the community, working together to help kids in and out of school. They decided to assemble an academic advisory board for the home. Anne Marie had a good idea what she and her staff wanted to accomplish—provide better academic support for the kids. They didn't know the best way to do it. So they formed the advisory board as a source of expertise and support.

Anne Marie and Mary identified several teachers and principals from the community who they wanted to invite onto the advisory board. They also put out word to the schools to see if others might volunteer. In the end, they assembled a board of seven practicing and retired educators. These educators did not join as part of their regular schoolwork, nor was joining part of the agreements the home had with the elementary school district for kids to attend the districts' schools. These educators joined simply because they wanted to find a way to help. I became a member of the advisory board as the home's program director. The home's education coordinator also became a member.

The first meeting of the advisory board was held in the main conference room at the home. Anne Marie and Mary welcomed everyone, and they spent a few minutes explaining what the home wanted to accomplish. They talked about how the advisory board might help. We went around the room, introduced ourselves, and shared our thoughts about what we each might contribute. The teacher members spoke mostly about classroom curriculum and instruction. Marge, the elementary district's literacy coordinator, spoke about her experience and expertise in literacy curriculum development and implementation. Becky, the principal of an elementary school in the community, spoke about how she could contribute in the areas of program leadership. She said that she could help us think about staffing and financing and about how the programs and supports we might develop could be coordinated with those at the schools the kids attended. Once we finished the introductions, the group began discussing problems the kids might be having academically and brainstorming courses of action.

Over the next several meetings, we engaged in vigorous discussions and debates. The advisory board helped us develop a number of strategies to better support our kids academically. One of the most important initiatives was the development of a Summer Reading Academy. Mary and Becky worked with us to develop a strategy for developing the academy. They helped us think through the resources and supports we would need to make the academy a success. And they helped us develop a budget and funding plan. Importantly, Mary, Becky, and Marge gave us access to contacts in their professional networks, from educational experts, such as reading specialists, to potential funders. They helped us draft funding proposals and develop plans to evaluate the academy's success. Through a connection that Marge had with a small college in the area, we were able to locate the academy there. Another board member helped us raise money to pay stipends to college students to work with our kids.

The advisory board met for five years—its school leader and teacher members voluntarily contributing their time and effort throughout. The academic supports and the Summer Reading Academy that it helped develop continue to this day, now nearly a decade later.

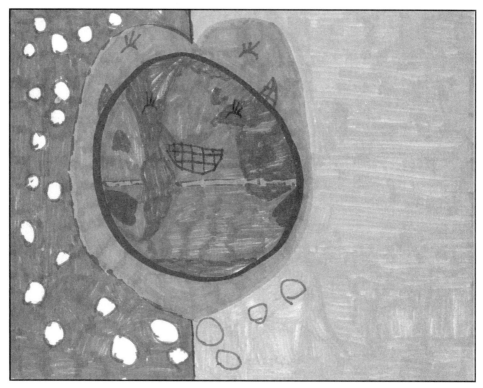

**Happy, Loving World. Henry Herbert, Grade 4**

# Bibliography

Abbott, P., & Meerabeau, L. (1998). Professions, professionalization and the caring professions. In P. Abbott & L. Meerabeau (Eds.), *The sociology of the caring professions* (pp. 1–19). New York, NY: Routledge.

Antrop-González, R., & De Jesús, A. (2006). Toward a theory of critical care in urban small school reform: Examining structures and pedagogies of caring in two Latino community-based schools. *International Journal of Qualitative Studies in Education, 19*, 409–433.

Benner, P., & Gordon, S. (1996). Caring practice. In S. Gordon, P. Benner, & N. Noddings (Eds.), *Caring giving: Readings in knowledge, practice, ethics, and politics* (pp. 40–55). Philadelphia: University of Pennsylvania Press.

Benner, P., & Wrubel, J. (1989). *The primacy of caring: Stress and coping in health and illness.* Reading, MA: Addison Wesley Longman.

Biddle, B. J., & Saha, L. J. (2005). *The untested accusation: Principals, research knowledge, and policy making in schools.* Lanham, MD: Scarecrow Education.

Bloom, P. (2018). *Against empathy: The case for rational compassion.* New York, NY: Ecco, HarperCollins.

Brechin, A. (1998). Introduction. In A. Brechin, J. Walmsley, J. Katz, & S. Peace (Eds.), *Care matters: Concepts, practice, and research in health and social care* (pp. 1–12). Thousand Oaks, CA: Sage.

Coles, R. (1989). *The call of stories: Teaching and the moral imagination.* Boston, MA: Houghton Mifflin.

Denning, S. (2011). *The leader's guide to storytelling.* San Francisco, CA: Jossey-Bass.

de Royston, M. M., Vakil, S., Nasir, N. S., ross, k. m., Giving, J. K., & Holman, A. (2017). "He's more like a 'brother' than a teacher": Politicized caring in a program for African American males. *Teachers College Record, 119*, 1–40.

Donaldson, G. A., Jr. (2006). *Cultivating leadership in schools: Connecting people, purpose, and practice.* New York, NY: Teachers College Press.

Fishman, E. (2017, June). Welcome to refugee high. *Chicago Magazine.* https://www.chicagomag.com/Chicago-Magazine/June-2017/Welcome-to-Refugee-High/

Frost, P. J., Dutton, J., Worline, M., & Wilson, A. (2000). Narratives of compassion in organizations. In S. Fineman (Ed.), *Emotions in organizations* (pp. 25–45). London, England: Sage.

Garmston, R. J. (2019). *The astonishing power of storytelling: Leading, teaching, and transforming in a new way.* Thousand Oaks, CA: Corwin.

Harris, S., Ballenger, J., & Cummings, C. (2015). *Standards-based leadership: A case study book for the principalship* (2nd ed.). Lanham, MD: Rowman & Littlefield.

Itkowitz, C. (2016, April 4). Kids don't have to be lonely at recess anymore thanks to this little boy and his "buddy bench." *The Washington Post.* https://www.washingtonpost.com/news/inspired-life/wp/2016/04/04/kids-dont-have-to-be-lonely-at-recess-anymore-thanks-to-this-boy-and-his-buddy-bench/?noredirect=on

Khalifa, M. A. (2018). *Culturally responsive school leadership.* Cambridge, MA: Harvard Education Press.

Kinnick, K. N., Krugman, D. M., & Cameron, G. T. (1996). Compassion fatigue: Communication and burnout toward social problems. *Journalism and Mass Communication Quarterly, 73*, 687–707.

Kleinman, A. (2019). *The soul of care: The moral education of a husband and a doctor.* New York, NY: Viking.

Kouzes, J., & Posner, B. (2012). *The leadership challenge.* San Francisco, CA: Jossey-Bass.

Kowalski, T. J. (2012). *Case studies on educational administration* (6th ed.). Boston, MA: Pearson.

Kruse, S. D., & Louis, K. S. (2009). *Building strong school cultures: A guide to leading change.* Thousand Oaks, CA: Corwin.

Lortie, D. C. (2009). *School principal: Managing in public.* Chicago, IL: University of Chicago Press.

Mayeroff, M. (1971). *On caring.* New York, NY: Harper Perennial.

Mintrop, R., & Zumpe, E. (2019). Solving real-life problems of practice and educational leaders' school improvement mind-set. *American Journal of Education, 125,* 295–344.

Mintzberg, H. (2019). *Bedtime stories for managers.* Oakland, CA: Berrett-Kohler.

National Policy Board for Educational Administration. (2015). *Professional standards for educational leaders 2015.* Reston, VA: Author. Retrieved from http://npbea.org/wp-content /uploads/2017/06/Professional-Standards-for -Educational-Leaders_2015.pdf

New York Principals. (2014, April 21). *Letter to parents about testing.* An open letter to parents of children throughout New York State regarding grade 3–8 testing. Retrieved from http://www .newyorkprincipals.org/letter-to-parents -about-testing

Noddings, N. (2005). *The challenge to care in schools: An alternative approach to education* (2nd ed.). New York, NY: Teachers College Press.

Noddings, N. (2013). *Caring: A relationship approach to ethics and moral education* (2nd ed.). Berkeley: University of California Press.

Palmer, P. J. (1998). *The courage to teach: Exploring the inner landscape of a teacher's life.* San Francisco, CA: Jossey-Bass.

Perry, B. D. (2002). Childhood experience and the expression of genetic potential: What childhood neglect tells us about nature and nurture. *Brain and Mind, 3,* 79–100.

Peterson, E. H. (1994). Teach us to care and not to care. In S. Phillips & P. Benner (Eds.), *The crisis of care: Affirming and restoring caring practices in the helping professions* (pp. 66–79). Washington, DC: Georgetown University Press.

Randall, W. L., Clews, R., & Furlong, D. (2015). *The tales that bind: A narrative model for living and helping in rural communities.* Toronto: University of Toronto Press.

Romm, T., & Mahler, S. (1986). A three dimensional model for using case studies in the academic classroom. *Higher Education, 15,* 677–696.

Sanders, L. C. (Ed.). (2004). *The collected works of Langston Hughes: Vol: 6. Gospel plays, operas, and later dramatic works.* Columbia: University of Missouri Press.

Schein, E. H. (2013). *Humble inquiry: The gentle art of asking instead of telling.* San Francisco, CA: Berrett-Koehler.

Schön, D. A. (1987). *Educating the reflective practitioner.* San Francisco, CA: Jossey-Bass.

Shapiro, J. P., & Stefkovich, J. A. (2010). *Ethical leadership and decision making in education: Applying theoretical perspectives to complex dilemmas* (3rd ed.). New York, NY: Routledge.

Sikora, L. (2019, November 5). Mental health worries rise at OPRF, school convenes Parent U. *Wednesday Journal.* https://www.oakpark.com/News /Articles/11-5-2019/Mental-health-worries -rise-at-OPRF,-school-convenes-Parent-U/

Singer, R., & Klimecki, O. M. (2014). Empathy and compassion. *Current Biology, 24,* R875–R878.

Smylie, M. A., Murphy, J. F., & Louis, K. S. (2020). *Caring school leadership.* Thousand Oaks, CA: Corwin.

Stevens, H. (2019, June 8). Oak Park 1st grader with autism didn't want to face the last day of school, so his principal asked if he could walk him there. The boy was delighted. *Chicago Tribune.* www .chicagotribune.com/columns/heidi-stevens /ct-life-stevens-saturday-oak-park-autistic -boy-principal-hero-0608-story.html#share =email~story

Stewart, Sonia, M. (2018). *All children are our children: A pearl in the heart of the city.* Lexington, KY: Self-published.

Taylor, D. L., Cordeiro, P. A., & Chrispeels, J. H. (2009). Pedagogy. In M. D. Young, G. M. Crow, J. Murphy, & R. T. Ogawa (Eds.), *Handbook of research on the education of school leaders* (pp. 319–369). New York, NY: Routledge.

TED Radio Hour (2019, March 29). Monique Morris: Why are black girls more likely to be punished in school? https://www.npr.org/templates/tran script/transcript.php?storyId=707191363

Thompson, A. (1998). Not the color purple: Black feminist lessons for educational caring. *Harvard Education Review, 68,* 522–555.

CORWIN
A SAGE Publishing Company

**CORWIN HAS ONE MISSION:** to enhance education through intentional professional learning.

We build long-term relationships with our authors, educators, clients, and associations who partner with us to develop and continuously improve the best evidence-based practices that establish and support lifelong learning.

# Solutions YOU WANT | Experts YOU TRUST | Results YOU NEED

**EVENTS** >>> **INSTITUTES**

Corwin Institutes provide large regional events where educators collaborate with peers and learn from industry experts. Prepare to be recharged and motivated!

**corwin.com/institutes**

**ON-SITE PD** >>> **ON-SITE PROFESSIONAL LEARNING**

Corwin on-site PD is delivered through high-energy keynotes, practical workshops, and custom coaching services designed to support knowledge development and implementation.

**corwin.com/pd**

>>> **PROFESSIONAL DEVELOPMENT RESOURCE CENTER**

The PD Resource Center provides school and district PD facilitators with the tools and resources needed to deliver effective PD.

**corwin.com/pdrc**

**ONLINE** >>> **ADVANCE**

Designed for K–12 teachers, Advance offers a range of online learning options that can qualify for graduate-level credit and apply toward license renewal.

**corwin.com/advance**

**Contact a PD Advisor at (800) 831-6640 or visit www.corwin.com for more information**